IN SEARCH OF AUTHORITY

In Search *of*

AUTHORITY

An Introductory Guide to Literary Theory

by Stephen Bonnycastle

second edition

broadview press

Canadian Cataloguing in Publication Data

Bonnycastle, Stephen
In search of authority: an introductory guide to literary theory
2nd Edition

Includes index
ISBN 1-55111-083-0
I. Literature - Philosophy. I. Title
PN45.B65   1996 801   C 95-932624-3

Broadview Press
Post Office Box 1243, Peterborough, Ontario, Canada K9J 7H5

in the United States of America:
3576 California Road, Orchard Park, NY 14127

in the United Kingdom:
B.R.A.D. Book Representation & Distribution Ltd.,
244A, London Road, Hadleigh, Essex. SS7 2DE

Cover: Michelangelo *Sistine Chapel* ('Dividing the light from the
darkness'). Photo by Adam Woolfitt; ©Nippon Television
Corporation, Tokyo 1991.

The excerpt from page 233 *The Prince and the Magician* is from THE
MAGUS by John Fowles. First edition copyright © 1965 by John
Fowles, Ltd.; revised edition and foreword copyright © 1977 by John
Fowles, Ltd. By permission of Little, Brown and Company.

Book design by George Kirkpatrick

PRINTED IN CANADA

Contents

For Will, Adam, and Daryl

A man with one theory is lost. He needs several of them, or lots! He should stuff them in his pockets like newspapers.

Bertolt Brecht

Theory is not truth. It is a vehicle for bringing about desirable change. Vocabularies are tools, not mirrors.

Francis Bacon

It was long since there had been so stormy a meeting. Parties were formed, some accusing Pierre of Illuminism, others supporting him. At that meeting he was struck for the first time by the endless variety of men's minds, which prevents a truth from ever presenting itself identically to two persons. Even those members who seemed to be on his side understood him in their own way, with limitations and alterations he could not agree to.

L.N. Tolstoy

Introduction

I HAVE WRITTEN THIS BOOK with a specific audience in mind, and my idea of that audience has nourished the book at almost every point. Originally I imagined my readers as undergraduates in a university course in literary studies, but I hope that this book will appeal to a wider group than that. I am writing for people who have an interest in literature and some experience of reading it with pleasure, but I am assuming that my readers do not know very much about literary theory. This field has developed remarkably in the last thirty years, and some observers would say that the most exciting developments in literary studies in recent years have taken place in this area. I feel that literary theory has a lot to offer general readers, and that one measure of its value is that a number of key ideas (such as "subtext," "deconstruction," and "grand narrative") which originated in literary theory now commonly appear in newspapers and magazines. Another index of the increasing significance of theory is its institutionalization in university programs and academic conferences.

But most books and articles on literary theory are written for specialists and other knowledgeable people, often in highly technical language. As a result they can be frustrating and hard to understand for students and for the general reader, like technical articles in scientific periodicals. Some critics see this as a fatal flaw in theory itself, but I feel that often theories can be explained simply, and shown to be relevant to our experience of everyday life. That is my aim here.

Although this book is written for beginners in literary theory, the first edition reached many of its readers because of reviews by experts, or because professors put it on reading lists for university courses. So I am conscious of having two audiences with differing concerns. The two groups deserve different introductions. No one needs to read both.

For Beginners

Exploring a new field can be both exciting and daunting, sometimes at the same time. It may be simply dull and boring, with no romance to enliven the experience, and no hint of new powers and perspectives that may enrich your life. One of the attractive things about beginners, as D. T. Suzuki observed in *Zen Mind, Beginner's Mind*, is that their feelings are very much engaged in what they are doing. People who already "know," who expect to find nothing new, often seem as though they are anaesthetized. Unlike beginners, they often do not respond with feeling to what they read.

Most teachers value an eager anticipation in their students as they begin a course, and an appropriate range of emotions with which to begin the study of literary theory would include excitement and high expectation. Someone new to literary theory can anticipate a challenging and rewarding exploration of new ideas and issues, which will deepen his or her understanding of literature and of other areas, such as human psychology, religion, and philosophy.

Literary theories propose solutions to problems which arise in the reading and study of literature, and it is only fair to say that they will have little interest for you if you have not had some rewarding exposure to literature. If you are not engaged by any of the following problems, then you probably will not feel the importance of finding solutions to them. Literary theories touch on some highly controversial issues:

- Does a work of literature have a single, correct meaning, or a number of possible meanings?

- How does an author – Shakespeare, or John Irving, for instance – become generally regarded as a "great author"?

- What happens when a reader is deeply changed by reading a work of literature?

- How is a person affected by intense admiration for a certain author?

- What is the best way to find out more about a book you care deeply about? Will knowing about the life of the author help you?

- How does the language we speak affect who we are? Do people who speak French, or Mandarin, live in a different world from English speakers, because of the language in which they think and express themselves?

- How does literature help us understand people from cultures very different from our own? Can we see, through literature, the plight of people who are vastly underprivileged in comparison to ourselves?

- Can literature function like a religion, and provide values and a sense of wholeness for an individual?

Many of these issues are energetically debated in a number of contexts today. The arguments are often detailed and sophisticated exchanges which can be exciting to watch and participate in, a bit like taking part in the Olympics or a Stanley Cup playoff. They occur primarily at conferences and in the pages of literary newspapers such as the *Times Literary Supplement* and the *New York Review of Books*, with echoes in some daily newspapers.

It is an assumption of this book that the experience of literature needs to come before the investigation of theory. I am also assuming that readers will feel that reading certain works of literature can be very rewarding, especially when the reading is challenging – as when you read and try to put together in your mind some long or complex work, like Tolstoy's *War and Peace* or W. B. Yeats's "Meditations in Time of Civil War." The satisfaction involved in this process can be as intense and rewarding as that of having an intimate relation with another person, or playing a sport well, or knowing another culture thoroughly. It is unnecessary to say this for many readers, because they know it already; but some people find themselves forced into studying literary theory when they have experienced little satisfaction in reading. This is a bit like having to study music theory before you have been moved by a song or a symphony.

Many literary theories are not very complex or hard to understand. Some are, but often the difficulty lies in adopting a set of assumptions which do not fit in easily with common sense. In this book, there are five main ideas which will be new and perhaps hard to assimilate for some readers. They are:

- The idea of paradigm and paradigm change. This occurs when you give up one set of assumptions (conscious and unconscious) and adopt another. Two examples are when you convert from one religion to another, e.g. from Christianity to Judaism, and when you change the way in which you read literature. The process of paradigm change is discussed in Chapter 4.

- The idea that a natural language, such as English, is systematic, and that speaking it has a big effect on how we see the world, what we notice, and what we ignore. This is easier to see if you speak more than one language and feel that your world changes when you switch languages, e.g. from English to German. This is the central insight behind structuralism, which is discussed in Chapter 6.

- The idea that cultures and ideologies are *constructed* rather than natural, and so they embody assumptions about life (which may seem arbitrary, silly, or even evil to people from outside the culture). Most North Americans believe that it is "natural" to allow individuals to own private property, but this idea is a construction of our culture. Many cultures have a built-in assumption that women should be dominated by men.

- The idea that if you don't like something in your culture, then you may want to take your culture apart, or deconstruct it. Then you could substitute (or construct) something else. Deconstruction is discussed in Chapter 8.

- The idea that an individual, or a culture, in the process of development can progress through four stages which can be distinguished from each other by the kinds of feelings involved and the way in which wholes are constructed. Briefly these might be called the stages of the lover, the analyst, the leader, and the deconstructor. These four stages are based on a theory of history developed in the 18th century by Giambattista Vico, and they are discussed in Chapter 9.

Many people find the second of these ideas the hardest to grasp — that the language we use influences, and in part constructs, the way we see reality. This idea, developed by the Swiss linguist Ferdinand de Saussure around 1920, caused a revolution in linguistics, and then spread to many other fields, thereby effecting what is sometimes thought to be the most fundamental shift in thinking in the humanities in the 20th century. It is as important as the idea of relativity in physics (postulated by Einstein about the same time), and similar in its meaning: everyone who takes it seriously needs to become a relativist, because it implies that *the world you see is relative to the language you speak.* In literature, you cannot get outside language, and so you cannot reach some absolute vantage point from which you could make objectively true judgments.

Part of the point of this book is to make the case for a liberal point of view, that people, and groups of people, are different from one another (sometimes because they speak different languages), and that to live a good life we need to take account of these differences, and not attempt to eliminate them by trying to find a set of absolutely true beliefs. In *A Portrait of the Artist as a Young Man*, Stephen Dedalus, aged about 10, says,

> God was God's name just as his name was Stephen. *Dieu* was the French for God and that was God's name too; and when anyone prayed to God and said *Dieu* then God knew at once that it was a French person that was praying. ...still God remained always the same God and God's real name was God.[1]

"God's real name was God." This is a striking statement of absolutism, and we can see how appealing it is – it simplifies the world to think that there is one correct point of view, and that we can be certain of our correctness. But this attitude – that one has attained an absolute objectivity – can be enormously harmful, and results in many kinds of abuse, from discrimination against women and victimization of children, to racism. I feel that the principal ethical benefit afforded by literary theory is that it can combat absolutism and fundamentalism, and help people live with tolerance and openness in a varied world.

Another assumption of this book is that feelings usually are prior to, and more important than, ideas, and that to ignore feelings is liable to alienate you from others and from your true self. Often books of literary theory, and the professors who write them, and teach theory, act as though the feelings of the learner didn't matter. But most people learn best when they feel relaxed, confident, and engaged, and (conversely) learn poorly when they feel overwhelmed with difficult theories and new facts. I have tried to keep this principle in mind throughout the book, though I am sure that I have not always adhered to it.

We are in a period, in the 1990s, of shifting boundaries in the intellectual world. Academic areas, such as English literature, are no longer as clearly defined as they were forty years ago, and indeed the very idea of literature has expanded to include forms of writing which were once not considered literature at all: diaries, biographies, sermons, and political speeches, for instance. New programs in cultural studies propose a much wider field of inquiry than literature departments used to claim as their territory. Part of the interest of literary theory now is that it crosses many boundaries, and so it can bring people together. The same ideas (of postmodernism, for instance) can be found organizing thinking in areas as diverse as politics, geography, architecture, music, and film studies. To learn about literary theory is to learn a powerful, new, ecumenical language which engages with the most recent developments in the humanities and the social sciences. It is a key, perhaps a very effective key, to unlock the world around you.

It is now time to turn to the introduction for people who are knowledgeable about literary theory. If the section which you have just read engaged you on the right level, the next section may seem opaque to you. If that is the case, it would be best to move now to Chapter 1.

How has the rise of literary theory affected literary studies? (An Introduction for the *Cognoscenti*)

The issue of the *Times Literary Supplement* for July 15, 1994, was devoted to assessing the current status of literary theory in universities and the wider world of literature. It contained general articles by Terry Eagleton, Denis Donoghue, Hillis Miller, and Lorna Sage; reviews of two new encyclopedias of literary theory; reviews of books on theory by Stanley Fish and Pierre Bourdieu; and a series of short responses to the question, "How have literature and criticism benefited, or suffered, from the rise of critical theory?" The respondents included Terence Hawkes, John Sturrock, Elaine Showalter, John Bayley, Camille Paglia, and Jerome McGann. There was even a brief, polite note from Jacques Derrida saying that the subject was too vast, and the time too short, for him to be able to contribute.

This issue of the *TLS* provides a good survey of the various attitudes toward the rise of literary theory to a dominating position in the academy. A number of contributors feel that theory has had a positive effect on the study of literature: that it has made English departments more interesting than they had been in the 60s (John Sutherland), that we could now see more clearly how the institution of literature works (John Sturrock), and that our understanding of works of literature can now be more complex and more satisfying (Robert Alter).

There is good representation, too, of many of the kinds of opposition to theory. From the beginning, in the 1960s, there has been a continuous line of fundamental hostility: theory is too abstract, too French, or too antihumanistic to do justice to literature. A number of other reasons for disliking theory developed as it became more and more successful: that it took up too much time to read; that it occupied too much space in the curriculum; that it was deliberately obscure, and alienated general readers; that it was deliberately self-inflating, and placed critics "above" creative writers; and that it promoted a hermeneutics of suspicion, interrogating works of literature like criminals rather than celebrating their insights and life-enhancing qualities.

A further problem has emerged with the enormous increase in the amount of theoretical writing which is published: it has now become fragmented into many separate discourses (postmodern theory, postcolonial theory, and queer theory, for example) which have little in common with each other. As Terry Eagleton says,

> There is no "theoretical paradigm"; theory is just a porous space opened up by an upheaval in the discursive division of labour, in which a whole lot of ways of speaking with almost nothing in common with each other proceed to argue the toss over an object ("art") whose definition is part of the problem. It is not an academic discipline, but the symptom of a crisis in our current disciplinary carve-up.[2]

Another sign of this fragmentation is the view that we are entering a post-theory period, in which attention is being increasingly paid to local issues and sub-fields of theory, and less to the grand, over-arching theories. The work of Edward Said is a case in point: in 1970 he was dealing with general issues such as structuralism and deconstruction; in the 1990s he is much more concerned with the politics of culture in particular geographical areas, such as Palestine.

One aspect of the hostility to theory is clearly expressed by John Gross, a former editor of the *TLS*, who says that literary theory does offer intermittent insights, but that

> the price that has to be paid for them is a hundred times too high, *if they*
> *can only be acquired at the cost of accepting everything that comes with them.*
> The body of theory that has accumulated over the past few years, taken
> as a whole, seems to me a monstrous excrescence, a paltry substitute for
> the experience of literature. [Italics mine][3]

But, we could reply, there are too many works for anyone with
broad interests to keep up with them all: too many new novels, too
many studies of romanticism, too much literary theory. You need somehow to select the wheat from the chaff, and the role of a book such as
this one is precisely to help in that process.

Gross is, however, pointing to a surprising shift in the way literature
has been studied over the past 30 years. In 1981 David Lodge said that

> Nobody professionally involved in the world of literary scholarship and
> academic criticism in England or America can deny that the most
> striking development of the last twenty years has been this massive
> swing of attention towards Continental structuralism. There are, of
> course, still strongholds of dissent and resistance, still plenty of academics
> in England and America (and elsewhere) who have convinced
> themselves that if they keep their heads down long enough the whole
> structuralist fuss will blow over; or who, more valiantly, man the
> ramparts in defence of empiricism, humanism, the New Criticism, or
> whatever. But if the allegiances of the brightest young university
> teachers and graduate students are any guide, that battle has already been
> lost (or won, depending on your point of view).[4]

Although structuralism does not command the attention it used to, its
offshoots, such as narratology and deconstruction, have, if anything,
even more influence than the original movement. It would be an interesting project to try to determine in some detail why this shift has taken
place.

The best explanation, in my view, is that theory holds the promise of
demystifying criticism, clarifying it, and promoting discussion and understanding. There is a hint of this in John Bayley's contribution to the
TLS symposium on how theory has affected literary studies. He also
touches on a number of common reasons for hostility to theory:

Those who can't write, teach; those allergic to teaching literature teach literary theory. ... The theorist seems to be doing something more demanding, as well as more exciting, than the teacher who patiently takes his students through the beauties of *Beowulf* or of *Paradise Lost*.

So theory today tends to be a substitute for the demands of reading, and a short cut not so much to knowledge as to a sense of power and superiority. ... Reading and discussing books once seemed too agreeable a way of getting a degree; theory cuts out the pleasure factor, and what could seem the aimless geniality of talking about books. It also makes a strong appeal to students for whom reading is a nuisance rather than a pleasure. ... *Authority is what matters, but not in the modes of custom and tradition.* Theory must be new, but strictly controlled both by political correctness and a Gallic domination of the abstract. [Italics mine][5]

Good theory, I feel, *can increase* both pleasure in reading and the quality of discussion, becaues it helps focus issues; but Bayley is right to say that theory can increase a person's authority. This, however, is not as damning as he feels. Most students and teachers want some authority, and it is hard to determine in advance what constitutes impropriety in taking short cuts. Some biologists felt that Watson and Crick were using model-building as a short cut when they discovered the helical structure of DNA in 1953. This particular short cut led to enormous progress in the field of molecular biology.

I would like to give a brief account of my developing interest in theory in the 1970s, to show why, to some of us, it was exciting, promising, and productive. Although I had several professors as a student in the 1960s who were excellent scholars and committed teachers – including John Bayley – I was often overwhelmed by the amount of information which they felt I ought to acquire, and confused by a plethora of different and unstated underlying assumptions about the study of literature. Perhaps the most daunting of these was the idea that the meaning of a text was embedded in history and in the biography of the author, and that to really understand literature, I would have to somehow absorb a seemingly infinite amount of historical information.

During the seven years which separated my undergraduate and my graduate work, I taught at two universities, one in France and the other in Canada. Although structuralism was flowering in France while I was there, I was oblivious to it – in the early stages, a revolution is often invisible unless you are looking carefully for it. But when I came to write my thesis, in 1973, the work of Roland Barthes (the first outstanding literary critic to use structuralism) provided a set of ideas which unlocked the subject I was working on. I wanted to understand the idea of personal growth contained in four romantic autobiographies (those by Rousseau, Wordsworth, Coleridge, and Stendhal), having noticed that for my four authors it was the author's sense of his own development that incited him to write an autobiography in the first place. In those days a structure was often defined as a "system of transformation" – and that was just the idea that I needed to make sense of what my autobiographers were describing. I was also riveted by the possibilities contained in Barthes's article on the structural analysis of narrative (published in 1968), and the opening up of the study of the experience of the reader in *Le plaisir du texte* (1972). A third key idea provided by Barthes, later developed by John Ellis and Frank Kermode, was that the meaning of a work of literature could change over the centuries, and that it is a defining characteristic of literature that it still is interesting and important even when it is taken out of the historical and geographical context in which it was written.[6]

Perhaps the most striking element in my response to these theoretical ideas was *relief*. What had seemed a jungle of information – historical, biographical, textual – could be clarified, could be seen to possess an inherent structure, which was understandable. The key ideas were complex, but they were also very liberating. And this seems to me to be the main justification for studying theory: it can allow you to understand something which, without the theory, may seem opaque. So John Bayley would be right to say that I liked learning about literary theory because I felt more powerful afterwards; but his notion that theory forecloses pleasure is, in my case at least, utterly incorrect. It can increase pleasure enormously.[7]

Was my experience typical? I do not know. But if we think about the surge of interest in theory in a broader, more pedagogical context, it makes sense that theory could be a relief to students if it clarified the activities, the aims, and the methods used in their courses in literary studies. This would also be a welcome development for most professors.[8]

Nine Assumptions behind This Book

I have included this list to help readers decide whether this book is likely to be helpful to them, and so they can see in advance where they might disagree with it.

1. **A reader has a right to expect some joy.** I agree with Ezra Pound when he says that

> What thou lovest well remains. The rest is dross.

Works of literature, and writing about literature, ideally should contain joy, or at least pleasure, even when they deal with painful subjects. You should feel the writer's (or the critic's) joy. If you can't, you should question whether he or she is worth reading. A lot of theory and criticism is stultifying because there is no evidence of pleasure in it.

2. **The death of the author:** the interesting meaning behind this phrase (coined by Roland Barthes in 1976) is that the author does not control the meaning of a text which he or she has written. Texts often take on new meanings when they migrate to new times and places. This is the process known as dissemination. This does *not* mean that texts can be made to mean anything.

3. **The importance of the individual:** one of the main beliefs purveyed by post-structuralism is that the individual is not the source of meaning, and that a better way to consider the individual is as a site where different transpersonal codes or ideologies operate. This belief can slide into a kind of determinism, and a denial of the freedom of the individual to make decisions, take action, and have feelings. This kind of extreme determinism is utterly foreign to my experience of life and literature. I have almost always felt that I had areas of freedom in which to make choices. Any theory of literature which denies this would be utterly irrelevant to me, and I would not waste any time on it.

4. **Reading literature is a subjective experience.** We can try to achieve greater objectivity by entering into discussion and seeing if our experience matches that of other readers. (I think that negotiating agreement among individuals is the most important process that occurs in lit-

erature classes. It is always accompanied by discovering irreconcilable differences.)

5. **It is dangerous to assume you are being objective.** Obtaining the agreement of others is very satisfying, partly because it establishes a common ground for further discussion. But anyone who demands the agreement of others because he or she is being "objective" is making a grab for power. Professors often get away with this tactic with students, because they already have a lot of power; but they should avoid using it. Treating a text historically does not mean that you are dealing with it objectively.

6. **The poverty of historicism:** I feel that literary studies are often robbed of their power because in most universities they are conceived of as conveying knowledge about the past. This historicist approach to literature is sometimes used to justify paying attention to facts and texts that have little importance today. What is worse, texts that do matter today, such as *Hamlet* and *The Prelude*, are treated as though it were their historical content – or what they say about the life of the author – that is significant, and not their current meanings, which are alive and forceful today. Historicists like to work in museums and to assume the roles of curators and guides. I enjoy museums, but I think that the real power of literature is felt when the reader consumes the text and incorporates parts of it for a lifetime. (It is important to take account of the process of digestion – and transformation – that is involved when this happens.)

7. **A wise reader will be wary of specialists.** It follows from my misgivings about historicism that I feel critical of a common assumption about literary study, that at its best it is done by specialists. University professors, and those who want to become professors, are encouraged in a variety of ways to become specialists. I think that this process usually warps the mind in an unfortunate way, and that specialists need to guard against this professional deformation, and certainly they should not encourage it in undergraduates. If the main social function of literature in society is to provide an arena for the examination of values (and I think it is), then specialists will often miss the most important points for the public-at-large in pursuit of issues which highlight the importance of their specialized knowledge.

8.   **We need to nurture our communities of learning.** The fundamental aim of the institutions of literature, such as university courses and programs, periodicals, books of criticism, and conferences, should be to create active and exciting communities. The production and handing down of knowledge, and the transmission of ritual and dogma, though important, are (in my view) of secondary significance.

9.   **The usefulness of theories:** often literary theories change our views of a work of literature by proposing new distinctions, or new categories, for looking at the work. This is a bit like putting on a new set of glasses: suddenly you see *some* things more clearly. Coleridge did this when he elaborated the distinction between fancy and imagination, as did Barthes when he proposed a typology of the pleasures of reading (see p. 175). Freud did this when he developed his ideas of the ego, the super-ego, and the id. Derrida did this when he articulated the idea of logocentrism by distinguishing between our attitudes to speech and writing. You cannot prove that distinctions like these are absolutely right; but you may feel that a particular distinction is valid and helpful to you as a reader. A lot of hostility to literary theory comes from people who feel that setting up categories like these usually distorts experience. I think sometimes it does, but at other times new categories can be very helpful in seeing and understanding the world.

Of these nine assumptions, the goal of building satisfying communities – in the classroom, in the university, at conferences, and through publications – seems to be the seed which generates all the others, or at least gives them a common character. Many aspects of academic life interfere with community-building: rising enrolments, the pressure to publish books and articles, the rewards of specialization, and the competition for jobs and promotion. Often reputations are made at the expense of community life, as they are at the expense of family life. I think we need to keep our priorities clear, or the whole enterprise of teaching literature will suffer.

Because this is a book for beginners, I have not tried to cover the field of literary theory completely. I have avoided a number of areas that seem too complex to present in a book of this kind. Although I have made use of the ideas of Sigmund Freud and Carl Jung, there is no chapter on psychoanalytic or archetypal criticism, because I think they require a kind of experience and tact that is hard to acquire, especially in the first half of life. I mention Northrop Frye only in passing, for similar reasons. He is a giant in 20th-century criticism, but his theories are based on his legendary breadth of reading, and although some of his ideas seem quite simple, I have found them difficult to use without being reductive of the experience of reading literature. I think they are hard for beginners to use well. In addition Frye's work seems quite independent of the currents of recent critical theory; he almost seems now to belong to another era than our own. I also have not dealt with queer theory, Lacanian psychoanalysis, or reception theory. These gaps, and others, reflect a lack of knowledge on my part. I would like to fill them some day.

Pronouns pose problems, especially for someone writing with a specific audience in mind. I have often used "you" as a rough equivalent of the British "one," and so my "you" could usually be changed to "we." I have also tried to write in a non-sexist way, partly by alternating between masculine and feminine pronouns.

I have incurred many debts in writing this book, and it is a pleasure to acknowledge them. My university, the Royal Military College of Canada, granted me a sabbatical that was essential to completing this book, and I am grateful for the support and advice of my colleagues in the Department of English. Michael Hurley and Lorne Shirinian have been particularly helpful. Mrs. Addie Searle and Mrs. Vivien Stanfield have cheerfully processed thousands and thousands of words on my behalf. I am grateful to Fraser Petrick and his Grade 5 class at Winston Churchill Public School in Kingston for producing many excellent imitations of Van Gogh, four of which appear on page 213. Krista Johansen helped with documentation, and Bryn Harris provided her enthusiasm, her editing skills, and a great deal of sound advice on the text. Janelle Jenstadt was a valued research assistant. Adam Bonnycastle invented the book's subtitle, and helped convert me from Nota Bene to WordPerfect 6. Daryl Tremain has made many helpful suggestions about wording and clarity. The suggestions of Don LePan, the President of Broadview Press, have improved the book in many ways, as have the attentions of Barbara Conolly and Martin Boyne, its editors, and George Kirkpatrick, who designed the book.

I first thought of writing a book like this one when I was editing *The Journal of Literary Theory* (originally called — a sign of the times — *The Journal of Practical Structuralism*) and attending the annual meetings of the Theory Group of the Association of Canadian University Teachers of English in the early 1980s. Colleagues involved in both these ventures wanted to make theory accessible to undergraduates, and this provided a stimulating arena for discussing the role of theory in teaching. Linda Hutcheon, Pamela McCallum, and Heather Murray have been especially helpful. Susan Drain offered me the opportunity to try out some of my ideas at Mount St Vincent University, as did Russell Perkin at St Mary's University. Joseph Gold has encouraged me in many ways, and taught me about bibliotherapy. Gerald Prince and Didier Coste helped me understand narratology. Peter Taylor of Queen's University has provided me with many helpful ideas about education and life. Enid Rutland gave me a detailed commentary on the first edition of the book, and suggested that it would be more accurately entitled *In Search of Empowerment*. I feel this as a compliment, but I have an attachment to the original title and the pun it contains. I hope most readers will detect my antipathy to authoritarianism and the patriarchy. I am grateful to many students at RMC/CMR, in both the Honours English program and the Engineering program, for responding to the materials in this book in a variety of forms. They have confirmed my belief that dialogue is an essential element in a liberal arts education and that theory can promote dialogue.

This is a book about teaching and my sense of the possibilities inherent in the classroom. My intuitions about this subject emerge from my experience with my own "great" teachers. The earliest of these are my parents, Mary Andrews and Larry Bonnycastle, now on the threshhold of their tenth decades. At Upper Canada College in Toronto I had two wonderful English teachers. Mr Howard in the Prep School, and Mr Sadleir in the Upper School, made classes exciting because they knew how to get us to argue passionately with each other – even, sometimes, about grammar, but, more importantly, about more important subjects. George Whalley of Queen's University inspired awe and affection in many of his students, perhaps somewhat as Coleridge inspired awe in him. I entered a new world – a world of wonders – through knowing him for twenty years. I now realize that I knew without any doubt, almost as soon as I met him, that I wanted to live in his world. This removed a lot of confusion from my life. I never met the final teacher in this list, but he had a similar effect on me through his books. This was Roland Barthes. It was a compelling adventure to follow his development as a critic in the 1970s. He too was inspiring, in the radical quality of his thought, his clarity, and his evident caring for his students. I am staggered when I think how a single teacher can alter a pupil's life.

Finally, this book would not have been possible without the friendship of three people whose lives have been intertwined with mine for many years: David Glassco, Ralph Heintzman, and Paul Scott Wilson. They, and the three people to whom this book is dedicated, have created for me my understanding of dialogue.

S. B.

Notes

1. James Joyce, *A Portrait of the Artist as a Young Man* (Harmondsworth: Penguin, 1960) 16.

2. *Times Literary Supplement*, July 15, 1994, 15.

3. *Times Literary Supplement*, November 15, 1991, 16.

4. David Lodge, *Working with Structuralism* (London: Routledge and Kegan Paul, 1981) vii-viii.

5. *Times Literary Supplement*, July 15, 1994, 9.

6. John Ellis develops this view in *The Theory of Literary Criticism: A Logical Analysis* (Berkeley and Los Angeles: University of California Press, 1974). In *Forms of Attention* (University of Chicago Press, 1985), Frank Kermode writes:

   The process of selecting the canon may be very long but, once it is concluded, the works [included] will normally be provided with the kinds of reading they require if they are to keep their immediacy to any moment; that is, to maintain their modernity. They quickly acquire virtual immunity to textual alteration, so the necessary changes must be all interpretive; and all interpretation is governed by prejudice. Consequently, the need to remain modern imposes upon the chosen works transformations as great as any they may have undergone in precanonical redaction. (75)

7. One important model for reaching a theoretical understanding, for me, occurs in John Fowles's *The French Lieutenant's Woman,* when Charles

discovers that it *is* possible to have an intimate relation with Sarah. Before this he has a theory in his mind that such a relation is unimaginable with someone from Sarah's class. Slowly, agonizingly, this theory is displaced by another, with the whole process aided by his knowledge about evolution. So the birth of a new theory can be filled with joy.

8. In *Illusion and Reality: The Meaning of Anxiety* (London: Dent, 1984), a book which has influenced me in many ways, David Smail, a British psychiatrist, explains that the suffering of his patients might be reduced if they could understand the causes of their anxiety – if they had a *theory* which would make it understandable.

> It seems to me that it is precisely through a *theoretical* framework that the nature of psychological distress can best be confronted, and to some extent alleviated. ... An adequate theory – i.e. an explicit set of ideas or concepts – is exactly what most people have no access to when trying to get to grips with "symptoms" of their psychological malaise, and this is why such "symptoms" seem, often, so mysterious. (1)

He goes on to explain how a theory can highlight the fact that, in living normal social lives, we participate in daily rituals of boasting, pretence, and competition, which seem almost *designed* to produce anxiety in large numbers of people. Without the theory, this important fact may be hidden from view.

CHAPTER ONE:

Why Study Literary Theory Now?

NO ONE HAS TIME to read everything. For those of us who want to understand literature, this is a significant problem. There are hundreds of authors who demand attention, and who hold out the promise of contributing to our knowledge of literature. Then there is the vast mass of critical material: commentaries on the work of authors, biographies, and histories of literature. With all of these books calling out to us, why would we want to turn our attention to literary theory? What will it give us? Why do we need it?

This chapter provides answers to these questions. We can imagine them arising in a concrete situation if we think of a second-year honours course on the English Romantic poets, with the following description in the university calendar:

ENGLISH 250: The English Romantic Poets   3 hours/week
This course concentrates on the poetry of Blake, Wordsworth, Coleridge, Shelley, Keats, and Byron. Students will study the meanings of their major poems in the contexts in which they were written. Attention will be paid to important critical ideas developed in the Romantic period, and to the idea of romanticism itself. Students will write two essays during the year, on subjects related to the course.

It is easy to imagine a student poring over this description, trying to wring from it a sense of what the course would actually be like. Probably he would have little knowledge of Romantic poetry, and the prescribed anthology might well seem daunting, with all its long poems. On the other hand he would be engaged in the excitement of starting a new course, with a new professor and a new group of students, which is not unlike the excitement of joining any new group – a hockey team, a choir, or a student council, for instance.

This course might be taught in two very different ways, and the distinction between them is crucial to understanding one of the defining problems in the modern world, and a central problem in English studies: relativism. Do poems have a "right" meaning? Or does the meaning of a poem change depending on who reads it?

The course description for English 250 defines it in terms of the material to be studied – the works of the six main Romantic poets. The vast bulk of their work was written between 1795 and 1825, and once you have a certain amount of knowledge about that work, you could probably pass the exam in the course on the Romantic poets at any university in the English-speaking world. The problem is to get enough knowledge inside your head.

But there is a second way to define the course, which is not mentioned in this calendar entry, and it raises problems of a different order. These problems make the study of literature controversial and exciting. They are: what are we going to *do* with the poems on this course? What kind of knowledge are we going to assemble about them? How does a student's experience of reading the poems – alone, on one particular evening, for instance – relate to the concerns of the course? And how are the poems that will be studied chosen from the vast mass of poetry written during the thirty years in question?

The difficulty raised by these questions is that there is no general agreement about the answers to them. If you brought together a dozen experts on the Romantic period, they would disagree sharply about these matters, and even if you locked them in a room for two weeks they would not reach a common conclusion. To give you an idea of what they would be fighting about, I will indicate three different positions they might take. (There are many others, too.) As a text we will use one of the masterpieces of Romantic poetry, "Kubla Khan," by Samuel Taylor Coleridge:

> In Xanadu did Kubla Khan
> A stately pleasure-dome decree:
> Where Alph, the sacred river, ran
> Through caverns measureless to man
>   Down to a sunless sea.

So twice five miles of fertile ground
With walls and towers were girdled round:
And there were gardens bright with sinuous rills,
Where blossomed many an incense-bearing tree;
And here were forests ancient as the hills,
Enfolding sunny spots of greenery.

But oh! that deep romantic chasm which slanted
Down the green hill athwart a cedarn cover!
A savage place! as holy and enchanted
As e'er beneath a waning moon was haunted
By woman wailing for her demon-lover!
And from this chasm, with ceaseless turmoil seething,
As if this earth in fast thick pants were breathing,
A mighty fountain momently was forced:
Amid whose swift half-intermitted burst
Huge fragments vaulted like rebounding hail,
Or chaffy grain beneath the thresher's flail:
And mid these dancing rocks at once and ever
It flung up momently the sacred river.
Five miles meandering with a mazy motion
Through wood and dale the sacred river ran,
Then reached the caverns measureless to man,
And sank in tumult to a lifeless ocean:
And 'mid this tumult Kubla heard from far
Ancestral voices prophesying war!.

    The shadow of the dome of pleasure
    Floated midway on the waves;
    Where was heard the mingled measure
    From the fountain and the caves.
It was a miracle of rare device,
A sunny pleasure-dome with caves of ice!

    A damsel with a dulcimer
    In a vision once I saw:
    It was an Abyssinian maid,
    And on her dulcimer she played,
    Singing of Mount Abora.

Could I revive within me
Her symphony and song,
To such a deep delight 'twould win me,
That with music loud and long,
I would build that dome in air,
That sunny dome! those caves of ice!
And all who heard should see them there,
And all should cry, Beware! Beware!
His flashing eyes, his floating hair!
Weave a circle round him thrice,
And close your eyes with holy dread,
For he on honey-dew hath fed,
And drunk the milk of Paradise.

If a historical critic were giving this course, he would tell you that the first thing to do with the poem is to place it in the context in which it was written. Normally this would involve relating it to our knowledge of Coleridge's life at the time, which is rich in pertinent information. He wrote the poem in his middle twenties, when he had already established a reputation for brilliance and wide reading. He was unsure, however, of how to make use of his talents in a career, and he may also have been partially addicted to opium. Coleridge himself said that he composed the poem while he was asleep or in a "reverie," after taking a common household medicine that contained opium. He also said that the poem was a fragment of a larger whole, which he had "written" in his sleep but which he could not remember in its entirety.

This background information raises some fascinating biographical questions. Was the poem actually composed, as it were, by Coleridge's unconscious mind, while he was asleep? How might it have been influenced by the opium he had taken? Many of the phrases in the poem are similar to, or the same as, phrases in books to which Coleridge had had access. Does this poem illustrate the power of Coleridge's mind to retain and integrate a vast amount of reading? Do the themes of the poem reflect the deep concerns Coleridge had about his own future — and the uses to which genius could be put? Kubla Khan is presented as a supreme autocrat, who can "decree" a pleasure-dome; this was not a possibility for Coleridge. But the poem criticizes this kind of power by suggesting that it is out of harmony with the forces of nature, and, in the last verse-paragraph, Coleridge presents another image of genius — the inspired poet, who enters a god-like state, and is surrounded by fervent admirers. This *was* a possibility – though distant and unreliable – for Coleridge. The real meaning of the poem, for the historical critic, would be the full meaning it had for Coleridge.

If a psychological critic were giving this course, she might say that the interest of "Kubla Khan" lies not in its connection with Coleridge's life, but in the way it articulates a commonly experienced dichotomy between two parts of a human being: the conscious, controlling, rational part, and the unconscious drives of sexuality and aggression. The poem suggests this contrast:

THE ENCLOSED PARK	THE ROMANTIC CHASM
control	lack of control
a civilized garden	the wildness of nature
safety	danger and violence
the secular life	the "holy," "enchanted" life
pleasure	sexual passion
social organization (to make decrees possible)	solitude
cultural creation (architecture)	natural "creation" (the fountain bursting out of the ground)

A psychologist would recognize Kubla's task of creating a cultural space within a natural setting as a job that each of us has to do in the process of growing up. She would probably point out that although Kubla's solution seems effective, the "ancestral voices prophesying war" suggest that some problems remain unresolved. She would also see that Coleridge's imagined visit to paradise (in the last verse-paragraph) is connected with an inspiring woman, with a feeling of exaltation, and with feeding – a concatenation suggesting the earliest bond between a child and his mother.

If the professor giving the course were a reader-response critic, he would say that the best way into the poem would be through the actual experiences of individual students sitting down to read the poem. He would ask such questions as: "Did you find the poem interesting or boring? Which attracts you more, the pleasure-dome or the mighty fountain? What does the 'lifeless ocean' suggest to you? Does the poem settle the problem which it raises about containing natural energy?" This professor would put the poem in the context of the life of the reader (*not* the life of the author) and ask, "How does this poem relate to the most important concerns in your life?"

When we see how these three hypothetical professors would proceed, we are faced with the problem that we have three experts, all with good credentials, who disagree radically about how to read the poem. They are asking different questions about it, and they are surrounding it with very different kinds of knowledge. The first uses a lot of biographical information about the author (material found in Coleridge's letters and notebooks, for instance); the second presents psychological material; and the third connects the poem with the life-histories of the students he is talking to. Sometimes this variation is called "the problem of approaches": each professor has a particular approach. But this term introduces a misleading metaphor, because it suggests that the three professors are all approaching *the same thing* – as though they were coming to a house in the country from different directions, the first from across a meadow, the second through the woods, and the third in a car on a paved road. This image suggests that once they get to the house, they will agree about what it is. But this is not the case: these three professors actually see different poems when they look at the same printed text. A better analogy would be three people talking about a fourth whom they all know well. In the process they discover that the fourth is somewhat different with each of them, partly because different aspects of her personality are brought out by each of the three people talking about her.

The Problem of Ideologies

In the long run, it is better to call this "the problem of ideologies" than "the problem of approaches." In essence an ideology is a system of thought or a "world-view" which an individual acquires (usually unconsciously) from the world around him. An ideology determines what you think is important in life, what categories you put people into, how you see male and female roles in life, and a host of other things. You can visualize your ideology as a grid, or a set of glasses, through which you see the world (see diagram below).[1]

Each ideology draws attention to certain features of the world, and hides or causes you to ignore others. The three professors described above have different ideologies, and so the courses they would give on the Romantic poets would be very different from one another. The historical critic draws attention to the author's life and ignores the reader's life; the reader-response critic pays no attention to the author at all, and concentrates on the reader.

The effects of ideologies can be seen at their clearest in religious conflicts. Imagine a woman raised in a thoroughly Christian culture, in which all the people she encounters are practicing Christians. It would be natural for her to assume that everyone is a Christian, and that Christianity provides the truth about the world. Now imagine this woman transported to a Buddhist monastery in Japan. If she could talk to the monks, she would quickly become aware that this new group of people was not operating with her ideology. They would not be impressed with the authority of the Bible, or especially interested in the life of Jesus. They would not understand what was meant by the idea of a God who took a personal interest in individual human beings. Furthermore, suppose that the Christian did not reject this new community outright, but instead decided to follow its way of life, and that she found new things in this world – practices such as meditation, the martial arts, or flower-arrangement – that are not important in a Christian culture. She

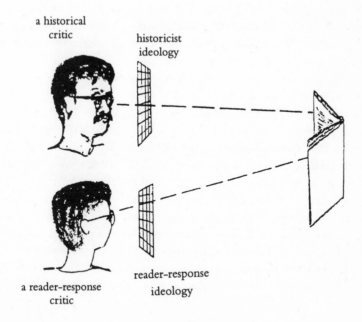

would begin to see that, to some extent, her ideology *creates* the world she lives in.

The main reason for studying theory at the same time as literature is that it forces you to deal consciously with the problem of ideologies. If you don't pay attention to theory, or if the professor doesn't put it on the course, that is like saying, "I'm going to ignore the fact that there are Buddhists in the world, and pretend that only Christians exist." This attitude might be considered irresponsible; at the very least it could leave you with a large gap in your knowledge, which could hamper your intellectual life later on.

One result of thinking about ideologies is that it introduces a lot of uncertainty into literary studies. It raises the question, "What knowledge is most worth having?" No one has found a satisfactory answer to this question, not even the experts. Many students don't want to cope with that kind of uncertainty early on in their university careers; they want "the truth"; they want "certainty." And there are understandable reasons for wanting to find the truth. Feeling you know the truth provides a lot of emotional security. Unfortunately "the truth" simply isn't available. If you are going to live intelligently in the modern world, you have to recognize that there are conflicting ideologies, and that there is no simple, direct access to the truth. Everyone must have met people who have chosen to embrace a very limited "truth" and so have avoided some complex but important areas of human experience.

So in a sense the "simple, plain truth," about Coleridge's poetry, for instance, is just not available. There are many truths, and the one you find will depend partly on the ideology you start with. If this situation sounds depressingly complex at the outset, it can later turn out to be both exciting and challenging. It means you can take your own part in the struggles for power between different ideologies. It helps you to discover elements of your own ideology, and understand why you hold certain values unconsciously. It means that no authority can impose a "truth" on you in a dogmatic way – and if some authority does try, you can challenge that "truth" in a powerful way, by asking what ideology it is based on. It means that you can choose which groups you want to belong to more effectively, because you can see the effects of the group's ideology. Theory is subversive because it puts authority in question.

Theory as a Map

Another way of thinking about theory in relation to a particular English course is to say that it can provide a map for what you are going to do in the course. If you are going to spend a month travelling in Europe, you need a map – to see how the various countries are related to one another geographically, and to see how you can get from one city to another. That doesn't mean that you only want to look at the map, or that the map is the reality. You carry a map with you because it is useful, and because it allows you to get the information you want quickly. Similarly, in studying literature we don't want to concentrate on theory exclusively. Most of our time will be taken up with reading works of literature, and writing and talking about them. But when we are unsure of what we are doing, or confused about the fundamental aims of the course, we take out the map.

The Bias of This Book in Presenting Theory:
A Reader-Centered View

The problem of ideologies arises because it is impossible for anyone to see the world objectively. What you see is coloured by your ideology. You can tell when teachers are aware of this problem; they will often make an effort to say what ideology they are using, or what their background is, which has led them to see things in a particular way. My presentation of literary theory is not meant to be objective, so I would like to briefly indicate what my main concerns are. This book presents a particular view of literature and literary theory; readers should know the assumptions which lie behind that view.

When literature is read, three main entities are involved: the writer, the text, and the reader. This is a simplification of a more complex situation (publishers and booksellers also play a role, for instance), but it corresponds to many people's intuitions about reading. The author and the reader meet in the text. With poems or novels that mean a lot to us, we often have the feeling of being in a direct and intimate relation with the author through the medium of the text. We could illustrate this with the diagram below.

We can say initially that there are three different ideologies of literary criticism, each one emphasizing one of the items in this diagram. Author-centered criticism is largely concerned with works of literature

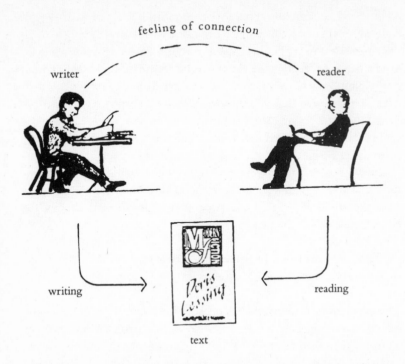

as expressions of the author's state of mind. Above all, this kind of criticism places emphasis on understanding what was going on in the author's mind, and what her intention was in writing the work. The meaning of the work is what it meant to the author. Often this kind of criticism is inspired by a great admiration for the author, who is seen as someone we would be fascinated to meet. In this approach, there is a certain disregard for both the text and the reader. The text (a poem, for instance) is often supplemented with biographical information so the critic can determine its meaning. The reader is hardly considered at all – his or her feelings, background, intuitions, and sex are made to seem irrelevant in comparison with the author's experience. The role of the reader is to conform to the author's state of mind. Often critics operating with this ideology like to see themselves as "transparent": they provide a window on the work they are discussing, they clear away obstacles, and they try to let us see the author as clearly as possible.

Text-centered criticism tends to ignore both the author and the reader in order to concentrate on "the words on the page." This kind of criticism focuses on issues such as regularities and patterns which can be seen in the text, and on how a poem solves the problems which it raises. Some structuralist analyses of literature fall into this category. Text-centered criticism goes along with a strong feeling of reverence for individual works of art – the kind of feeling nourished by the Aesthetic movement of the 1890s, for instance. If the author is considered in a text-centered analysis, it is not the actual, historical author, but the author who can be constructed from the evidence in the text. The reader is conceived of in an idealized way, as a kind of perfect receiver of the text.

Reader-centered criticism begins with the experiences of individuals when they read texts. A reader-response critic would maintain that a poem does not exist in a real sense as "words on the page." It only takes on an existence when it enters the mind of someone reading it. Furthermore, it can never enter the mind of a reader in a neutral, objective way, because we all give slightly different meanings to the individual words we read, and we put them together in different ways. The way you interpret the word "mother" will have a lot to do with your experience of your own mother – modified, to some extent, by your knowledge of how other mothers behave. So reader-response critics are especially interested in accounts of how people have actually responded to texts they have read. If I am a reader-response critic, my idea of what a poem means will be built up from reports by readers on how they have felt about and understood a poem.

A state of ideological conflict exists between these three types of critic – the author-centered, text-centered, and reader-centered. This book is based on the assumptions of reader-centered criticism.

If literature is worth studying in university, and worth spending a number of years on, that is primarily because of the experiences and skills it imparts to the people who do the reading and studying. Reading literature should feel like an important activity – otherwise it isn't worth doing. I feel that the best way to relate to literature is to pay a lot of attention to our individual responses, and I think this provides the best base for developing connections between different readers in the classroom. When we draw on our responses, we connect with our own immediate experience, and we can talk about how works of literature influence our own lives.

Author-centered critics and historical critics dominate the literary profession. This is illustrated by the fact that most university courses are defined in terms of the authors or the historical period covered. A lot of excellent work is done with this literary ideology. My main objection to it, when it dominates English departments, is that it tends to be authoritarian, and to maintain that the meaning of a work of literature is objective and external to the reader. This attitude often squashes readers and their responses, in the interests of "being faithful to the author's intention" or "being accurate historically." But literature does not live through accuracy about the past; it lives through the enthusiasm of readers.

Text-centered critics are useful in making us look carefully at the words on the page in front of us. I think, however, that they make a fundamental error if they assume that they can interpret these words objectively. Whenever interpretation is taking place, there is someone (a particular person) interpreting, and that person has his or her own agenda and ideology, which play a major role in constructing what is read. If we want to understand what happens when literature is read, we have to take account of the subjective element in the process.

One of the main achievements of literary theory in the past twenty years has been to direct more attention to what the reader experiences. A lot of criticism today is concerned with how readers make sense of books, and why some books are highly valued by a lot of readers. So my presentation of literary theory in this book is colored by my concern with the details of how readers interact with books and with each other. An author-centered critic and a text-centered critic would each give a very different account of contemporary literary theory, and I think it would be a less interesting one.

A Literary Theory about Reader-Response and the Curriculum

To conclude this chapter I want to provide an example of a literary theory, and show how it can shed light on what happens in English classes. Books can be arranged in many different ways. In encyclopedias, books are discussed under the author's name, and authors are listed alphabetically. Author-centered critics often classify books by their historical period, so that Sidney and Shakespeare go with Jonson and Donne. Text-centered critics often classify works according to genre or style, so that Shakespeare can be grouped with Shaw, and Donne with Dylan Thomas. The system of grouping which I will propose is based on reader response, and it applies, in the first instance, to your own experience of reading books.

Think of ten books you have read, and put them in categories according to your response to each one. What I call response #1 is one of interest, involvement, and fascination, but the key element is the feeling that you want to *read the book again* – that it would give you pleasure to reread it. You may not have the time, but if you do feel the desire to reread it, then the book goes into category #1.

Response #2 occurs when you feel, after finishing a book, that you might want to reread it if you were able to take a course related to it. After finishing Tolstoy's *Anna Karenina* you might feel moderately interested by the novel, but know that for it to become really involving for you, you would need to gather some other information: a knowledge of 19th-century Russia; familiarity with other books by Tolstoy and other Russian authors of the period; and perhaps some knowledge of Tolstoy's life, and how it is transmuted to become the life of the hero, Levin.

Response #3 is boredom. You feel it is unlikely that you will ever, under any circumstances, be really interested in reading the book again. Of course it is hard to be sure about this, but nevertheless we often have that feeling, and it feels quite different from a #2 response. Often we don't finish books which inspire a #3 response.

The interest of this literary theory lies in what it allows us to say (and perceive) about courses in literature.

I believe that literary education depends crucially on the student having a #1 response to a number of books, and that courses should be designed with this in mind. We could say that books which arouse a #1 response in a lot of readers are alive and well on their own, as it were – they don't need a support system. Books that elicit a #2 response usually need to be kept alive in a sort of museum – which often means a university course. Without that supporting environment they would not be read or appreciated very much. Books that cause a #3 response are dead, and it is very difficult to revive them.

It is a fair description of some university courses that the books assigned are ones to which the professor has a #1 response (and so she rereads them eagerly), but they cause a #3 response in the students. A course like this functions perfectly well according to the university regulations – lectures are given, essays and exams are written, and grades are assigned. The professor finds the process very interesting, perhaps, but the educational value from the students' point of view is very limited.

Although most people might agree that there is little point in putting books that elicit a #3 response on courses, there is an interesting debate as to whether it is better to use #1 books or #2 books. Some professors would argue that #1 books can live on their own, and that it is better to concentrate on books that evoke a #2 response. This approach has the advantage of putting students through the experience of not being able to understand a book, learning the material on the course, and then being able to understand the book in the end. The feeling of "growth of understanding" is a moving and powerful experience for many students, and some would say it is the essence of university education.

Although this view has a certain validity, and any course should contain a few #2 books, the most lively courses, and those with the most long-lasting effects, are based on books that evoke a #1 response on first reading. Students are willing to talk about these books in class, and they generate a lot more energy than #2 books. A class working with #1 books is self-propelled; a class working with #2 books is always waiting for the professor to explain things – and there is always the possibility that, even after everything is explained, the book may remain relatively unengaging for the student. In a commentary on the myth of Parsifal, a psychiatrist has written:

> It is important to remember that a myth is a living thing and exists within every person. You will get the true, living form of the myth if you can see it as it spins away inside yourself. The most rewarding thing you can do with this or any myth is to see how it is alive in your own psychological structure.[2]

In a sense this is also true of books that generate a deep and lasting response in the reader. When you read something that is important to you, it *does* "spin away inside yourself." I think that a #1 response is an even more powerful spur to growth and learning than a #2 response. You want to understand the work better because it involves you in some profound way.

Grouping responses to books into these three kinds sheds light on the recurring problem of whether you should read a book before or after going to the lectures on it. With a #2 book, you are better to hear the lectures first; then you may get more out of your reading. But with a #1 book, it makes more sense to read it first, so you can enjoy the freshness of your own response, and use it in discussion in class.

This literary theory looks like a "classification of responses." Typically, literary theories propose typologies, or ways of classifying things. It is not necessary to decide whether a particular theory is right or wrong. The test is whether or not it is *useful*, whether it helps us understand our experience, and define our goals, better. If this theory allows you to explain the difference between interesting and dull university courses, then, as Brecht says, you will want to keep it in your pocket as long as you are studying literature.

Canon-Formation: Why Do Some Books Become Classics?

We can use the distinction between the three kinds of responses to look at a central issue in literary studies, and one which is rarely considered in the undergraduate curriculum. Each year thousands of books are written and published. A tiny number of these books will continue to be read a hundred years from now and (if present conditions continue) most of these books will be on university courses. How does this selection process occur? Who chooses? For what reasons?

We can ask these questions about the course on the English Romantic poets discussed earlier. In this course six authors are studied. It would be fair to say that the works of these authors form the canon of English poetry in the Romantic period. But hundreds of other poets published works in Britain between 1795 and 1825. Why do Blake, Wordsworth, Coleridge, Shelley, Keats, and Byron continue to be read in university courses, while all the rest are more or less ignored?

There is a good reason why students don't normally ask this question. If you don't know anything about the poets writing in this period, you have no grounds for criticizing the instructor's list of required readings. You have to take what is proposed to you on faith. But questions about canon-formation are nonetheless interesting to ask, because they make you notice a hidden but important side of what makes some authors "great."

Here are four ways of accounting for canon-formation in courses. The first is, "We study these poets because they wrote the best poems in the Romantic period." Notice that this answer assumes the "best" poems can be discovered by some relatively objective means. It is almost as though God had chosen the poems, and then made some announcement about it. (Think of the controversy – and lobbying – surrounding the choice of the best film of the year at the Academy Awards.

"Forget that book. This is __must__ reading."

The Role of the Bookseller in Canon-formation
(drawing by Levin; ©1983 The New Yorker Magazine, Inc.).

Why should choosing the best Romantic poets be any less complicated?)
Notice also that the professor occupies a position of authority in this answer. She knows which are the best poems, the student doesn't, and so
there can be no argument about it. The student hasn't a leg to stand on.

The second account of canon-formation runs as follows: "We study
these poets because in the general opinion of specialists in this field they
are the most rewarding poets to study." This answer admits that there is
a definite source of authority (there has been a collective decision on the
part of a group of English professors), and the decision is not timeless.
The list would have been different in 1880: Blake would not have been
included then. This explanation also implies that there could be changes
in the future, and that decisions about the canon are social or political
ones. If you could persuade a few thousand English professors that Felicia Hemans was a better poet than Percy Bysshe Shelley, she might replace Shelley on the reading list.[3]

A third answer is, "We read these poets because I like them best" – which makes the professor sound more egocentric, but at least clearly identifies the source of the decision. This explanation implies too that you might be able to argue with her, and in that way possibly change the reading-list.

A fourth explanation is, "I teach these poets because I find they are the ones students profit from and enjoy the most." Here again there is a political process at work; this answer suggests that students could change the canon of poets in effect in that particular course.

In any of these cases students can feel frustrated with the whole question of canon-formation, because they are not able to make suggestions until the end of the course. And at that point, why bother?

The answer is that in studying literature all of us inherit what is passed down to us by those who have come before. Almost all of our reading consists of literature selected – from a vast number of available works – by other people. It is natural to want to take part in that process of selection, even in a small way. The process itself is extremely complicated, involving writers (and all their helpers), publishers, reviewers, professors, students, booksellers, and the general reading public. But we can develop an approximate model of what happens.

It is reasonable to assume that professors teach certain poets because they find them exciting and rewarding to read and discuss. If they didn't, they would drop them off the course, and in time a different group of poets would be selected for the canon. According to this view of canon-formation, books are put on courses for reasons that are essentially similar to, and comparable with, a student's own experience of literature – that is, because they are enjoyable to read. This method of selection encourages dialogue between students and professors. If students don't like a work, they can at least ask why it excited the professor enough for it to be put on the course list. This interaction makes literature more accessible – it provides a human explanation for "great literature," and it creates a link between the student's responses to literary works and those of the professor.

There is considerable inertia in the process of canon-formation. Sometimes an author becomes canonized, and is regularly taught in university courses, even though very few people actually enjoy reading him. The professor thinks, "I don't like Shelley very much, but he is a major Romantic poet, so I need to teach him." The students may also have a #3 response to Shelley, but be hesitant about saying so. As a result a poet can remain a part of the canon long after the reasons for his belonging there have disappeared. What this theory of canon-formation suggests is that the student should challenge the professor over the inclusion of Shelley, and the professor should challenge the status of Shelley as a canonized author. (It is often boring being taught a book which the professor doesn't like.) But you have to understand the process of canon-formation in order to initiate any change.

It should be admitted that a certain loss occurs when you begin to understand how works become canonized. There is a loss of the glamour that surrounds the "great authors," who seem to inhabit a realm that is almost divine, and who possess the magical power of creating great art. You begin to understand that "great art" is given that status because of the approval of a complex social network of professors, publishers, and readers, and you also see that the elevation of an author to major status has a significant political dimension. But frequently we overvalue things that we have come to admire without understanding. The loss in this case is justified by the gain: we understand how "greatness" is achieved, and we see that we can play a part in the process.

Why Study Theory Now?

In any group in which talking is the main activity, it is possible to draw a useful distinction between content and process. "Content" refers to the information being discussed, while "process" refers to the human interactions involved in the course of the discussion. A student may volunteer to provide the details of Coleridge's relation with his wife, ostensibly to clarify one of his poems – that is the content. The process might be the attempt on the part of the student to show that he is serious about his work, or that he identifies strongly with the professor. In university classes we usually pay attention to the content but ignore the process – even when the process is significant.

One reason for studying literary theory is that it calls attention to issues of process, such as how authors and texts are treated, how professors and students treat one another, and how the professor distinguishes between excellent and merely satisfactory work in the course. (Usually this distinction is not just a matter of the student "working hard" – it involves knowing the ideology of the professor, and what seem to her to be the important, valuable questions to ask about the content of the course.) Literary theory raises those issues which are often left submerged beneath the mass of information contained in the course, and it also asks questions about how the institution of great literature works. What makes a "great work" great? Who makes the decisions about what will be taught? Why are authors grouped into certain historical periods? The answers to fundamental questions like these are often unarticulated assumptions on the part of both the professor and the students.

Socrates said that the unexamined life is not worth living. The analogous statement about university courses is that "the unexamined course is not worth taking." Literary theory at its best helps us realize what we are really doing when we study literature.

Notes

1. I am using the word "ideology" in a neutral sense, and assuming that everyone has and uses an ideology, whether or not they are conscious of it. Often the word is used in a pejorative sense, to indicate a set of ideas which falsify or distort the way the world "really is." In my view, people cannot see the world as it really is, in an unbiased way; we inevitably acquire an ideology in growing up. We can abandon our ideology, and we can modify it, but we cannot escape having an ideology. Although I don't think ideologies can be evaluated objectively, I find some ideologies much more attractive than others.

2. Robert A. Johnson, *He: Understanding Masculine Psychology*, 2nd ed. (New York: Harper Row, 1989) x.

3. Felicia Hemans (1793-1835) was "commercially the most successful English-language poet of the nineteenth century and, commercially, the most successful woman poet ever" (Peter Cochrane, *Times Literary Supplement*, 21 July 1995, 13). Her early death is mourned by Wordsworth in his "Extempore Effusion upon the Death of James Hogg."

Suggestions for Further Reading

Terry Eagleton, *Literary Theory: An Introduction* (Oxford: Blackwell, 1983).

Raman Selden and Peter Widdowson, *A Reader's Guide to Contemporary*

Literary Theory, 3rd ed. (Lexington: University Press of Kentucky, 1993).

Roger Webster, *Studying Literary Theory: An Introduction* (London: Edward Arnold, 1990).

The above are three short books which cover many of the same topics as this book. All three have useful bibliographies.

There are many dictionaries and encyclopedias dealing with literary theory and criticism. I have found these two particularly helpful. The first is short, up-to-date and has brief and often witty entries; the second is a big volume, with entries up to 2,000 words long.

Chris Baldick, ed., *The Concise Oxford Dictionary of Literary Terms* (Oxford, 1990).

Irena Makaryk, ed., *Encyclopedia of Contemporary Literary Theory: Approaches, Scholars, Terms* (University of Toronto Press, 1993).

John M. Ellis, *The Theory of Literary Criticism: A Logical Analysis* (Berkeley and Los Angeles: University of California Press, 1974). This book presents clearly and forcefully the view that literature functions in many different contexts, not just the context in which it was written, and that it is a defining feature of literature that it is still of interest when its original context has disappeared.

Roland Barthes, *Criticism and Truth*, trans. and ed. Katrine Pilcher Keuneman (Minneapolis: University of Minnesota Press, 1987). This is a short, polemical book, in which Barthes defends the practice of re-interpreting literature through methods unknown at the time it was written (for example, by producing a Freudian reading of Racine). It is a clear statement about what came to be known as "*la nouvelle critique*" in France, which was based on structuralism.

CHAPTER TWO:

Monologue and Dialogue
in the Classroom

IN A CLASS WHICH contains thirty or more students, it is likely that the professor will spend a good deal of her time lecturing. In a class of a hundred or more, lecturing would seem to be the only possible method of teaching. In this chapter I want to suggest that there is an inherent contradiction between lecturing and education, and propose that the most important skill which an arts student should take away from four years at university is the ability to engage in meaningful dialogue with others. This subject might seem to be a side-issue in an introduction to literary theory, but it turns out that the idea of dialogue is crucial to some of the main issues addressed by literary theory.

In a letter to the *Times Literary Supplement,* one reader presented a powerful argument for a fundamental change in our educational philosophy. He maintained that

> ...for too long academics have unthinkingly accepted that the proper
> basic intellectual aim of inquiry is to improve knowledge and
> technology. This philosophy of knowledge is, however, dangerously,
> harmfully irrational. Knowledge and technology are important; but
> what the modern world desperately needs is the capacity to resolve its
> global problems and conflicts more cooperatively and rationally than it
> does at present.[1]

This argument maintains that our greatest need now is to learn to live peacefully with one another, and that this depends on finding ways of discussing issues that will lead to acceptable solutions. Universities, this writer feels, should train people in methods of cooperative discussion and thought, instead of simply producing more and more specialized knowledge. I think he is right in what he says about the global situation, and I would add that much of our satisfaction in life depends on our skills in connecting with other people – skills of dialogue, we might call them.

The Problems with Monologue

By the time they have completed a year at university, students have had a lot of experience with monologue, given that lecturing is the basic method of instruction in most first-year courses. Some lectures seem to imply that the student's mind is like an empty barrel, and the purpose of the lectures is to fill it up with information. Often, though not always, lectures are fairly boring, and there is a good reason for this: when information flows in a single direction (from professor to student), no consideration is given to what the student is experiencing – whether the information is having any effect, whether it is coming too quickly or too slowly, whether it fits into the patterns of thoughts and feelings in the student's mind, or whether it answers any particular need or desire in the listener. Going to a lecture is quite like reading a book, with the disadvantage that you can't stop reading, or skip passages, when you want to.

Many of our conversations with others are really a succession of monologues. These can be quite interesting because of the alternation of speakers, and the chance for everyone to speak from time to time. Sometimes, though, a compulsive talker will give you a ten-minute lecture on some subject of little or no interest to you – and usually this becomes boring just like some university lectures. You aren't being treated like a person with individual interests and concerns; you are simply being used as an audience.

Why Dialogue is Interesting

Dialogue begins when we are able to intervene and redirect or modify what another person is saying. If two people are interested in the same subject, and they are willing to learn from each other, an engaging process can occur. The first person outlines his or her view of the subject (at an appropriate length – dialogue depends on subtle sensing of how the other is responding), and implicitly asks, "What do you think of my account of this? Can you give me a better account? If you can, then I will adopt it."[2] This is an invitation for the second person to add his or her perceptions to the common pool of ideas.

In a full-blooded dialogue, each speech of the conversation adds something new to the shared view of the subject, and the feeling of growth can be very exciting. You realize that two people in conversation are more than the sum of the two individuals: together they are able to do things, and make discoveries, which neither could achieve alone. If the subject under discussion is of definite interest to you, then the process can be fascinating. In my opinion, the experience of dialogue is one of the finest things that university education in the humanities has to offer. It can give feelings of wholeness, concentration, and deep connection with another person. The concept of dialogue can also be a paradigm for other activities; it is not so much an idea as an experience that can be charged with emotion and the feeling of discovery.

Dialogues vary in quality, of course, and some are more satisfying than others. If the subject being discussed doesn't interest you particularly, then the intensity will be low – although the exchange may still be a pleasant one. With some people you share a lot of background, and so you have common reference-points and can communicate easily; with others, who have very different life-experiences, communication may be almost impossible. Different people use language in different ways, and this may enhance or impede the interchange. Some people talk too much for you, some too little.

The British critic and novelist David Lodge has said, "Conversation is like playing tennis with a ball made of Krazy Putty that keeps coming back over the net in a different shape."[3] Racquet sports present a good analogy for dialogue. For an involving game the partners have to be willing to make an effort and be reasonably well-matched to each other. If there is a serious imbalance in ability, the game will be less satisfying.

In general in the humanities today dialogue is not highly valued. For one thing, it is risky and open-ended. You have to be willing to expose yourself to engage in real dialogue, and you cannot predict where it will lead you. An eminent critic, William Empson, has said, "The object of life, after all, is not to understand things, but to maintain one's defences and equilibrium, and live as well as one can; it is not only maiden aunts who are placed like this." Professors (it stands to reason) like to be in control, and so dialogue can seem unattractive to them. Besides, the university milieu is obsessed with writing books and articles, and these are usually monologic forms of discourse. If you think you are trying to develop knowledge, then you probably feel it should be permanent, objective, and encodable in a book, which will last forever. A powerful myth in universities is that knowledge is eternal – although the history of knowledge shows that it is always provisional and often superseded by new knowledge. The German artist Albrecht Dürer acknowledged this when he wrote, "I shall let the little I have learnt go forth into the day in order that someone better than I may guess the truth, and in his work may prove and rebuke my error. At this I shall rejoice that I was yet a means whereby this truth has come to light."[4]

In spite of academic distaste for it, dialogue has a distinguished history. Plato's dialogues present an early example of the form, although they do not seem very open-ended, because Socrates always has the upper hand. The tradition of dialogue – that you should be able to present your views on a subject clearly and succinctly, and then be willing to listen to criticisms of them – is much stronger in philosophy than in literary studies, perhaps because of the example of Plato. Of course the ability to write riveting dialogue is important in many plays and novels – as examples consider the exchanges between Birkin and Ursula in D.H. Lawrence's *Women in Love* or between Antony and Cleopatra in Shakespeare's play. By and large, literary critics do not seem to value dialogue highly, perhaps because they are anxious to have the final word.

Dialogue in the Classroom

Is it reasonable to expect dialogue to take place in the classroom? I think the answer is "yes," especially for classes with less than thirty students; but aiming for dialogue sets a high standard, for both professors and students, and the attempt can turn out to be frustrating. It is well worth making the effort, though, if only because the alternative (lecturing) is such a poor pedagogical method for most students.

If a professor tries to generate a dialogue in class about a controversial part of a book (such as the section on ghosts in *Zen and the Art of Motorcycle Maintenance*, in which the author, Robert Pirsig, maintains that scientific laws are as intangible as spirits in Amerindian culture), the class will generally divide into two groups: those who have read the section and thought about it, and those who haven't. The students in the second group essentially become spectators in the class; they aren't equipped to take part. The real participants are the students who are moved by the book to say something about the issue. Dialogue is liable to fail if there are not enough participants. The non-participants may be willing to listen to what the professor has to say, but they are normally much less interested in the opinions of their peers.

There are a number of practices that can help or hinder dialogue:

Practices that help dialogue:

1. Identifying the common interests of the group.
2. Finding problems that need attention.
3. Listening when other people speak.
4. Encouraging others, or restraining yourself, in order to balance participation.
5. Identifying ideological differences between members of the group.
6. Restating a point so its meaning is clear to everyone.
7. Emphasizing a willingness to negotiate. Distinguishing between what is sacred to you, and what is negotiable.
8. Asking, or explaining, why a certain process is occurring in the class.
9. Identifying what is happening when a strange interaction occurs (for example, when one person tries to annihilate another).
10. Scaling things up or down to improve discussion (i.e. using a microscope or inverted telescope).
11. Finding an analogy – even a bizarre one – that helps explain something (for example, a conversation is like a game of tennis).
12. Pointing out a passage in the book being read which illustrates a point well.

Practices that hinder dialogue:

1. Engaging in private dialogue, between students or between a student and the professor.
2. Monologue.
3. Drawing on private knowledge (of a book, play, film, and so on) too much, without making that knowledge available to the rest of the class (e.g. by telling the story).
4. False objectifying (that is, expressing feelings as objective facts

about the book or the world).

5. Projecting extremes onto other people (e.g. making their position look ridiculous by taking it to an extreme which they would not accept).

6. Offering your view, and an absurd alternative.

7. Allowing an *argumentum ad hominem* (Latin for 'the argument against the person'; for example, "Smith was an alcoholic, so his view must be wrong," when, in fact, his view might be correct).

8. Dropping cynical one-liners that cut off the exchange of dialogue.

One of the greatest impediments to dialogue is the tendency of people with too much knowledge to swamp others with their learning. Professors are the most likely to do this, because they have spent much of their lives gathering knowledge, and talking fills up class time, but some students like doing it as well. One of the main pedagogical reasons for limiting discussion (in a particular class) to a single text is to give students an opportunity to be almost as well-prepared as the teacher.

Dialogue as an Analogy: The Relation between the Reader and the Writer

A basic problem in literary studies is to establish a model for the relationship between the reader and the author being read which balances the weight given to the experience of each of the two people involved. Until twenty years ago, it seems that these power struggles were usually resolved by allowing the author to dominate the reader. Reader-response criticism is to some extent a reaction to that unfair settlement, and it seems to neglect the past in favor of recording in minute detail the responses of contemporary readers.

A similar problem of relating the present and the past arises in the writing of historical accounts. Is it possible to simply give an account of "what actually happened"? Almost everyone agrees that with important historical events this is not possible. A historian has to *select* what will be given, and that selection, or the sieve used to make that selection, will reveal an ideological bias. In Chapter 9, on Vico, the argument will be presented that in order to construct a narrative sequence, the historian has to make fundamental choices that may lock him into a certain view of human events. So although history may be about the past, it sees the past from the present, and is coloured by the ideology of the author. One classical historian, M.I. Finley, has gone so far as to say that history is essentially "a dialogue in the present, about the present."[5]

The best model I have been able to discover to regulate the relation between the author and the reader is the model of dialogue. It is as though you are having a conversation with the author. If you abase yourself before the author, and see everything her way, then reading may come to resemble religious prostration before a dominating god. On the other hand, if the reader is only interested in his own experience, then he will not really connect with the author, and miss what she has to say. Of course, in a meaningful relation with an author, there will be a large area of overlap and agreement, where conflict will not be evident. But generally speaking I think readers should try to create a condition of dialogue with an author, where neither is squashed, and the reader feels liberated through the relationship. A visual illustration of the three possibilities (the reader ignoring the author, being dominated by him, and establishing a dialogue) can be found on page 213, in the imitations of Vincent van Gogh's paintings by four children.

Polylogue as a Model for Culture

If dialogue is a process that occurs between two people, polylogue occurs when several people participate. The American critic Kenneth Burke uses the model of what might go on in a seminar to shed light on the way culture itself operates:

> Imagine that you enter a parlor. You come late. When you arrive, others have long preceded you, and they are engaged in a heated discussion, a discussion too heated for them to pause and tell you exactly what it is about. In fact, the discussion had already begun long before any of them got there, so that no one present is qualified to retrace for you all the steps that had gone before. You listen for a while, until you decide that you have caught the tenor of the argument; then you put in your oar. Someone answers; you answer him; another comes to your defense; another aligns himself against you.... However, the discussion is interminable. The hour grows late, you must depart. And you do depart, with the discussion still vigorously in process.[6]

Polylogue seems to be a good model for the processes by which an academic field or a culture evolves, and it makes sense to try to achieve an analogous polylogue in the classroom, because the effort can help move the participants toward an understanding of how culture works.

Dialogism and the Work of Mikhail Bakhtin

If you want to use the idea of dialogue as a basis for understanding the world in a broad way, the work of the Russian thinker Mikhail Bakhtin is very suggestive and illuminating. He was a student in St. Petersburg during the Russian Revolution, suffered through the major upheavals which followed it, and survived the years of repression under Stalin. His major themes, articulated between 1924 and 1947, could serve as an excellent introduction to many of the central issues in literary theory since 1960.

The word "dialogism" has been coined to provide a label for Bakhtin's thinking about language, literature, and the way they are embedded in social life. Unlike the structuralists, whose views we will encounter in Chapter 6, Bakhtin saw language not as a system, but as a series of particular, singular utterances, arising from individual people living in specific places. These utterances occur in conversations or arguments between people, who don't always agree. So the meaning of what a certain person says on (for instance) October 24, 1917 *depends on the conversation he is taking part in*. The meaning depends on the relation of the utterance to a particular ongoing dialogue. Bakhtin felt that becoming a "self," or knowing your "self," was achieved through being able to be an "author" in this situation – being able to speak out, in dialogue with others who hold different opinions or beliefs.

Bakhtin thought that even single words and sentences were inherently dialogical. He felt that a word was a "shared territory," shared between the speaker and the listener, and that the meaning of a word could change as the social experience of the speakers changed. Similarly, a literary work can be thought of as a territory shared by the writer and the reader. Its meaning will change when the work is read in a later period, or in a culture different from the one in which it was written. This view of the meaning of utterances (and works of literature) is thoroughly relativistic. Another way of expressing Bakhtin's idea is to say that literature is like a figure on a background. If the background changes (this often happens when the listener or reader changes), the meaning will also shift.[7]

Bakhtin's experience of political life in post-revolutionary Russia (among other things) led him to draw a distinction between the dialogism of normal social life and the authoritarian attempt to impose (or allow) only one way of thinking or speaking, which he called "monologism." Life is various and chaotic; and some groups strive to impose order by allowing only one ideology to flourish. We could transplant this distinction and use it to mark the difference between authors who are authoritarian, dominating, and try to allow only one point of view (their own), and other authors, like Shakespeare and Dostoevsky, who normally incorporate several conflicting points of view in their works, and don't try to settle conflicts between their characters in a final way. Bakhtin thought that the novel was the literary form which best allowed a variety of languages and ideologies to be expressed, while he thought the lyric poem and the epic were inherently monological forms of literature.

E. M. Forster's novel *A Passage to India* provides a good illustration of the distinction between the monological and the dialogical, and also shows the importance of the concept of "otherness" which is crucial to this distinction. In Forster's novel, the British administrators in Chandrapore do their best to stay aloof from the native Indians, and pretend that they can live in a monological world – their own little England. The Moslems are presented as being very different from the British in their friendships and their social interaction, and the Hindu Brahmin philosopher, Professor Godbole, is made to seem almost incomprehensible at times. But three of the British characters try to bridge the gap and engage with the Moslems. The novel is made up of a series of misinterpretations caused by cultural differences, interspersed with a few moments of illumination when members of different cultures hear each other and are partially understood. One message of the novel is highly Bakhtinian: that although engaging in dialogue with people who are very different from yourself can be threatening, it can enrich life greatly. Pursuing monologism, on the other hand, can lead to the death of the soul.

Bakhtin had a strong sense of how we live in a sea of words, which he called the logosphere. Words flow around and through us almost all the time, and give expression to our inmost desires and fears. Monologism drastically limits what we can say, and perhaps even what we can think to ourselves. Bakhtin especially valued the forces which upset rigid authority, and one of these, he thought, was the spirit of carnival, in which kings and beggars exchange roles and costumes, and social relations appear in startlingly new perspectives. The freedom and liberation of carnival, combatting the authority and decorum of monologism, can be used to represent one of the primary tendencies of literary criticism in the late 20th century: the desire to subvert the dominant ideology (whether it is seen as bourgeois, capitalist, or patriarchal), and to develop new languages and new critical methodologies which will allow us to see the world in a new way, and mold it closer to our hearts' desires.

For example, the impulses behind feminist literary criticism are quite easy to grasp for most people: the recognition that women see the world in a different way from most men, and speak differently from them. Many women are therefore determined that these differences should not be ignored, marginalized, or squashed. Feminism says, you would see the world differently if you were a woman. Deconstruction says, you would see the world differently if your language were altered in certain ways. Multiculturalism makes a similar point about cultural differences. Part of the challenge of living in the late 20th century is that dialogue, and dialogism, have become essential in an increasingly complex and diverse society. Dialogue (as opposed to monologue) in the classroom can help us prepare to live more fully in our own times.

Notes

1. Nicholas Maxwell, Letter to the *Times Literary Supplement*, 7 December 1984, 1415.

2. Karl Popper, "Towards a Rational Theory of Tradition," *Conjectures and Refutations: The Growth of Scientific Knowledge*, 4th ed. (London: Routledge and Kegan Paul, [1963] 1972) 127.

3. David Lodge, *Small World* (Harmondsworth: Penguin, 1985) 25.

4. Quoted by Popper, 2.

5. M.I. Finley, *Aspects of Antiquity* (1968; Harmondsworth: Pelican, 1972) 15.

6. Kenneth Burke, *The Philosophy of Literary Form: Studies in Symbolic Action* (Louisiana State University Press, 1941) 110-111.

7. Another way in which the meanings of words can shift is when they are "double-voiced," i.e. spoken as though they had quotation marks around them. We then recognize that they may carry a meaning other

than the one which the speaker intends, because someone else has said them in another context, with another meaning. This usually happens in ironic speech, but it may happen in more complex situations, too. If an older person says to you, "To thine own self be true," is he giving you sincere advice, or is he consciously quoting the pompous, interfering Polonius, and so undermining his own counsel? An analogous problem can occur for the speaker (as opposed to the listener), when, uncertain of how to respond, he produces a phrase or a sentiment which he has heard somewhere else before. Who, in this instance, is speaking? This introduces the question, a fertile one for structuralists and post-structuralists, of how (and to what degree) our selves are created by the language (and the literature) which is there, in place, before we arrive on the scene, and which (to some extent) structures our thoughts and our feelings.

Suggestions for Further Reading

Michael Holquist, *Dialogism: Bakhtin and His World* (London and New York: Routledge, 1990).

David Lodge, *After Bakhtin: Essays in Fiction and Criticism* (London and New York: Routledge, 1990), especially the essay "After Bakhtin," 87-99.

CHAPTER THREE:

Literature and the Ideology of Science

WE LIVE IN A WORLD dominated by science. The reigning ideology in North America makes most of us believe – even without our thinking about it – that the most solid and real kind of knowledge is scientific knowledge, and that the most important researchers work in scientific fields. Most of us think that our lives have been greatly changed by scientific developments, and that the quality of human civilization will continue to improve because of new developments in science and technology.

The prestige of science has a powerful effect on literary studies. Your view of literature will to some extent depend on your relation to the sciences, and that makes it important to explore the ideology of science early in this book. It is easy to feel, for instance, that in comparison to the knowledge given by science, the knowledge offered by literature is "soft" and suited to second-rate minds. In most universities it is easy to switch from science to arts, but if you want to move in the opposite direction you have to go back and start at the beginning. Scientific knowledge is thought to be "objective," and therefore universally valid; knowledge in the humanities has a greater degree of subjective content, and so it is hard to be certain that it is absolutely solid.

Within universities there is often a barrier between the arts and the sciences, or between the arts and engineering. Students in one field tend to pride themselves on being different, and better, than their counterparts in the other field. This is the result mainly of the competitive nature of human groups, and the need many people feel, especially in the first half of their lives, to be connected with a superior group and manifestly not connected with a group considered inferior. The same tendencies can be seen in the conflicts between other pairs: Catholics and Protestants, Pro-life and Pro-choice groups, and capitalists and socialists.

As students of literature, we need to acknowledge the enormous contributions of science and technology to our lives, and then examine the real differences and similarities between the arts and sciences. The differences will give us a sense of our particular field of action, and the similarities will show us ways in which we can be more effective in what we do.

Although the rise of the sciences has marked our lives in fundamental ways, not all of these developments are attractive or desirable. Our living conditions, our modes of communication and transportation, the quality of our health care, and the dissemination of great works of art have all changed radically in the last hundred years, thanks to new developments in science and technology, and for most people these changes have improved life in significant ways. At the same time, in the 20th century we have been able to engage in wars that are unparalleled in brutality and human suffering; we have created unattractive and sometimes dangerous working conditions in many industries; and with nuclear weapons we have made the extermination of the human race a possibility.

The prestige of science is largely based on these changes, and even the changes for the worse are impressive because of their scale. But it is interesting to consider areas in which science has had little effect, and problems science has failed to solve. How do we relate to our friends? How do we express our feelings? How do we choose whether to marry, or have children? Why do half the first marriages in North America end in divorce, and why are half the children in our schools being raised by only one parent? How should children be raised? Why is there so much drug abuse? What ideology should we live by? What are the claims of the religious life on us? What are our obligations to other people in society, both at home and around the world, and especially those who live under terrible conditions of famine, sickness, or exploitation?

Some of these areas have been affected by scientific and technological progress – birth control has influenced how marriages work, and friendships can be conducted over great distances in ways that weren't possible two hundred years ago. But we still have to make decisions – some of the most important decisions in our lives – without any guidance at all from science. It is possible, however, to get some guidance from a good novel. Someone thinking about marriage might be deeply influenced by the relationships presented in *Anna Karenina* – the failure of Anna's relation both with her husband and with her lover, and the success of the relation between Levin and Kitty.

Science has nothing to say about some of the most important problems in our lives, because those problems depend on feelings and values, and because they are a matter of choosing to be connected with other human beings – spouses, friends, mentors, clubs, churches, and all the other groups in which people who have similar concerns get together to support and help one another. I think that our happiness depends to a very large extent on these connections, and literature has a lot to say about them. One of the best reasons for studying literature is that it allows us to try experiences out imaginatively to see if they feel right. This can be a helpful guide for making real choices in life.

The Similarities between Science and Literature

If we think of ourselves as students of literature, and different from scientists and engineers, it is logical to attribute negative qualities to members of the other group. The Swiss psychoanalyst Carl Jung calls this process "projection," because the individual projects things in his own mind onto other people who are seen as being different. Often the qualities projected are important aspects of the individual which he does not want to acknowledge or recognize in himself. One of the goals of psychoanalysis is to help patients withdraw the projections – that is, for the individual to stop projecting onto the other, and see the other as he really is. One way to embark on this process is to look for the similarities between yourself and the other; and scientists and students of literature are similar in significant ways.

In an essay about how traditions work, the Austrian philosopher of science, Karl Popper, explains a fundamental similarity between the purposes of science and those of literature. He puts them both in the context of classical Greek thought, which was often expressed in the form of a myth, sometimes with religious overtones. Popper is thinking of the tendency of the Greeks to explain natural phenomena, such as thunder and lightning, by saying that Zeus was angry, and so he was throwing lightning bolts at someone he wanted to punish. Popper says that basically scientists and myth-makers are trying to do the same thing: they are trying to explain why things happen the way they do. But there is a crucial difference (here it appears as a difference between science and religion), which is the development of a critical attitude:

My thesis is that what we call "science" is differentiated from the older myths not by being something distinct from a myth, but by being accompanied by a second-order tradition – that of critically discussing the myth. Before, there was only the first-order tradition. A definite story was handed on. Now there was still, of course, a story to be handed on, but with it went something like a silent accompanying text of a second-order character: "I hand it on to you, but tell me what you think of it. Think it over. Perhaps you can give us a different story." This second-order tradition was the critical or argumentative attitude. It was, I believe, a new thing, and it is still the fundamentally important thing about the scientific tradition. If we understand that, then we shall have an altogether different attitude towards quite a number of problems of scientific method. We shall understand that, in a certain sense, science is myth-making just as religion is. You will say: "But the scientific myths are so very different from the religious myths." Certainly they are different. But why are they different? Because if one adopts this critical attitude then one's myths do become different. They change; and they change in the direction of giving a better and better account of the world – of the various things which we can observe. And they also challenge us to observe things which we would never have observed without these theories or myths. [1]

This account of science "softens" it, by pointing out that scientific explanations evolve, and that scientific doctrines are open to question and can be revised in the light of new information. Here Popper is emphasizing the importance of dialogue. Basically science progresses through one person proposing a hypothesis, and another one criticizing it.

What has this to do with literature? Literature, too, gives accounts of things. It tells us, for instance, how Hamlet manages to emerge from depression and engage with the real world around him – and the status of *Hamlet* in our society implies that we think it is a valuable account. One reason a work of literature becomes a classic is that it presents a powerful and important human experience in language. But the canon of the accepted classics is always open to change, just like the body of accepted scientific theories. If we are interested in the vitality of the canon of accepted classics, and how new works become integrated into it – a central question in literary studies – then science, and the social structure which maintains it, can present a number of helpful models and procedures. For instance:

(i) Science has been successful at bringing together people who have the same interests and who are trying to solve the same problems. These are the people who can really help each other through dialogue. Researchers in literature tend to be grouped around historical periods and individual authors, rather than around shared problems, and this sometimes makes exchange more difficult. Two Milton specialists may be interested in very different problems related to Milton, and so have virtually nothing to say to each other.

(ii) Scientists make a clear distinction between contemporary problems worth solving and the history of science. In literary studies, the historical and the contemporary are blended in a way that is confusing. One result is that there is little general consensus about what the important contemporary problems in literary studies are.

(iii) Scientists try to distinguish between central and peripheral problems, between the problems that are vitally important to solve, and the problems that are of much less significance. This allows them to mobilize the resources to work on the big problems. In literary studies this distinction is not made, and so the energy of groups cannot be focused in the same way.

(iv) A ground rule of science is that scientists will be honest in what they report. Anyone who is found falsifying results will cease being treated as a member of the scientific community. One possible corresponding requirement in discussions of literature would be strict honesty about feelings and responses to works of literature. This may be more difficult than reporting scientific findings accurately, but it is a goal worth pursuing.

(v) In science there is a high value placed on the development of broad, revealing hypotheses. Often these turn out to be wrong, but they represent progress when they are articulated, and there is no shame attached to being wrong in an interesting way. A similar attitude would be valuable in literary studies, too; critics and teachers often seem to be primarily concerned with details about texts or the lives of authors that have no general relevance or applicability.

In pointing out these five ways in which critics could learn from scientists, I am not saying that criticism itself should be scientific or that science is a higher activity than studying literature. Nor am I saying that the two fields are fundamentally the same. There are both similarities and differences. The similarities are related to the fact that the two are fields of study, supported by a complex social network of professors, students, and researchers. The primary difference is the fact that science tries to be objective, while literary study involves subjectivity and personal response, even if these are not acknowledged.

Two Kinds of Community

The question of honesty is a significant one for a class that runs on dialogue. Often professors and students are unwilling to discuss their personal responses to a work of literature, because these responses would bear on important issues in their own lives – so it would make them feel vulnerable. What you might be willing to discuss with a close friend you might prefer to be silent about in a literature class.

Often we don't show ourselves as we really are to other people. We want to make a good impression; we want others to think we are strong, intelligent, sensitive, in control of our lives, and so on. Most of us want to be admired, or at least liked, and so we tend to construct a public self we hope will elicit the desired response. In university classes, in addition, it is often easy to guess the kind of response or comment the professor wants, and to provide what is expected.

This sabotages the whole process of dialogue, and that is why the tradition of honesty in science is worth promoting in literary studies. A dialogue in which one or more people are faking their responses can only be frustrating; it can't lead anywhere. After experiencing classes in which discussion is based on dishonesty and faking (which often reduces honest people to silence), it is a pleasant surprise to step into a group in which people are open and willing to talk about their own problems, difficulties, and uncertainties. It is reassuring and relaxing to find that other people have confusions in their lives too – it can make an individual feel less unusual. It is also much easier to care about people who are willing to be honest and to expose their vulnerabilities.

A university class is not usually the place in which we feel we can reveal our inmost secrets, and sometimes students are ostracized when they take advantage of an open group to swamp others with their emotions. But it is hard to generalize about groups of this sort, because what occurs depends entirely on the membership. A group that can accept the play of personal feelings is much more stimulating than one that avoids them by placing an implicit taboo on personal contributions. Learning what we can and cannot say is an important aspect of participating in groups. Certainly the quality of interaction in a group will be greatly improved if the members don't feel that they have to present an idealized self-image, and if they feel free to confess to inadequacies, misunderstandings, and even a general lack of comprehension about what is happening in class. Often these feelings turn out to be shared by other members of the class. If that is the case, the confusion can effectively freeze the class and make interesting dialogue impossible.

Frankness about individual responses to works of literature is important if a discussion in class is to be successful, but no professor can force students to be open. When a class discussion works well, however, it provides an experience of personal sharing and discovery that cannot be duplicated in a science class, or in any humanities course that systematically avoids dealing with what is personal and subjective. So while there is a lot for students of literature to learn from science as a field of inquiry, the two fields cannot be helpfully compared on the basis of the knowledge they generate. Literary studies deal with significant human questions that science does not consider, and discussions of literature can provide an experience of shared subjectivity that is rare and can be both exciting and illuminating. Although in some ways our world is dominated by science, the mandate of literary studies is large, important, and easy to justify. It is a mark of the current power of scientific ideology that this justification is not widely understood and accepted.

Note

1.   Karl Popper, "Towards a Rational Theory of Tradition," *Conjectures and Refutations: The Growth of Scientific Knowledge*, 4th ed. (1963; London: Routledge and Kegan Paul, 1972) 127.

Suggestions for Further Reading

David Smail, *Illusion and Reality: The Meaning of Anxiety* (London: Dent,
1984). One of the main themes of this very interesting book is that
scientific ideology encourages us to think that we ought to see ourselves
objectively – which discounts feelings and intuitions, and can produce
anxiety. (See note 8 at the end of the Introduction, on page 25, for
further information on this book.)

CHAPTER FOUR:

Paradigms, Paradigm Change, and Interpretation

ONE IMPORTANT WAY IN WHICH the study of science can help us understand literature and the problem of ideologies is by showing that science itself has divisions which are like ideological splits, and which are a necessary and natural part of its ongoing development. This thesis first became well known because of a fascinating book written by Thomas Kuhn in 1961, called *The Structure of Scientific Revolutions.*[1] One critic has said that it "is arguably the most frequently cited work in the humanities and social sciences in the past twenty-five years."[2] Ironically, but understandably, its main thesis has been much more warmly received in these areas than in the sciences themselves. My purpose in this chapter is to give an outline of Kuhn's argument, and show why it is illuminating about the study of literature.

Kuhn says that if we look at the history of science, we can see that most scientific activity falls into one of two categories – normal science, and revolutionary science. Normal science, Kuhn says, is done by a community of people which is held together because its members share certain assumptions about what they are doing and what the world is like. They share what is called a *paradigm*. As an example, we can think of European astronomers prior to 1600, who generally shared the belief that the Earth was at the center of the universe and the moon, the sun, and the planets revolved around the Earth in circular orbits, or orbits that could be constructed out of circles. The outer edge of the universe was a celestial sphere, which held the stars in place. It was as though the universe was located inside an enormous black basketball, and outside the ball was heaven, where the Lord of Creation held his court, surrounded by angels and archangels.

The Catholic church was directly involved in astronomy because there were important connections between Christianity, the Biblical account of creation, and what astronomers said about the universe. The church maintained that the universe had been created for human beings, and so their home (the Earth) had to be at the *center* of the universe. Another belief influencing astronomers was that the most perfect and God-like form of motion was circular, and while it was clear that there were all kinds of non-circular motion on Earth, it was thought that all motion between the orbit of the moon and the celestial sphere was perfectly circular. The planets were thought to be held in place by glass spheres. These rotated slowly because of complicated invisible clockwork, which in turn caused the planets to move.

Although there were no telescopes before 1600, astronomers kept careful records of the movements of the planets, and when their observations did not suggest circular orbits for the planets, they constructed elaborate circles-upon-circles to account for the paths of the planets. This is a good example of how the geocentric or Earth-centered paradigm influenced thought. Astronomers did not simply see what was there in the sky; they constructed what they saw out of what they expected to see. The theory came before the "facts," and helped to construct them.

Around 1530 Copernicus wrote an account of the solar system that placed the sun at its center; the Earth and the other planets went around the sun, and the moon around the Earth. This new paradigm fitted in much better with the data which astronomers had collected, but Copernicus was aware that the heliocentric (or sun-centered) view of the solar system had revolutionary implications, and he refused to publish his views during his own lifetime. In 1616 Galileo had a head-on collision with the church because he openly promoted the Copernican paradigm, and supported it with observations made with the newly invented telescope.

Galileo's argument with the church represents a paradigm conflict, in which two fundamentally different models of the solar system competed for supremacy. It is clear enough to us now that Galileo was right, but it was not at all clear to most people in 1600. To switch from one paradigm to the other caused major disruptions and upset the faith of many people. Astronomers working with the Earth-centered model had evolved complicated explanations of the movements of the planets; for them, switching to the Copernican model meant throwing out years of work and starting over. The church objected to the heliocentric paradigm because it seemed an insult both to humanity and to Christ that they be displaced from the center of divine creation. It was also difficult for the church to accept correction at the hands of astronomers, when it claimed to have certain knowledge in this area.

As the heliocentric paradigm began to gain adherents, the science of astronomy entered what Kuhn calls a "revolutionary" phase, which is very different from the period of "normal" science. During a revolutionary period, there are two or more competing paradigms – two models of the solar system, in this case – and it is not clear which is preferable. Each paradigm has advantages, and one of the main advantages of the old paradigm is that most people understand and accept it. Each paradigm is based on "facts," but since the paradigm itself defines what counts as a fact, the "facts" supporting each paradigm are different. Galileo was the first to discover the moons of Jupiter, by using a telescope. This proved to him that Jupiter was not kept in place by a glass sphere, because such a sphere would be broken by the moons crashing through it. But for the papal authorities, the existence of these moons was not a fact; they thought the moons appeared only because of the telescope – perhaps they were even painted on the lenses in some way.

It is a regular feature of paradigm conflict that the two parties do not agree on what the facts are. This situation is especially complex because there is no higher authority to settle the matter. A similar situation often exists when a married couple separates. If you listen to both the husband's and the wife's accounts of what went wrong in the marriage, you usually discover that they don't agree about the significant facts of the case. Each person sees a different marriage. Neither can see the whole picture.

A further aspect of paradigm conflict is that it usually involves strong feelings, particularly anger and frustration. This is not just an intellectual matter. When your fundamental beliefs about the world are attacked in some way, you tend to feel insecure and upset, and this can put defenders of the old paradigm in a rage. If you are promoting a new paradigm, then you feel excited by your new discoveries made with its help, and it can be bitterly disappointing when they are not only not welcomed, but actually denied.

The uncertainty involved in revolutionary science, with its paradigm conflicts, can be appreciated if we think in political terms about the

global opposition between capitalists and communists in the years between the end of the Second World War and 1989. In this case there
were two competing groups, one led by the United States and the other
by the Soviet Union. They were proposing very different patterns for
the organization of society. Each hoped to gain adherents by changing
people's minds about how they wanted to live. The extremists in each
camp wanted to defeat the opposition completely – to remove it from
the world. If you were living in North America, you probably didn't
feel much need to choose between the two, because you didn't have any
real alternative to the society in which you were living. The situation
was different, however, in a country such as Nicaragua, where there was
an ongoing struggle between the two paradigms. In 1989 the communist countries in Eastern Europe found they had a choice, and chose to
start changing their paradigm toward capitalism and free enterprise.

Once you become aware of the existence of paradigms, and how they
influence the way people think about the world, you can see that the
"truths" about the world – about religion, politics, and even science –
are not absolute truths; they depend on particular paradigms. You cannot look at the world except through a paradigm, and what you see depends on the paradigm you are working with. If your father is a busi-
nessman in a capitalist country, you may simply assume that it is
acceptable for one person's income to be a hundred times that of another person. If you were a papal astronomer in 1500, it was a fact that
the earth was at the center of the universe.

Problems with Paradigm Differences

Another example of paradigm change brings us closer to home, because it
has significant implications about the nature of education. What is the
mind? How do we conceptualize or visualize the mind, and how does this
influence our ideas of mental development? In the 18th-century the mind
was often considered to be like an empty blackboard (a *tabula rasa*). During
the course of a person's life, experiences and sensations left marks on the
blackboard, and knowledge was a result of those marks. This paradigm is
characteristic of the empiricist philosophers, who wanted to emphasize
that knowledge comes through experience ("there is nothing in the mind
which is not first in the senses," they said), rather than directly from God
through revelation. During the 19th century, romantic poets and thinkers
objected that this paradigm made the mind too passive –it made it seem as

though the mind could be shaped any way the shaper desired, by simply providing the appropriate experiences. The empiricist paradigm seemed to lead to determinism, according to which a person was *merely* the product of his or her experience. In opposition to this, the romantics proposed a new model for the mind – it was seen as an organism (such as a flower) that grows according to its own *inner* laws. It is affected by its environment (if there is no water, a flower will die), but it contains in its seed the pattern of its ultimate development. This paradigm implied that the educator had to take account of the individual natures of his students; there was no point in trying to educate a rose to become a cob of corn. Ideally, according to this paradigm, the teacher should provide a nourishing setting for each student. In the 20th century a new model for the mind emerged – the computer, which introduces the image of programming as an analogy for education.

It is still possible to find educators who believe in each of these paradigms, or behave as if they did. Very often a good education depends on choosing teachers whose paradigm is consistent with what you want to happen. Different phases of education will require different paradigms, as well. An 18th-century paradigm would seem appropriate for "learning the facts" of history, while the plant or the computer analogy would be better for learning about historiography – the study of how books of history are written. This subject will be discussed in more detail in Chapter 9, with reference to the Italian historian Giambattista Vico.

Paradigms and Dialogue

If you accept the idea that you are always looking at the world through a set of assumptions, or a paradigm, then you have to admit that knowledge cannot be absolute. Anything that you know, you only know relative to the paradigm you are using. You cannot expect someone working in a different paradigm to agree with your knowledge. You cannot force him or her to agree with you by an appeal to the facts, since facts emerge as the result of the operation of a particular paradigm.

Some people do not want to acknowledge the existence of paradigms, because they want to have access to absolute truth. There are understandable, though not very admirable, reasons for wanting access to some absolute truth. Life is much easier if you have truth at your disposal – many difficult decisions are eliminated, and often you can use your truth to gain power over other people. Students are often willing to submit to an absolute authority because they aspire to achieve a similar kind of authority themselves. Many professors find their students yearn for "the truth," and it can be tempting to fabricate one.

There are, however, many advantages to doing away with absolute truth. The action tends to make people more tolerant and open to others with whom they disagree. You don't want to burn people at the stake if you understand the operation of paradigms, and it also helps you understand how communities or cultural subgroups work, because they are generally built up of people who share a paradigm in a particular area of life. As with a group of scientists doing normal science, people who share a paradigm can make assumptions about one another, converse rapidly, and make use of a local idea of what constitutes "facts" and "the truth."

Recognizing the existence of paradigms has a fundamental effect on the way a person engages in dialogue. When you are talking with another person, you become aware that there are basically two distinct possibilities: either you share a paradigm, or there is a paradigm conflict between you and the other person. You need to proceed in very different ways in these two cases. When you share a paradigm, you can move much more quickly, you can predict better what the other will say, and you can count on your evidence being accepted. Your dialogue can be tight, precise, racy, and witty. You can willingly accept a good deal of toughness and anger because you share a basic commitment with the other person.

If you sense that there is a paradigm difference between you and the other person, then you have to be much more tentative, careful, and open, and you have to listen extremely carefully to understand what the other person is saying. You can't assume that the other person is experiencing the world the way you do, and you have to make a much greater effort to get into the other person's world, and feel what it is like. You have to expect that the other's truths will not be valid for you. You need to be curious about the other person's world if the conversation is going to be worthwhile, because it is not liable to shed much light on your own immediate experience. You need to assume that there will be fundamental differences between you, and, if the dialogue is going to continue for long, you will eventually have to identify the paradigm differences and work out some kind of compromise over them.

Paradigms and Interpretations

One way of recognizing the existence of paradigms and their influence on how we see the world is to say that we are always interpreting the world around us, and that we can never be sure that we are seeing it as it actually is — especially in complex situations such as meeting a new person, reading a new book, or starting an English course. We are filtering what we see through our paradigm or our ideology, and we can't get at reality in its raw state.

I want in this book to use "interpretation" in a very broad way, and maintain that whenever we read a book or a poem we produce an interpretation of it. Even if we only register boredom, that is a significant interpretation of what we have experienced. (Boredom is not simple, and often it is a way of shutting out troubling experiences.) The single most significant aspect of interpretation, in my view, is the degree of importance we ascribe to the book. We usually remember little about a book that bores us. Some books temporarily hold our interest, but we take nothing away from them. Some books engage us, and we remember things about them for a long time. Some books (these are the really significant ones for each of us) actually change the way we see the world, and we never revert to our earlier paradigm. Sometimes the Bible has this effect on people who are converted to Christianity, but the same effect occurs with secular literature too. The influential French critic Roland Barthes reports that Marcel Proust's long novel, *A la recherche du temps perdu*, formed his mind in fundamental ways, and William Wordsworth's poetry, especially "Tintern Abbey" and *The Prelude*, had a similar effect on me. It is often interesting to know what books have formed the minds of critics and teachers with whom you come in contact.

A professor or a student may produce an essay or a lecture on the subject, "What does *The French Lieutenant's Woman* mean?" This will be an interpretation in the narrower sense of the word; it will cover the main events in the book and assemble them in a more or less interesting way. But what is selected as a "main event," and how these events are put together, will depend on the writer's interpretive paradigm. The interpretation cannot be innocent or objective. Any critic who claims to be transparent, innocent, and simply presenting the object "as it is," is deluding himself.

I have used Kuhn to prepare for the main point of this chapter — that in literary studies there are a number of different interpretive paradigms, and they operate in much the same way as do Kuhn's paradigms in science. Different critics and professors work with different paradigms, and anyone wanting to participate in the literary community has to learn how to deal with this difficulty.

Students sometimes encounter this problem when they realize that they are expected to write different kinds of essays for different professors, and that an essay that received an A from one professor might receive a low B from another. Some professors like a lot of quotations and footnotes; some don't. Some like a tight, logical argument; some prefer more flow and feeling. Some professors are interested in the personal opinions of their students, and some want objectivity.

Encountering these variations can be a frustrating and alienating experience for students, who are likely to complain that the department has not worked out a common policy on these matters. But what the students are encountering is not just a fragmented department, but the fragmentation of the modern world. There is no general agreement about what is true or important, and this dissension is present in many aspects of academic life. The idea of paradigms helps you cope with this situation, and allows you to see the freedom inherent in it. For in some ways it is easier to serve several masters than just one. When there is a diversity of authorities there is a degree of choice, and the possibility of working out the details of your own paradigm.

Paradigms as Social Constructions

Someone might object to this whole theory of paradigms by saying, "What this really shows is that everyone has a different experience of the world, and so everyone ends up with his or her own individual paradigm. This means that we have nothing in common, and we can't communicate properly, because we are always involved in paradigm conflicts."

That is a skeptical point of view, and for some people it may accurately express how they feel about their relations with others. My own reply is that I am not a skeptic, because there are some communities whose paradigms I am happy (or at least willing) to accept and share. Paradigms are social constructions, like natural languages. There is no point in speaking a language that only you know; you want to speak languages that allow you to communicate with other people. Recognizing the importance of shared paradigms, and valuing the communication that can occur when a paradigm is shared, can give you a new respect for communities, and a willingness to tolerate the restrictions they impose.

Having said that, I should admit that most people seem to feel that the full meaning of their lives cannot be realized in any one community, or set of communities. A student who goes to class with one group of people, drinks beer with another, and plays on the basketball team, probably feels that some essential part of herself never receives expression in any of her social engagements. Identifying and making public that essence can be a powerful incentive for reading and discussing literature. Here we touch on the theme of the search for authority – the search for an author who has authority for you.

Paradigms for the Interpretation of Literature

The rest of this book will be concerned with presenting different ways in which literature can be interpreted. Historical criticism, new criticism, structuralism, deconstruction, and feminist analysis are all different types of interpretation, and present different paradigms for understanding literature. Essentially these theories inhabit different worlds, although there is some overlapping and interconnection. Each has its own ideology; each proposes a different model for the relationship between human beings and the world we live in. Reading the work of a structuralist, a historical critic, and a feminist on *Hamlet* is like visiting three different countries. Each type of critic approaches the text with a particular set of concerns and desires, and finds material in the play which responds to his or her overtures.

According to Thomas Kuhn, a field of inquiry does not become a mature science until a dominant paradigm emerges and everyone using other paradigms is seen as doing marginal or trivial work. Before that, the field is in a *preparadigm* state, and it has the following characteristics. There is a huge variety of activity; people feel free to work in their own idiosyncratic ways; communication between members of the profession is relatively poor; and people writing books and essays usually feel the need to "begin at the beginning," because there are no shared assumptions to count on. This is a good description of the state of literary studies in the mid-1990s: there are a large number of schools of criticism, and a lot of mavericks who don't want to belong to any school. There is an incessant debate over fundamental issues, and a good deal of competition between the various schools to produce a paradigm that will subsume the others. Perhaps in fifty years a dominant paradigm will have emerged, and work in literary studies will seem less chaotic. At the moment, the only option seems to be to live with the chaos, to try to enjoy it, and to keep an eye out for the emergence of a master paradigm. "May you live in an interesting time" is an ancient Chinese curse. This is an interesting time in literary studies, when everything seems up for grabs.

A Woman and a Man Reading *The French Lieutenant's Woman*

To illustrate how a paradigm difference between two people can produce different readings of a single text, I want to sketch the responses of a woman and a man — we will call them Emily and George — to John Fowles's novel *The French Lieutenant's Woman*. Not all men and women would necessarily focus on the issues that arise in these accounts of the book, but some might.

George found the book fascinating almost from the first page, because it dealt with problems he had pondered a good deal in the course of his life. How do you decide if you want to get married? If you commit yourself to marriage, what should you do if you find yourself falling in love with another woman, who makes you realize that your commitment to your fiancée is built on an insecure, and perhaps eroding, foundation? What role does mystery play in drawing you to another person, and does that mystery inevitably disappear as you become familiar with a woman? In a practical rather than theoretical manner, George found himself identifying strongly with Charles Smithson, the hero of the novel, who was embroiled with exactly these questions. At the opening of the novel, Charles, the son of a wealthy aristocrat in Victorian England, is engaged to Ernestina Freeman, whose father is a member of the rising middle class and the owner of a successful department store. Ernestina is pretty in a conventional way and dresses stylishly, but her education has left her narrow-minded and self-centered. Shortly after the book begins, Charles finds himself attracted to another woman, Sarah Woodrough — the "French lieutenant's woman" of the title — who is lower-class, poor, poorly dressed, eccentric, and possibly insane. Charles thinks of himself as her protector and helper, but gradually he is drawn into a sexual relationship with her, almost against his will. He then has to deal with the conflict in his allegiances.

For George, the central action in this book is how Charles deals with the problem of commitment to another person. Everything else in the book radiates from it. The subplot, concerning the marriage of Charles's servant, echoes and amplifies the main plot. Dr Grogan, the older man who advises Charles at key points in the novel, leads the life of a man who has chosen not to marry.

Emily also found *The French Lieutenant's Woman* intriguing, but from another point of view. She had always felt squashed and hampered by the restrictions placed on girls and women, and she was not attracted by the standard roles of housewife and mother. She sympathized with Ernestina, who had been smothered in much the same way as Emily had been; Emily saw that Ernestina was much less liberated and energetic than she might have been, and Emily could guess how this had come about. But it was Sarah who really interested her. Sarah had had few advantages in life, apart from her strong mind and passionate nature, and society was closing in all around her. Her main problem was not whom to marry, but how to lead an interesting and involving life without becoming ensnared in the traps that society, and particularly men, set for her. Emily saw that Sarah deliberately deceived people so that they could not pin her down and that in order to retain her freedom she willingly accepted the disguise of insanity. Even in her developing relation with Charles, to whom she was very attracted, Sarah employed deception in order to involve him, and she later led him on in order to make him face his real feelings about his engagement to Ernestina. Emily sympathized with Sarah's need for independence, and she could understand why Sarah had chosen to disappear just when Charles was ready to declare his love for her and ask her to marry him.

The main action in this book is different for George and Emily, and the parts that arouse their greatest interest are not the same. They could almost be said to be reading different books — although the same text has passed beneath their eyes. In reading something as long as a novel, it is impossible to give equal attention to everything, or to remember everything with equal force. The structures of the novel remaining in the minds of George and Emily after they had finished reading the book were radically different. To compound this problem, the novel has two endings. In the first Charles and Sarah end up together, presumably about to marry, and we discover they have a two-year-old child, conceived on the one occasion on which they made love. In the second ending they separate; the child is not theirs; and Charles has to make his way into the world again, alone, after an enormous detour. The novel George has read is better completed by the first ending, because Charles has dedicated himself to finding and marrying Sarah, at the cost of great personal suffering: he deserves her. But for Emily the second ending is preferable, because the novel has essentially been about Sarah's emancipation. At the end of the novel Sarah has found a community of artists who respect her and treat her well; it would be a betrayal of her whole project to enter into marriage with a dominating aristocrat who seems to think that the main purpose of a woman's existence is to bear children.

Suppose George and Emily are asked to resolve their differences in an English class. What can they achieve together? Is there anything they can gain from each other? Or are they simply living in separate worlds?

This is a real problem, and it is typical of the crisis in criticism and interpretation in the 1990s. Any easy solution is bound to be unsatisfactory. The rest of this book will add new dimensions to the problem, but not solve it.

Notes

1.   Thomas Kuhn, *The Structure of Scientific Revolutions*, 2nd ed. (Chicago: University of Chicago Press, [1961] 1970).

2.   Stanley Fish, "Rhetoric," in *Critical Terms for Literary Study*, ed. Frank Lentricchia and Thomas McLaughlin (Chicago: University of Chicago Press, 1990) 210.

CHAPTER FIVE:

Historical Criticism and New Criticism

THE PURPOSE OF THIS CHAPTER is to set the stage for the rise of literary theory in the 1960s. This is a very condensed and schematic account of the development of English studies in the university setting. My aim is not to give a complete account of what happened, but to present two paradigms for the study of literature, both of which are alive and functioning today. Together they would account for at least 70 percent of the teaching done in honours literature programs at North American universities in the 1990s. Students will probably find most of their professors operating in one, or both, of these paradigms.

Historical, or Life-and-Times, Criticism

The main paradigm for literary studies today is provided by historical criticism. According to this paradigm, which was briefly described in the first chapter of this book, the meaning of a work of literature is the meaning it had for the author when he or she wrote it, or the meaning which was understood by the original audience. If you want to know what *Hamlet* means, you need to assemble a lot of the pertinent historical information. You will want to find out as much as you can about the life of Shakespeare and the thought of his period. There are a number of references to God in the play, so you will want to know what the Elizabethans thought about God. You will want to know what they thought about ghosts, and whether the information that the ghost of Hamlet's father gives to Hamlet is likely to be true or false. It would help to know what Shakespeare's society thought about regicide – when was it permissible to kill a king? We know that *Hamlet* was written for performance in a particular theatre and by a particular group of actors – how might the location and actors have influenced the ways in which Shakespeare wrote the parts?

Once you assemble a good deal of this information, you begin to see what Shakespeare may have had in mind when he wrote the play. Some information is lost forever, so your reading can never be perfect. It becomes clear, however, that you could spend five years or so gathering the relevant historical materials, and another ten mastering them. Understanding *Hamlet* properly begins to seem almost like a life's work; and since you cannot afford anything like this amount of time, you need to depend on your professor to tell you the most important information. (Your professor, unless she is a *Hamlet* specialist herself, depends on another set of experts.)

The authoritarian nature of this paradigm is readily apparent, and lecturing is an appropriate mode for teaching in it. There is a virtually infinite amount of information, and the people who have it convey the important material to the people who want to know it. It is not clear in this paradigm why the student should read the play at all, since his ideas about it will undoubtedly be wrong, and his responses inappropriate in many ways. Sometimes courses based on this paradigm do not involve a lot of reading of *literature*, although there may be a great deal of work on what critics have said about the works of literature, and on lecture-notes.

The impulse to set up literature courses in this way comes, in the best instances, from the professor's genuine admiration for an author. The author is seen as a great man or woman (or at least a significant one); the works studied contain great thoughts, and what the professor really wants to do is to climb inside the head of the author and live the author's life as completely as possible. Charles Augustin Sainte-Beuve, an eminent 19th-century worker in this paradigm, said:

> Literature, literary production, as I see it, is not distinct or separable
> from the rest of mankind's character and activity. I may enjoy a work,
> but it is hard for me to judge it independently of my knowledge of the
> man who produced it. I am inclined to say, *tel arbre, tel fruit* – the fruit is
> like the tree. Thus the study of literature leads me naturally to the study
> of human natures....
>
> There are never too many ways to go about learning to know a
> man – man is a complex creature, by no means pure spirit. What were

his religious ideas? How was he affected by the spectacle of Nature? How did he behave towards women? What was his attitude towards money? Was he rich, poor? What was his routine, his daily life? Finally, what was his vice or weakness? Every man has one.[1]

Most readers must feel something like this when they encounter an author they admire intensely. You want to know more about the writer, and so you go to biography and history, to the experts who have the information you want.

This paradigm proposes a structure for literature as a whole that is historical, and one of the main reasons for a training in this paradigm is to give students a feeling for the grand progression in English literature from medieval times through Shakespeare, Milton, Pope, Wordsworth, Arnold, to Yeats and Lawrence. It is simply a fact of English studies today that this paradigm dominates most university departments and the publishing of most books and periodicals about literature. With a few exceptions, university courses are organized according to historical periods, experts in those periods are hired, and books and articles are written about authors, groups of authors who knew each other, and historical periods.

Although a great deal of valuable work is done in the historical paradigm, it suffers from three striking internal contradictions. The first is that although it represents a thoroughly historical approach, it usually places "great" authors on a transcendent level, and sees their works as "immortal" or "timeless," often because the author has been able to say something that is considered "eternally true" about the human condition. There is often a strong moral impulse behind the work done in this paradigm, and some critics feel that the rise of English as an academic subject was partly caused by the decline of religion. As religion became less and less vital as a moral force in England, educators were on the lookout for another way of improving the morals of the general public, and the study of English literature emerged as the successful candidate.[2] But it is not clear how a historical account of literature can judge some works to be timeless or eternal. Any judgment of that sort must be made in specific historical conditions, and so be limited by those conditions.

The second contradiction is that although the paradigm is fueled by intense admiration for certain great authors, it proposes and underwrites projects for gathering knowledge that have little to do with this admiration, and even seem to work against it. If you want to understand *Ham-*

let, it seems reasonable to collect all the Elizabethan plays about revenge, and find out as much as possible about their authors. This can be an enormous task, occupying the lives of many scholars, even though the works and their authors inspire little admiration, and in fact now seem hardly worth reading. An academic industry is set up (one operating with great energy today) that produces an endless stream of materials. Instead of illuminating *Hamlet*, by and large this activity fills libraries with books and articles that only a few people want to read.

The third contradiction is the failure of the historical paradigm to leave room for the reader. Essentially the reader is supposed to be transparent – to make himself or herself conform as closely as possible with the mind of the author. But most people don't want to be invisible – they want to gain authority and presence themselves, and they are attracted to authors who possess these qualities. They also usually want their responses to matter. In the historical paradigm those responses are hidden – although it is clear that what makes the experts declare that certain works are "great" must be related to what those experts feel when they read the works in question.

As in Thomas Kuhn's model for the development of a science, the contradictions or inadequacies in the dominant paradigm caused some people to develop a new paradigm to overcome those contradictions. That paradigm, called "practical criticism" or "the New criticism," became important in Britain and North America between 1930 and 1950. It never displaced historical criticism from the center of the stage, however. There were two rival paradigms in operation, and there was a good deal of friction between them. ("New Historicism" developed in the 1980s and became another competitor with "life and times" criticism. This movement is described in Chapter 12.)

Practical Criticism and the New Criticism

The new paradigm concentrated not on the author, but on the "words on the page." The basic method of practical criticism, as it was developed by I.A. Richards in England, was to give students a set of three or four fairly short poems, with no indication of who wrote them, when they were written, or how good they were. The students were asked to read the poems several times and write down their responses to them, saying what they liked, what they didn't like, what they didn't understand, what the poems reminded them of, and so on. These statements demonstrated to Richards (and to the world, when he published them) how difficult it was to read poetry "correctly," how few people could do it, and what kinds of mistake were most common. A course in practical criticism taught you to pay close attention to the details of the text, to identify different styles of language, to avoid certain errors in reading, and sometimes to "date" passages – that is, to assign an approximate date for when the poem might have been written.

Practical criticism is authoritarian, although in a different way from historical criticism. Professors have authority not because of what they know – the information at their disposal – but because they are skilled at reading. They can elicit and present the main feelings and ideas in a poem, and show their structure and interrelations, better than most people, and their students can learn these skills from them. There are interesting analogies with learning how to listen to music better, or how to get more out of paintings.

A moral element entered this paradigm of criticism with the hypothesis that the best poems and novels give us the deepest and fullest relation to life. In order to read and appreciate these texts (which are often complex) we need to be versed in the skills offered by a course in practical criticism. Practical criticism arose after the First World War, in Britain, when the ideology of the British Empire had been discredited by all the senseless slaughter, and reflective people were looking for a new basis for their values. As Terry Eagleton stated,

> English was an arena in which the most fundamental questions of human existence – what it meant to be a person, to engage in significant relationship with others, to live from the vital centre of the most essential values – were thrown into vivid relief and made the object of the most intensive scrutiny. *Scrutiny* was the title of the critical journal launched in 1932 by the Leavises [two critics at Cambridge], which has yet to be surpassed in its tenacious devotion to the moral centrality of English studies, their crucial relevance to the quality of social life as a whole.[3]

In this way English studies became very practical indeed. Instead of being anchored in the life of the author, a great work was considered to be alive in the present, in the sensibility of a trained reader who had read it. The value of reading rested not simply in enjoying the book; the reader could make better choices about his or her own life after reading it.

New Criticism was the American variant of practical criticism, and it worked within much the same paradigm. "New Critics" concentrated on outstanding poems and read them with great care. They were especially interested in features such as paradox, conflict, and the tensions between opposing elements or ideas, and how these could be resolved harmoniously. A fine poem was thought to be similar to a "well-wrought urn" or a "verbal icon," and it was expected to present an arresting solution to some important problem.[4] Formal patterning was considered important; poetry was often expected to induce a contemplative, accepting frame of mind, as some music does.

Practical criticism and American New criticism had some clear pedagogical advantages over the historical paradigm. Narrowing the focus of attention from the sweep of history to the words on the page made the primary material of literature more available to the students, who could then take part in the process of exploring and discussing the meaning of a poem rather than simply listening to a set of lectures. The new paradigm allowed the students' responses to come into the classroom, even though they were likely to be mildly rebuked or set straight much of the time. The emphasis on skills of reading rather than a mass of seemingly arbitrary information was enlivening, and it helped students in their work to feel that somehow they were connecting with the central issues in their civilization.

There were two problems with this paradigm. One was that the skills of the good reader were often not specified, so that the professor seemed like a magician producing wonderful readings of texts that otherwise appeared opaque to the students. A series of dazzling readings might be instructive, or it might induce in the student an unhealthy passivity – the feeling so often experienced by students: "The professor can do it, but I don't know where to begin." There was no doubt that the professor's historical knowledge helped her avoid incorrect readings, but this was seldom acknowledged.

The second and more serious problem with practical criticism was that it provided no means of connecting works of literature with each other, or with anything else for that matter. Because its general approach was to have students read works in isolation, the result tended to be fragmentary. A four-year university course could hardly consist only of a large number of empirical readings of texts. A larger structure had to be found to relate works to each other, and usually this came from the historical paradigm. Within courses, practical criticism was employed; but the courses themselves were still organized historically. This sort of compromise was more or less inevitable until a new paradigm emerged.

The rise of a new paradigm in the 1960s placed this problem in the foreground, and proposed several solutions to it. The first important solution, which attracted widespread attention and (some experts would say) revolutionized literary studies, was provided by structuralism. The fact that this broad intellectual movement originated in France was almost to be expected. It seems the French take intellectual life much more seriously than do English-speakers, and they are famous for revolutions. Practical criticism and New Criticism were more empirically-based, depending on "facts" and on readings of individual texts. This suited the down-to-earth Anglo-Saxon mind. In a sense the advent of structuralism marked the inauguration of a new field known as "literary theory." To this upheaval we can now turn our attention.

Notes

1. Charles Augustin Sainte-Beuve, "On Sainte-Beuve's Method," *Sainte Beuve: Selected Essays*, trans. and ed. Francis Steegmuller and Norbert Guterman (Garden City, New York: Doubleday 1963) 281-2, 290.

2. Terry Eagleton, *The Function of Criticism* (London: Verso, 1984) 55-67.

3. Terry Eagleton, *Literary Theory: An Introduction* (Oxford: Blackwell, 1983) 31.

4. Cleanth Brooks, *The Well-Wrought Urn* (1947; New York: Harvest, 1963) and W.K. Wimsatt and Monroe Beardsley, *The Verbal Icon* (1954; London: Methuen, 1970) are two well-known books in the tradition of New Criticism.

CHAPTER SIX:

Structuralism

THE DEVELOPMENT OF STRUCTURALISM represents the most important 20th-century change in ways of dealing with literature; indeed some scholars think that the rise of structuralism constitutes one of the major turning-points in intellectual history. With structuralism came a new paradigm with a new model for thinking about literature – and about cultural production generally. That model is language.

When you first begin to look at the world in terms of this model, what you see changes, in some significant ways. Structuralism was by its very nature a cross-disciplinary phenomenon, affecting linguistics, anthropology, history, literature, philosophy, psychology, and psychiatry. It inspired excitement and admiration in some people, and hatred and loathing in others. Both responses are understandable, and once you have read this chapter you should be able to decide which is closer to your own.

Historical criticism sees literature as the product of the author's mind, and new criticism treats a work as an isolated experience of the reader. Both of these paradigms seem justified by common sense. Authors do write poems at particular moments in their lives. Often when readers read poems, they have the feeling (especially with good poems) that the poem occupies a kind of ideal space, that it transcends normal experience, and that the reader's relation to it has a mystical quality. New criticism is based on this kind of experience of literature.

Structuralism proposes that a work of literature is like a language, and it views language in a particular way. You need to get a feel for this view of language in order to grasp what is new about structuralism. It was developed by the Swiss professor of linguistics, Ferdinand de Saussure, early in the 20th century; he was the inventor of structural linguistics, which is where the name "structuralism" comes from. Saussure said that if you look at how a language functions at any given moment in time, it can be seen as a *system* that offers you a set of categories for understanding the world. At first it is hard to see that this is the case with your own language, so I will give an example from French. If you are talking to people in France, you are obliged to put them in one of two categories – those you say *vous* to, and those you address in the second-person familiar, *tu*. This poses some real difficulties for a person coming to terms with the French language as a mature adult. To say *tu* to a person implies a considerable degree of intimacy with him or her; you open yourself to the rebuke of the other addressing you as *vous*. On the other hand the person might be insulted if you used *vous*. So you have to distinguish, publicly, between those people you are close to and those you are not so close to. (This is not such a problem for native speakers, who can master the system as children.)

Any language, a structuralist would say, presents us with a vast array of categories – but the act of dividing up the world into categories influences how we see the world, and even what we are able to perceive. It is said, for instance, that the Inuit have twenty-six different words for "snow," and as a result they can distinguish varieties of white that seem the same to a person whose mother tongue is English.

How does this approach help us to understand works of literature? A structuralist might say that a novel, for instance, can best be seen as creating a set of categories for understanding the world – and a set of typical relations between those categories. The best way to describe such a novel is to identify the various categories and the relations between them. Structuralists are not concerned with how the author came to write the book or what it meant to him, nor are they interested in the feeling of exaltation that some books give to certain readers. They want to understand "the language of the novel," and how this language works. An example will help make this clear.

The Jewel in the Crown, by Paul Scott, is a fascinating and involving book. It is concerned with the British in India, and it shows how the British Empire and its ideology influenced life in one Indian city during the Second World War. We are given a detailed view of how the white people live, in their own separate section of the city, and we see how they control the rest of the population. We are also given glimpses of life among the Indians. It is clear in the novel that both the English and the Indian populations are or-

*"Well, I don't see any point in looking any farther.
It was probably just one of those wild rumors."*

Structuralism in action: at its best, structuralism gives you a new perspective, and allows you to see patterns in a text which are normally hidden from view. How do the patterns in the English language affect what we are able to say, and see? How much are we aware of them?(Drawing by Charles Addams © *The New Yorker Magazine.*)

---

ganized into caste systems, and the castes determine what an individual is and is not able to do. Most of the characters in the book live within the boundaries of their own race and caste. But about five characters, including the two protagonists, Daphne Manners and Hari Kumar, cross the caste boundaries regularly, and mix with both Indians and whites. They do not live according to the prescribed social norms. *The Jewel in the Crown* suggests, in very clear terms, that such people are both more moral and more vital than those who stick to their own social groups, because the former have the courage to act in conflict with the prescribed norms. They also place themselves in considerable danger by ignoring these norms, and three of them suffer severely for having done so.

A structuralist critic would say of this book that one of its principal structures is the division of people into three groups: whites who live with whites, Indians who live with Indians, and individuals who mix with both groups. Like a language, the novel offers us these three categories for thinking about the people in the world. It says a number of things about how these three groups interact. We might say that the main subject of the book is how defined social groups affect our lives, and especially how they shape relations of power and love in our lives. Hari and Daphne fall in love with a particular intensity because they are not limited by castes in the way most people are, but their freedom leads to problems as well as joys.

The attraction of this kind of structural analysis is that it allows you to state in a concise way the generating principle of the book. You penetrate beneath the surface of the work and grasp the key idea in it. This is rather like finding out what makes a person tick — a person you find stimulating and mystifying. A skilled psychiatrist is good at seeing these patterns in a person's behaviour. A good structuralist critic is skilled at seeing these patterns in individual texts — and the main analogy which he or she is constantly using is the model of language. When you become familiar with the patterns present in language itself, you begin to see them cropping up in unexpected places.

A New View of Language

Saussure invented a new way of looking at language, and he went through a good deal of agony in doing so — as do many people who become involved in the early stages of a paradigm change. When Saussure received his training in linguistics, the field was defined in a fundamentally historical way. Its principal subject-matter was the ways in which languages have developed over long periods of time. An example would be the changes which occurred in popular Latin during the early Middle Ages to transform it into the various romance languages, such as French, Spanish, Italian, and Portuguese. Historical linguistics is concerned with the development of syntax, the alterations in the meanings of words over time, and gradual shifts in pronunciation.

All these matters have a diachronic basis: they concern changes that occur as time passes. Saussure argued that certain important aspects of language remained hidden if the linguist looked at it diachronically. In a letter in 1894 he wrote:

I am fed up with...the general difficulty of writing even ten lines of good sense on linguistic matters. For a long time I have been above all preoccupied with the logical classificiation of linguistic facts and with the classification of the points of view from which we treat them; and I am more and more aware of the immense amount of work that would be required to show the linguist *what he is doing*.... The utter inadequacy of current terminology, the need to reform it and, in order to do that, to demonstrate what sort of object language is, continually spoils my pleasure in philology.... This will lead, against my will, to a book in which I shall explain, without enthusiasm or passion, why there is not a single term used in linguistics which has any meaning for me.[1]

To deal with this frustration, Saussure developed a new paradigm for linguistics. Instead of looking at language diachronically, he proposed to study it synchronically – that is, he wanted to look at language as it functions *as a system* at a particular moment in time.

Most people don't think of language as being systematic. The common-sense attitude toward language is that it acts as a kind of transparent window on whatever is being talked about. If I describe my trip to Germany last summer, my words are supposed to let you see, more or less, what I saw. If I describe my outrage at political corruption in Ottawa, my words are meant to let you see what is in my mind. When language is used well, you don't notice it very much – it allows you to see beyond it. It is like the windshield of a car. What Saussure was suggesting, however, was that language modifies what we see, because it creates the categories we use when we describe things. My description of Germany has something to do with what was there, but it is also influenced by what I can and cannot say in the English language – and what I can and cannot see because English is my mother tongue.

While most structuralists would admit that language to some extent refers to the world outside, they would insist that we can only see the world through the categories and relations that our language emphasizes. So a language (such as English) is very much like a paradigm in science: you have to use a paradigm to see the world, but the particular paradigm you are using determines what you see. And many people are not conscious of using a paradigm at all.

Some structuralists are interested in comparing different languages to see how those languages affect the user's vision of the world. English, for instance, has sentences that are based on the pattern of subject-predicate, or subject-verb-object. This tends to make users of English think in terms of individuals taking action (the active voice) or being acted upon (the passive voice). Suppose you spoke a language which emphasized not the opposition between action and passiveness, but the harmony between the individual and his or her environment, in which action was seen as initiated by the person *and* the object (which seems to be acted upon) simultaneously. Then you might think of your life in a very different way than you would as a user of English. Instead of being primarily concerned with free will and asserting yourself in a hostile environment, you might be more concerned with cooperating with the people and things around you. And your language would have been crucial in causing this difference.

Structuralism Is, and Is Not, like Science

Structuralism often has a scientific feel to it, which is partly due to the fact that it is based on linguistics, a social science. But in fact the new paradigm for criticism suggested by structuralism is very different from the scientific paradigm, and it is important to see why, because the new paradigm actually liberates the humanities to pursue their own goals without having to pretend to be scientific.

We need to go back to considering the "system" of language. The English language has a grammar, a set of rules, which indicates how correct sentences ought to be constructed. Anyone who knows English well can distinguish between a well-formed and a badly-formed sentence, even if they could not quote the actual rule of grammar that is at stake. Unconsciously, they have a mastery of the system they are using. To call it a system makes it sound as though it were scientific in some way. But this system is unlike scientific systems *because the rules can be broken.* People break the rules of grammar all the time, and usually this does not alter the system of correct English. It simply means that the speaker is not a member of the social group that habitually uses correct English. Members of that group can, if they want, break the rules to achieve a desired effect, without changing the rules. In science, any exception to a rule means that the rule is invalid.

Saussure expressed this difference between linguistics and science by distinguishing between *langue* and *parole*. The word *parole* refers to an individual speech-act – that is, to what a particular person says on a specific occasion, obeying (or breaking) the rules of grammar. *Langue* refers to the system that is inherent in the language being used. Saussure said that if you try to understand *all* the speech-acts in a language, you are doomed to failure, because many of them are idiosyncratic, and don't follow the prescribed rules. But if you can separate *langue* from *parole*, you can discover some very important rules that operate in the system of *langue*. One of those rules is that the rules can be broken, which indicates a fundamental difference between the rules of grammar and the laws of science.

How does this difference liberate the humanities? Before the rise of structuralism, much work in the humanities proceeded on a quasi-scientific basis, that is, on the assumption that what was important in humanistic knowledge was assembling facts and forming valid generalizations. But in a subject like English literature there are almost no watertight generalizations, and so you are left with a lot of facts or information which may be very limited in their interest. The same could be said of history. And it is interesting to notice how work in English literature done in the historical paradigm seems to have a cause-and-effect basis. The effect is the work of literature; to find the cause you investigate the life of the author and the times he lived in.

With the advent of structuralism, it became clear that the humanities were not limited to studying diachronic cause-and-effect relationships. They could also study synchronic systems as they appear in human creations and action – systems that, like a language, divide the world up into categories and establish the relations between them. This is to ask not "What are the causes of this work of literature?" but "What ideology is present in this work of literature? How is that ideology articulated in characteristic patterns of language and thought? What are the important implications of this ideology?" These questions don't concern facts and scientific truths; they are about how human beings act, and (often) how they form themselves into groups. Breaking the rules is perfectly possible, although it may prevent you from belonging to particular groups of people.

Structuralists use the idea of language as a model for understanding social practices, and rules of grammar provide a particularly helpful analogy. Many activities have implicit rules which an educated person is aware of even though she may not pay much conscious attention to them. There are rules about what dishes can be served in combination in a formal dinner, and rules about the sequence in which they appear. Anyone serving dessert before the main course would be thought eccentric. Serving the salad before the main course is considered barbarous in France, although it is acceptable in polite society in North America. There are also rules about what clothes can be worn together in business circles, while breaking these very rules may be required by other social groups. All these rules can be seen as the "grammar" of eating or of dressing.

What is so attractive, a critic might ask, about the model of language and an obsession with grammar? It seems narrow-minded, technical, and disconnected from the important issues in life — especially emotions.

What is especially interesting about language is that we all possess remarkable sophistication in using it, and we are endlessly original in what we produce when we write or speak. We can distinguish between correct and incorrect usages when we hear and see them, but we do this unconsciously. There is a system in place, but you don't have to be aware of the system in order to use it perfectly well. The model of language offers the possibility of moving from the surface level of comprehension (for example, from understanding all the words and sentences in a book) to a deep level where the generating principles of the work can be described and its essence grasped. That is an exciting possibility if you are engaged in the study of literature.

If language structures our world and our perceptions without us being aware of it, there is a possibility of understanding ourselves much better if we can raise this system to consciousness. In a similar way, a scientist might be much better off if she could understand the fact that she is using a paradigm rather than just blindly practicing science in an unselfconscious way. But for someone confronting his or her use of language, the questions can have fascinating personal significance. Language is the means by which we know (or divine) the most intimate and essential aspects of ourselves and the people we care about. Structuralism has influenced some kinds of psychoanalysis by focusing on the verbal nature of the unconscious mind, and on how language affects our conscious activities.

What does structuralism tell us about our feelings? It will appear to some readers that it takes a highly intellectual approach to literature, and so stifles or ignores the emotions. But at its best structuralism helps us understand our feelings and the assumptions on which they are based. Feelings are not simple and unitary; they depend on many factors drawn from our past and our expectations of the future. They depend on our ideology. Structuralism allows us to explore some of these complex interconnections. It also encourages us to raise ideological issues and explore them, because the system behind a language is a good means of approaching ideologies. Ideologies, like languages, are largely hidden from consciousness, and pervade every aspect of our lives.

As an example of how structualism can shed light on our emotions and their relations to ideology, consider the response of a student reading *The French Lieutenant's Woman* for the first time, when he comes to the end of the book, and discovers that there are two radically different endings. The student I am thinking of felt intensely frustrated that there was no clear winding-up of the book, and that he did not know what actually happened in the end. Did Sarah Woodruff and Charles Smithson get married, or not? Why does the author make such an effort to say that one ending is just as probable as the other?

A structuralist would analyze this response as follows: the student reading this book was used to novels that had clear endings, and usually the endings solved the problems which the novels had posed. In the same way that we expect a good sentence to have a subject and a verb, this student expected a good novel to have one ending, and a satisfying one. It was part of this student's ideology that the best novels give you a complete picture, and take things through to their conclusions, yet here was a widely acclaimed novel that had broken this rule. This student thought that well-formed lives reached proper conclusions, too – he looked forward to a career ending with a position of some responsibility and honour, and to acquiring some wisdom in old age, which would help him face the problem of dying. To help him plan his moves in the future, he sometimes thought of his own life in a fictionalized way, writing (as it were) the novel of his life.

A structuralist would say that the classical novel usually *does* reach a satisfying conclusion – that is one of the rules of the genre. But with the rise of postmodernism, authors have begun to question their god-like status, and stopped feeling obliged to lay out everything for the reader. So the "open ending" has come to be an acceptable conclusion for a book, and it has even been defended as being more lifelike than the closed ending, because life itself is usually open-ended: we are left with choices to make, and often we are unsure about which of several courses of action to choose. What this reader was looking for in a novel was that sense of satisfying finality which was lacking in his own life, and when he was denied it, he felt frustrated.

The French Lieutenant's Woman breaks the rules of the classical novel in this respect. But that does not mean that the rules no longer exist. It is still possible to write classical novels, and most recent novels have closed endings. But Fowles, and many other postmodernist writers, have created a new set of rules for "postmodernist fiction," and those rules are a reflection of a new ideology, in which the author explicitly leaves a major part of the creation of the work of art to the reader. My student was frustrated because the book's ideology did not mesh with his own. But he was glad (in a way) that this book had made him aware of his own ideological assumptions in this area, and after rereading it he found it easier to accept the new convention.

Expanding the Scope of Analysis beyond the Individual Work

So far we have considered structuralism as it might apply to the analysis of a single work of literature, and I have suggested that a novel or a poem provides us with something like a small language for describing some kinds of experience. This is the most useful aspect of structuralism for most undergraduates, because they can readily apply it in essays and in understanding works of literature. But many structuralists are highly ambitious thinkers, who want to expand their horizons beyond the limits of single individual works. One reason why structuralism seemed an attractive alternative to New Criticism was that it permitted "larger" questions to be raised.

It is possible, for instance, to expand your horizons to include all the works by a given author. Then you would be looking for structures, or oppositions, or categories, that run through the whole of an author's *oeuvre*. You could spend several years developing a structuralist analysis of a major author's work. Often this kind of analysis is related to finding patterns in the author's personality, although structuralists prefer to think about "texts" rather than about authors. Nevertheless, the fact that Wordsworth consistently opposes the value of living in the country with the human frustration involved in living in big cities seems to indicate something substantial about his own phobias. A frequent image in Stendhal's novels is that of someone looking down from a height to see a pattern in the world below. Does this indicate that Stendhal liked the feeling of distance, or does it reveal the kind of understanding that comes from seeing things from a distance as opposed to being plunged into the middle of events? If a structuralist analysis can shed light on the prevailing ideology in an author's work, then it seems a short step to ascribe this ideology to the author. The main point, however, is not that Stendhal the man had a certain way of seeing the world, but that a certain ideology is present (as an organizing principle) in his works.

It is possible to extend the scope of structuralist analysis to a whole genre, and to define a genre in terms of certain repeated structures. Vladimir Propp, one of the Russian formalists, did a famous analysis of the Russian folk tale, in which he pointed out that these tales follow consistent patterns. Similarly, some popular literary forms, such as the romance novel or the detective story, are based on simple, identifiable structures, and on character roles that can be easily described in general terms, such as the hero (or "quester"), the "object of the quest," the "persons blocking the quest," and the "persons aiding the quester."

A final expansion of this kind of analysis would be to analyze the discourse of a whole period, and find constant categories and structures of oppositions which characterize it. In the romantic period in England many authors put a particularly high value on exceptional and intense experiences. Wordsworth often talked about "spots of time," when he had a vivid recall of an earlier event; Coleridge sometimes privileged intense feelings of guilt; and Keats was often concerned with "timeless moments." These unusual experiences can be contrasted with the normal happenings in everyday life. One kind of structural analysis would be to investigate this kind of opposition in the literature of a period.

The ultimate ambition of a manic structuralist would be to identify the basic structures in the human mind itself; structures that (ideally) might account for the general patterns in human culture everywhere. Not many undergraduates will be involved in this kind of search, and it may seem futile to many people. Perhaps at this point it is wise to remember Paul Valéry's observation: "L'homme est fou par ce qu'il cherche, et grand par ce qu'il trouve."[2]

Why Structuralism Can Seem Dehumanizing

In some notable cases structuralism can seem dehumanizing and rebarbative. There seems to be something "inhuman" about structures – they sound almost machine-like, obsessively repeating themselves, whether in a single work, in the *oeuvre* of a single author, or in the whole of a culture. We don't like to think of ourselves as caught in a repeating pattern, and we especially think of creative writers (at the level of genius) as being able to transcend such patterns to make something new and fresh.

Structuralist analysis often does identify limitations in the work of an author – perhaps limitations not evident before – and this may have the effect of convincing us that the author is less free than we had thought. Structuralist analysis may be a bit like psychoanalysis, in that it highlights patterns that the subject may not have known about. Robertson Davies's character David Staunton discovers this kind of thing in *The Manticore*, which is an account of his psychoanalysis in Zürich. Staunton's analyst points out the patient's tendency to isolate himself from others, and to assume a romantic and mysterious role as a courtroom lawyer; she also makes him realize he is using alcohol to deaden the pain in his life. Staunton seems less impressive in some ways when he has been through analysis, but the reader can see that he has come to have a much better grip on his own life.

It is a definite thrust of structuralism to show that authors follow certain patterns, but it is a mistake to think that patterns are necessarily limiting. If you think of the patterns imposed on action in the game of tennis, you will see that within those patterns there are an infinite number of shots, and tennis does not become boring because of restrictions about where you can hit the ball. On the contrary, these restrictions in one sense create the possibility of playing the game, and enjoying yourself in that way.

The same is true of language. Languages have definite rules, but even when you obey those rules, you have virtually infinite freedom to create new sentences. Still, it is useful to know what the rules are. Then you know when you are breaking them, and what the consequences are likely to be.

Structuralism points, in a general sense, to ideology. Our ideology might be said to be made up of the rules we follow without knowing that they are rules, because they seem to represent the "natural" way of doing things.

Structuralists sometimes suggest (in a rather dehumanizing way) that individual people are "made up of" ideologies, and that if you describe the ideologies which make up a particular person in enough detail, you will be able to define that person completely. This would seem to suggest that an individual does not exist in his or her own right. A theme frequently repeated in structuralist writings is that "the subject has ceased to exist," because the subject is only the site of operation of various ideologies. It is important to look carefully at a statement such as this, so as to see what its real implications are. How threatening is it?

Most reflective people would admit that their identities are partly a result of their adherence or allegiance to certain ideologies or forms of thought. People with firm religious beliefs are usually quite happy to acknowledge this, but it is also true of people who are not conscious of adopting any particular ideology. Most arts students in North American universities are living in a liberal humanist world, and think in terms of liberal humanism, even though many of them may not be aware of this fact.

Even though we live within a set of constraints established by the language we speak, or the traditions and ideologies we have inherited, this does not mean that we do not have wide freedoms. The aim of structuralist analysis in this area is to point out that we are not completely free to do anything we like. A very revealing project is to work out the constraints that are actually operating in individual situations. For instance, when you read a novel and are very moved by it, that may feel like an intensely personal experience. But to what extent is the emotion you feel the result of certain easily definable assumptions that you share with the author about what can and cannot be done in a novel? There are certain limitations on what the author can do, and those limitations help him communicate with you.

Conclusion

The main effect of structuralism, when it developed in France in the 1960s, was to shift the emphasis in literary studies from history (and historical criticism), and from the words on the page (and New Criticism), to two new areas: ideology and interpretation. Since language was the new dominant image, structuralist critics were less interested in finding "the truth" of a literary text (what circumstances really produced it, or what it really meant); they were more concerned to find out what "language" a text was speaking – what categories it proposed for understanding the world – and what ideology that "language" presented.

Languages, like paradigms, are neither true or false. They cannot be evaluated in an objective way. They can, however be evaluated subjectively, according to how satisfying they are for a particular person (or group) to speak. An important aspect of your interpretation of a work of literature will be your decision about whether you want to adopt its language, or see that language as a possibly useful tool, or reject it completely. That decision will probably depend to some extent on the "language" you are currently speaking, and so interpretation becomes a matter of relations between languages.

"Relations between languages" may sound like a complex idea to use when understanding works of literature, but it held out two promises which were attractive: the complexity might allow (and indeed promote) a better understanding of literature, and it could take better account of the role of the reader in participating in the institution of literature. For whatever reasons, structuralism caught and held the attention of many of the best minds in the world of literary criticism. This does not mean that there was not resistance and opposition to structuralism; but from the 1970s on it has been a school, and an ideology, that we have to reckon with.

Notes

1. Quoted by Jonathan Culler in his *Ferdinand de Saussure* (1976; Ithaca: Cornell University Press, 1986) 23-4.

2. A full translation of this sentence might be: "A person may be considered insane if the object of his search is on a grand scale, but he will be considered great if he is successful in finding it."

Suggestions for Further Reading

Jonathan Culler, *Structuralist Poetics* (London: Routledge and Kegan Paul, 1975). This is a good, full, and detailed introduction to structuralism, written in a very clear manner.

Fredric Jameson, *The Prison-House of Language: A Critical Account of Structuralism and Russian Formalism* (Princeton and London: Princeton University Press, 1972).

Robert Scholes, *Structuralism in Literature* (New Haven and London: Yale University Press, 1974).

John Sturrock (ed.), *Structuralism and Since: From Levi-Strauss to Derrida* (Oxford: Oxford University Press, 1979). This contains good thirty-page essays on Claude Levi-Strauss (by Dan Sperber), Roland Barthes (by John Sturrock), Michel Foucault (by Hayden White), Jacques Lacan (by Malcolm Bowie), and Jacques Derrida (by Jonathan Culler).

CHAPTER SEVEN:

Structuralism (ii): Syntagmatic and Paradigmatic Relations

A HALLMARK OF STRUCTURALISM is that it is much more concerned with the *relations* between things than with things considered in isolation. It is the relations between things which establish the existence of a system, and the rules of the system determine what is likely to happen in that system.

This tendency is easy to see in the case of family constellations. In a family with three sons spaced two years apart from one another, it may be a rule of the system that the oldest boy normally dominates the other two, and tends to get his way when conflicts arise. Of course this person will have an identity apart from his siblings, but a large part of his identity may well be the result of his immersion in that family system for a long time. This kind of identity is sometimes referred to as "relational identity" – something created by (and to some extent dependent on) a system of human relations. In later life this oldest child may well find himself happiest when he can recreate the system in which he grew up – that is, a system in which he can dominate the people around him. Such a man might make an excellent chief executive officer in a company, but do poorly as a vice-president, because his relational identity makes it difficult for him to submit to the direct authority and supervision of another person.

Because structuralism uses language as the master model for understanding the world, it is especially concerned with *relations between words* and the systems in languages like English which regulate those relations.

In linguistics there are two fundamentally different kinds of relations between words, *syntagmatic relations* and *paradigmatic relations*. Although these technical words may seem somewhat formidable, the reward of learning how to use them is ample, because they introduce an extremely powerful distinction that can be applied to many situations in both literature and life.

The adjective "syntagmatic" comes from two Greek words that mean "to put together in the right order." The syntagmatic rules in English grammar (that is, the rules of syntax) tell you how to put words together in the right order so a sentence sounds correct. So a syntagmatic relation exists between any two items that are together, side by side, in a well-ordered grouping. Sometimes the grouping is spread out in a linear way, like a chain – this is true of sentences. In cases like these, there are syntagmatic relations between each link in the chain and those which come immediately before and after it.

It is possible to think of a number of groupings which have this chain-like structure. Someone once said that life consisted essentially of birth, copulation, and death. We might want to add more items to this chain, but it is clear that the order is important. It would be an error in the "syntax of life" to say that life consisted of death, birth and copulation. A second example could be found in the flight path of a plane making the journey from Toronto to Moscow. There would be a syntagmatic relation between the cities where it lands on the way to its final destination. A well-formed sequence would be: Halifax, London, Munich, Warsaw, Moscow. If two of these were reversed, you would suspect that something was drastically wrong with the flight – a highjacking, for instance. A third example of a syntagmatic chain could be found in the career path of a successful business executive. The chain would be made up of the positions which he or she filled in succession.

Paradigmatic relations have a very different quality from syntagmatic relations. We can think of a paradigm as a kind of model or a pattern, and a number of things which have the same basic form or pattern, or are made on the same model, have a paradigmatic relation to one another. The essence of a syntagmatic relation is *being next to*, or contiguity. The essence of a paradigmatic relation is *similarity*. So we could say that there is a paradigm for the literary genre of tragedy, and all tragedies that conform to this paradigm have a paradigmatic relation to one another. There is a generally accepted paradigm for "falling in love," and we can often recognize, with very little evidence, when this experience has happened in the life of someone we know. There is a paradigm for "sports cars," and we can feel the paradigmatic relation between an M.G. and a Corvette. Often when you have a choice to make in your life, such as which university to go to, the items you are choosing between have a paradigmatic relation to one another: you could substitute them for one another in the "sentence" which you are making up of your life, and the sentence would still be a "correct" one. Four years spent in a penitentiary would not be a good substitute for doing an undergraduate degree. It would make the sequence of your life seem much less impressive.

I will now turn to syntagmatic and paradigmatic relations in the formation of sentences. In order to make English sentences which are well-formed and effective in communicating, you have to engage in two kinds of mental activity, one syntagmatic and one paradigmatic. The syntagmatic activity is a matter of being able to construct the sentence as a whole, with (let us say) a subject, a verb, an object, and an adverbial phrase:

David	hurled	the stone	at Goliath.
[subject]	[verb]	[object]	[adverbial phrase]

The paradigmatic mental activity is a matter of choosing the appropriate item (from a number of possibilities) in each part of the sentence. "David" could be replaced by "the youth" or "the Israelite boy" – but not by "the man." "Stone" could be "pebble" or "small rock" – but it couldn't be "boulder."

There is medical evidence which suggests that syntagmatic and paradigmatic operations take place in different parts of the brain; some kinds of brain damage impair one kind of operation without affecting the other greatly. Although the distinction between syntagmatic and paradigmatic relations comes originally from linguistics, its importance for students of literature is that it allows us to describe the difference between the feelings generated by different texts. We can approach this area by applying the distinction to different kinds of mind.

Why Does This Matter? Syntagmatic and Paradigmatic Minds at Work

It helps to distinguish between syntagmatic and paradigmatic relations because different people make use of them in different ways, and some authors think and write in a more paradigmatic way than others. This tendency can have a powerful effect on their works, and on our responses to those works.

Suppose you meet a close friend whom you haven't seen since the day before, and you ask her to tell you what she has been doing. If she has a mind that tends to work in a predominantly syntagmatic way, she will probably run through what has happened to her in the last twenty-four hours in a sequential chain: "I got up early and had a game of squash, I went shopping for groceries, then I studied in the library. I had lunch, then Barry came over and we played bridge with two other friends." She will probably leave out trivial details, but the *sequence* of the events will dominate her presentation. If she has an extremely syntagmatic mind, when she expands on some incident, she will do it by going into finer detail about that item. "I studied in the library" could become "I returned some overdue books, went up to the reading room, got a book which I had been looking for off the reserve shelf, rubbed out the pencil markings which someone else had put in it," and so on. Normally people won't expand items unless you show some particular interest.

If your friend's mind tends to work in a paradigmatic way, she is much more likely to pick out particular experiences for emphasis, and then she will probably link them with other experiences which are similar. If playing squash was the high point of the day, then she might think of other games she has played that had been as exciting or exhausting. If playing squash and playing bridge seemed similar to her, she might remark on that. A paradigmatic mind is like a grasshopper, always moving vertically, looking for parallels, similarities, and contrasts; a syntagmatic mind seems more like a mouse making its way across a wheatfield, moving slowly and sticking to the same plane.

Although this example may make the syntagmatic thinker seem duller than the paradigmatic thinker, two qualifications are in order. The first is that any recounting of a day's experience will make use of both syntagmatic crawling from point to point and paradigmatic leaps that illustrate similarities and indicate patterns. Nevertheless there is a difference in feel between the two kinds of thinker.

The second qualification is that the syntagmatic, close-to-the-ground thinker is more likely to provide a concrete feeling of what is being described and a strong sense of context and texture. This gives you a better sense of *being there* – which may or may not be useful, depending on the case. A problem with some paradigmatic thinkers is that they leap around so much from point to point that they seem always to be in the air, never touching ground with reality. Philosophers sometimes give me that feeling, and, when they do, I often sense that their philosophies are liable to be irrelevant to me. Some literary theoreticians do the same thing, and lose touch with feeling or with the needs of the audience.

A person who is aware of the differences between syntagmatic and paradigmatic thinking, and who is reasonably flexible, can consciously choose which of the two kinds of thinking to engage in at any particular moment. Sometimes you may become aware that what you are saying needs to be more firmly grounded in concrete experience. That is the time to engage in syntagmatic thinking, which should help you to provide a concrete and physical sense of the situation you are describing. Sometimes, on the other hand, you may feel that what you are talking about is becoming clogged down in particular details, and that your account would be more illuminating if you related what you are describing to other, similar experiences – especially experiences that the other person might share. That is the time to shift to paradigmatic thinking. An important aspect of good essay-writing is knowing when to shift from one mode to the other. Usually near the beginning of an essay you will want to give a plan or a paradigm for the whole essay. Often just before the end of the essay you will want to indicate the broad significance of what you are saying by suggesting further paradigmatic leaps. In between you will probably want to present a closely reasoned argument, with a strong syntactical drive and a firm connection with the real world.

Paradigmatic Thinking, Obsession, and Allegory

There are both conscious and unconscious reasons for engaging in paradigmatic thinking. If some past event or experience has made a deep impression on you, it might provide your basic orientation to experience, and you might see what happens to you in the present in terms of what has happened in the past. Suppose you are a young man whose mother abandoned your father when you were in your teens – and further suppose that your older brother has also been abandoned by a woman. It would be likely that the paradigm of the abandoned man would make a strong impression on you, and you might always see relations between men and women as fraught with the danger of abandonment. This would tend to make you interpret events paradigmatically, by referring them back to the narratives of your father and brother.

The pattern could just as easily be a more attractive one. Suppose you ran a small business at your high school in a very successful way – you had the experience of getting a number of people to work together in a creative and satisfying way, which helped your clients and made money as well. This experience might become a part of a pattern that you try to repeat in your adult life, and it might be the basis for some very significant achievements. Your guide for what you were doing would then be the pattern you experienced as a teenager.

For some people important patterns in their lives may be supplied by literature itself. This was, for instance, the intention of the ancient Greeks, who used *The Iliad* and *The Odyssey* for teaching models of desirable behavior to adolescents. Roland Barthes reported that Marcel Proust's enormous novel, *A la recherche du temps perdu*, provided him with the essential framework for his understanding of life. Some professors choose course texts that they think can fulfill this function for students, such as Charles Dickens's *Great Expectations* or Mordecai Richler's *The Apprenticeship of Duddy Kravitz*. These are both stories of young men growing up, and they may prove irrelevant to many members of the class, especially (perhaps) the women in the class.

When does a pattern become an obsession? That is a difficult question, but people with obsessions are in some ways closed to new experiences because they cannot help but refer everything to those obsessions. If you are obsessed by the need for cleanliness and order, you will spend a lot of your energy trying to tidy up dirt and disorder. If you are obsessed by *Romeo and Juliet*, you may associate romantic love with death. But in both these cases, there will be a great deal of switching back and forth between the paradigm and experience. Obsession represents paradigmatic thinking taken to an extreme.

Allegory is a literary form that has some of the features of obsession about it. In an allegory a story is told on two levels at once – or, to put it another way, there are two stories with a paradigmatic relation between them. In *Animal Farm*, George Orwell tells a story about farmyard animals, but the novel is meant to reflect the events of the Russian revolution. Each narrative casts light on the other. A reader who is conscious of this parallel shifts back and forth (vertically) from one narrative to the other while moving through the story. Allegory is a powerful device, because an event on the farm can suggest by implication something

about the Russian revolution. Allegory is also an opportunity for a virtu-
oso display of literary talent, since it is difficult for the author to keep
both stories progressing in a convincing way, and at the same time have
the events in one story illuminate the events in the other. *Dr Faustus*, by
Thomas Mann, is a masterpiece of allegory, in which the descent into
madness of Adrian Leverkühn, the composer, is a way of talking about
the fall of Germany into the hands of the Nazis.

Paradigmatic Thinking and Metaphor

Metaphor represents one of the main ways in which paradigmatic thinking occurs in literature. When a writer uses a metaphor, she implies that
there is a similarity between two different things or events. When Macbeth says,

> Out, out brief candle!
> Life's but a walking shadow, a poor player
> That struts and frets his hour upon the stage
> And then is heard no more...

Shakespeare is using three metaphors, suggesting the following parallels
or comparisons:

> A person's life can come to an end suddenly, as candle can be blown out
> by a gust of wind;

> Life is insubstantial in the way that a shadow is;

> A man living his life is like an actor who has only a brief period on the
> stage. After life, or the play, is over, no more is heard from him.

These four lines from *Macbeth* suggest some of the emotional power of
metaphor, because this device can, in a highly condensed way, use
different images (the candle, the shadow, the actor's profession) to express how Macbeth is feeling about his own life.

Metaphor is one of the ways in which language is used "figuratively,"
that is, not literally. Metaphor always departs from the *literal* truth (life is
not really a walking shadow) in order to convey a particular feeling.
Some people criticize metaphor for not being logical (because it is not

logically correct to say that life *is* a walking shadow), but for poets it is often more important to convey feeling than to be logical or literal. The point of writing poetry (and prose, too) is often to influence readers' feelings as well as their thoughts, and so it is easy to justify the use of metaphor.

Most people do not use metaphor much in speaking, and it is striking when you hear a series of metaphors flowing through someone's speech. Sometimes this occurs when the speaker is taken up with by some particular field of activity – naval officers, for instance, sometimes use nautical metaphors a great deal, even when talking about things that have nothing to do with the sea. It is rare for people to use a wide variety of metaphors, and perhaps this is due to the importance we attribute to a banal form of scientific discourse, which strives to be logical and literal as much as possible. If you want to be "right," you probably want to be literal. But creative scientists, working at the fronts of their fields, can have highly metaphorical minds, and new discoveries are often the result of seeing information in a new way that is suggested by a new metaphor or a new model. So paradigmatic thinking can be important in science as well as in literature.

Metaphor and Metonymy

Metaphor stresses the vertical axis of language, substituting one image for another because they are similar. There is another figure of speech, known as metonymy, that is based on what might be called "horizontal substitution." The distinction between metaphor and metonymy is a powerful and interesting one. In metonymy you substitute for one word (or idea) another word that represents something nearby in space or time. If you say, "Washington decided to oppose free trade; Ottawa was furious," you are not referring literally to the two cities; you are using their names to indicate the two governments located in those cities. If you read a newspaper headline that says, "The Crown denies rumors about Prince Andrew," you know that "the Crown" is a metonymical substitution for the Queen or one of her representatives. A literary history might state, "The eighteenth century distrusted enthusiasm;" here metonymy works through a shift in time rather than in space. The literally true statement that corresponds to this one might read, "Certain influential thinkers and moralists who flourished during the eighteenth century distrusted enthusiasm."

The distinction between metaphor and metonymy is similar in some ways to the distinction between paradigmatic relations and syntagmatic relations.

VERTICAL	HORIZONTAL
similarity (or contrast)	contiguity in space or time
paradigmatic relations	syntagmatic relations
metaphor	metonymy

This general contrast between the vertical and the horizontal (or between metaphor and metonymy) has been used brilliantly by David Lodge, in a brief and suggestive article, "Modernism, Antimodernism, and Postmodernism."[1] According to Lodge, it is possible to map the literary history of the 20th century based on the swings back and forth between literature that is essentially metaphoric (for example, James Joyce and T.S. Eliot) and literature that is essentially metonymic (for example, W.H. Auden and George Orwell). Metaphoric writers sometimes use vertical parallels between what they are presenting and earlier works of literature (for example, Joyce modelled his *Ulysses* on *The Odyssey*); they emphasize formal perfection; and they see art as aspiring to the condition of music (which usually does not refer to the actual world in a concrete way). Metonymic writers try to imitate the actual world in their works; they are more concerned with truth than with formal perfection; and they see art as aspiring to the condition of history (which achieves much of its force through concrete references to the details of social and political life).

We could distinguish between metonymic and metaphoric writers in terms of the different feelings of entrapment that they sometimes convey. The metonymic writer tends to pay more attention to the details of the actual world than the metaphorical writer, and so she may seem more a captive of a particular place and time. A metaphorical writer often seems to imply that you can escape from any particular world along a vertical, paradigmatic axis. In *Ulysses*, Joyce is dealing with Dublin in 1904; but he is also recalling classical Greece and *The Odyssey*. With a metaphorical writer you might feel trapped by a particular set of parallels (which might represent the author's obsessions), but you are not trapped by a particular place and time. These two kinds of entrapment feel very different, and a person who likes metaphoric literature may feel claustrophobic when reading about some particular corner of the world, with all its arbitrary detail. An author who writes realistic, metonymic literature may use the arbitrary detail to break out of the limiting quality of mental obsessions, which run over the same paradigmatic tracks again and again.

The metonymic impulse appears clearly in a lot of modern advertising, in which a product is made to seem attractive because an attractive person is using it. An advertisement for Scotch cannot suggest its particular taste, so instead we are shown the beautiful, interesting, and successful people who drink it. The implication is a purely metonymic one: the glamour of an attractive person is transferred to the Scotch; and by drinking the same kind of Scotch (the advertisement implies) you can acquire some of that glamor yourself. The variations played on this theme in advertising show that metonymy is alive and well, although it is not frequently used as a figure of speech in conversation or even in literary language.

Certain writers subscribe to the validity of metonymy in much the same way that advertising agencies do. The 19th-century French novelist Honoré de Balzac is a case in point. He clearly believes that to a great extent an individual is defined by the things which surround her, and so, in *Père Goriot*, he begins with a long description of the boarding-house owned by Mme Vauquer. At one point he says,

> Madame Vauquer is at home in its stuffy air, she can breathe without being sickened by it. Her face, fresh with the chill freshness of the first frosty autumn day, her wrinkled eyes, her expression, varying from the conventional set smile of the ballet-dancer to the sour frown of the discounter of bills, *her whole person, in short, provides a clue to the boarding-house, just as the boarding-house implies the existence of such a person as she is.*[2]

Some people believe that a person can be adequately described by the house she lives in and the objects she possesses, so it is clear that a metonymic mind suggests a particular philosophy of life. At the opposite extreme is the religious mind, which sees the particular circumstances surrounding a person as relatively unimportant and envisages human life as presided over by a higher world, corresponding paradigmatically (to some extent) to this world.

The distinction between the metonymic mind and the metaphoric mind can be clearly seen if we contrast the paragraph by Balzac quoted above with the following paragraph by James Joyce. Here Stephen Dedalus is thinking about his own surname, which refers to the craftsman in Greek mythology who constructed two sets of wings that would allow him and his son to fly like birds and so escape from Crete, the island where they were being kept prisoners by a tyrant. Stephen Dedalus wants to do something similar to escape from the restrictions placed on him in Ireland, and so the story of the Greek Daedalus hovers above the narrative and acts as a paradigm for the story.

Now, as never before, his strange name seemed to him a prophecy. So timeless seemed the grey warm air, so fluid and impersonal his own mood, that all ages were as one to him.... Now, at the name of the fabulous artificer [Daedalus], he seemed to hear the noise of dim waves and to see a winged form flying above the waves and slowly climbing the air. What did it mean? Was it a quaint device opening a page of some medieval book of prophecies and symbols, a hawk-like man flying sunward above the sea, a prophecy of the end he had been born to serve and had been following through the mists of childhood and boyhood, a symbol of the artist forging anew in his workshop out of the sluggish matter of the earth a new soaring impalpable imperishable being?[3]

The paradigmatic feeling in this passage is strong, emphasized as it is by the telescoping of time, so that "all ages were as one to him." This allows the myth of Daedalus to come forward into the present, to act as a pattern for the development of Stephen Dedalus as the artist; and the medieval image of "a hawk-like man flying sunward above the sea" also comes to life. The paradigmatic mind jumps over time and space in search of parallels and similarities, and Stephen uses his own paradigmatic tendencies to liberate himself from the restraints imposed on him at home by his family, his religion, and his country.

How to Use the Distinction between Syntagmatic and Paradigmatic Relations

The distinction between syntagmatic and paradigmatic relations is particularly useful because it can help us distinguish between two habits of mind. The syntagmatic mind is tied more closely to the concrete world and the actual connections in time and space that exist there. The paradigmatic mind is tied more closely to parallels between different parts of experience. Since all minds need to operate with both kinds of relations, we are not talking about an absolute difference between two sorts of mind. What is at stake is a *relative* difference between minds, which is important because the difference influences how the mind sees and feels the world around it. So the distinction allows us to account for the difference in feeling between a predominantly syntagmatic mind and a predominantly paradigmatic mind, and between the kinds of literature produced by each. It can also allow us to see interesting contrasts between two different professors, or two different friends.

The distinction can also be used to change how you think (and write) about things. Once you are familiar with the difference between syntagmatic and paradigmatic relations, you can become aware of how you engage in them yourself – and where they serve you well, and where badly. You can become aware of your characteristic ways of dealing with certain situations. When you are obliged to attend a boring class or a tedious meeting, you may find that you have a tendency to escape from it paradigmatically by making a vertical leap to a fantasy world. It is interesting to become aware of habits such as these, and some concepts developed in structuralism can help you identify them.

Notes

1. David Lodge, "Modernism, Antimodernism, Postmodernism," *Working with Structuralism* (London: Routledge and Kegan Paul, 1981) 3-16.

2. Honoré de Balzac, *Père Goriot*, trans. Marion Ayton Crawford (Harmondsworth: Penguin, 1951) 33, emphasis added.

3. James Joyce, *Portrait of the Artist as a Young Man* (New York: The Viking Press and Penguin Books, [1916] 1982) 168-9.

Suggestions for Further Reading

David Lodge, "Modernism, Antimodernism, Postmodernism," *Working with Structuralism* (London: Routledge and Kegan Paul, 1981) 3-16.

CHAPTER EIGHT:
Deconstruction

DECONSTRUCTION, which is both a method of analysing literature and a set of assumptions about language, emerged in France (and was taken up in the United States) as a response to the development of structuralism. Structuralism produced euphoria in some critics and thinkers because it seemed to represent a great improvement on previous methods in criticism. It seemed to have a potential for certainty – it seemed as though when you had determined the structure of a work of literature, you would have it firmly and permanently in your grasp, and you could show that structure to other people with confidence in its objectivity. In structuralism, literary criticism and science seemed to be coming together.

Roland Barthes, one of the key figures in the development of structuralism in France, passed through what he called "a euphoric dream of scientificity." He had thought, for instance, that it would be possible to set up a system that would account in a thorough way for the structure of narrative. But as he moved into his poststructuralist phase, around 1970, he began to feel that any system would be too limiting to fully explain our experience of life or of literature. His writings became much more autobiographical, personal, and playful. Although all of his work is systematic in important ways, his poststructuralist writings pay more attention to particular experiences which elude systems. There is almost a sense of disappointment with systems, and a plunging into life itself. Barthes began to feel that systems were likely to be overbearing and restricting, and he sought out ways of subverting them. This process is an important aspect of deconstruction.

Deconstruction as Resistance to Authority

Deconstruction is often talked about as though it were primarily a critical method, but it is best understood as a way of resisting the authority of someone or something that has power over you. For instance, most people go through a phase during which they revolt against the authority of their parents and reject the models of life their parents have provided – which is part of an attempt to work out a style of life that will suit them. During this phase they need to deconstruct the authority of their parents. The word "deconstruct" originates in the German word *abbauen*, which simply means "to take apart" or "to unbuild."

You don't need deconstruction unless you are feeling oppressed. This is likely to happen when you discover that an authority (that you had previously become attached to) is inadequate, exploitative, or simply dishonest. Often we find ourselves linked to some authority-figure through an accident (being brought up by a particular set of parents) or through a commitment which we have made ourselves (choosing a professor to supervise a thesis), and then we come to feel that we need to get away from that authority for the sake of our own growth and development. It is at this point that deconstruction becomes valuable. It is not, in my opinion, very satisfying "on its own." It only is attractive when you want to *use* it.

What techniques does deconstruction provide to help you subvert the authorities that oppress you? I can best answer this question by describing a book that has had great authority for many readers, *Fifth Business*, by Robertson Davies.[1] It is also a novel that carefully presents a Jungian ideology, and that is open to deconstruction in an interesting way.

Fifth Business is about a competition between two childhood friends for success in the world and for power over one another. The hero of the book, Dunstan Ramsay, chooses for himself the path leading to psychological understanding: he becomes (in succession) a student of history, a schoolmaster, a scholar in the field of the lives of saints, and finally a psychologist with a deep understanding of why human beings act and feel as they do. Ramsay's rival gains his power through the business world. His career leads him to the chairmanship of a large conglomerate, and during the Second World War he is appointed to the federal cabinet. At the end of the novel there is a confrontation between these two characters, and Ramsay wins hands down. He is leading a fulfilling life among interesting friends, while his rival has become depressd (in spite of his success) and wants to commit suicide – a condition Ramsay is able to diagnose correctly.

Fifth Business seems to be a novel about the real world. It suggests that ultimately it is more rewarding to seek psychological understanding than to strive for wealth and public prestige. Furthermore, in its presentation of psychology, it is one-sided: it explicitly embraces the ideas developed by Carl Jung, and denigrates those of Sigmund Freud. In a way the novel is an extension of the conflict between Freud and Jung, the two founding fathers of psychoanalysis. The book amounts to a presentation of a Jungian ideology, and many people find it persuasive. Reading it was my first introduction to Jungian psychology, and I was very impressed with what I found in it. This kind of response is important, because if you do not feel a deep engagement with a book, you will probably not feel a need to deconstruct it later on.

Davies's novel takes many ideas from Jung, but I will mention only three. The first is the belief that sexual activity is not very important in a healthy life – it is less important, on the whole, than religion and art. The second is that human beings are fundamentally solitary. It follows from this that social experience is usually unsatisfying, and marriage is disappointing. The third idea is that it is wise not to decide in advance what you want from life; it is better to "co-operate with your destiny," and take advantage of the possibilities that unfold as your life develops. The hero of the novel is on the "right side" in these three issues, and his rival is on the wrong side. If you agree with what Jung has to say, you will probably find the hero to be an impressive and interesting character.

The urge to deconstruct this book comes when you begin to feel that it is not necessarily telling the complete and final truth about the world, and that its ideology is limited and one-sided. You need then to work out how the book has been made to *seem* more compelling than it actually is. One way to do this is to take it apart – to deconstruct it – so you can see how the impression of truth has been achieved. A particularly interesting technique has been used in *Fifth Business*.

Essentially the book is about Dunstan Ramsay's education. He has a sequence of teachers, and he moves on to the next when he has learned what one has to offer. His teachers include his parents, an isolated woman in the village where he grows up, a British woman who initiates him in love-making, a Jesuit priest, and a Swiss woman who directs a troupe that gives magic shows. The teachings occur mostly in a series of monologues: the teacher speaks, and Ramsay listens – and absorbs what is being said. The three main teachers are made to speak a Jungian language, so that Ramsay is instructed (and his attitudes formed) by a series of Jungian monologues delivered by authoritative characters. Nothing they say is ever challenged or questioned by a strong opponent, and so the book makes it appear that its Jungian ideology is "the truth about the world" – because it is dispersed among a number of authoritative characters.

When you realize that the book is *constructed* in this way, it loses some of its ideological force, and you begin to see it in a broader context. Why are Freudian ideas regularly attacked, and why are Jungian beliefs presented with such reverence? Why is real conflict and hard questioning never permitted? Why does the instruction occur with a docile pupil, who seems only too glad to listen quietly and accept everything he hears? When the novel is deconstructed in this way, it appears to contradict itself to some extent. If the ideas it presents are really powerful, they could stand up to some real resistance. The fact that there is no serious opposition makes the principal ideas seem weak rather than strong.

The desire to deconstruct a work of literature comes from (first) thinking that it contains the truth, and (secondly) seeing it in broader terms that make the book's truth seem much more limited, and its vision less authoritative. So although it is possible to teach deconstruction as a neutral "technique of literary analysis," such an approach actually makes little sense. Usually teachers want to make their students enthusiastic about the books on the course, and deconstruction is likely to have the opposite effect. Since 1966 deconstruction has been very much in vogue in the United States, and it seems to be a kind of rival to historical criticism, new criticism, and structuralism – which it is, since deconstruction challenges their claims to authority. But it is different from these other methods because deconstruction is almost always negative. Its philosophical underpinnings are fundamentally skeptical, i.e. it is based on the assumption that it is *not possible* to develop valid beliefs about the nature of the world and of human experience.

Radical Deconstruction: Deconstruction as Ideology

You can use deconstruction to subvert an authority that is oppressing you, but if you go to deconstruction in order to find a set of values or a philosophy of life, you enter a world that is anarchistic and solipsistic – a world in which each person is essentially alone and cannot communicate with others, and social groups fall apart because they have no coherence. This, I think, is an almost impossible world to live in, but it is an interesting one to know about.

We can gain entrance to the deconstructionist world most easily through the structuralist view of language. Structuralists maintain that language does not merely *represent* the world, it also organizes the world. Language is like a set of categories that imposes structures on the world. (This idea is more fully explained in Chapter 6.) So language is by no means transparent: it affects what we see when we look at the world. Someone who speaks English sees a different world from someone who speaks French, because some of the structures in the two languages are different. If you are able to speak two languages fluently, you probably feel that the language you use colours the way you see the world and how you operate in it.

Deconstructionists conclude from this observation (rightly, I think) that any truth couched in a particular language is affected or distorted by that language. This means that *nothing expressed in language is absolutely true.* So whenever you encounter an author or a group claiming to possess the *absolute* truth, you can always deconstruct their claim by saying that their truth is relativized by the very fact that it is expressed in a particular language. Another way of saying this is that the truth is *mediated* by language, since language is the medium through which truth is expressed.

Some religious groups and some authors (mostly of a romantic cast of mind) seem to believe that they possess an absolute truth, which they find expressed in sacred texts, poems, or novels. These people are particularly vulnerable to deconstruction. You can always say, "Your truth depends on your language, and your language is not absolute; it is only one of the many languages in the world." But it is very important to notice that this deconstructive strategy only works on *absolute* claims. As soon as an author replies, "My works do not present an absolute truth; they are simply the closest I (or my community) can get to the truth, using the language we have at our disposal," he is off the hook. But at least he has admitted that his truth is not absolute, and so it is open to criticism and possibly negotiation.

Deconstructionists agree with structuralists in noting that language often works through binary oppositions, such as male/female, center/margins, rich/poor, white/black, win/lose. In these particular cases, the first term is often considered superior to the second term, and so a rich white male who has won his way to a significant position in an important center of population has more power and influence (usually) than a poor, black woman who lives in the country. Oppositions such as male/female, with values attached to them, are important elements in particular ideologies, and they are often masked in some way, or assumed to be "reasonable" rather than arbitrary.

Deconstructionists are quick to spot these binary distinctions, and to ask what they are based on. Often they find that the oppositions are based on power relations and that one section of society, holding arbitrary power, uses the distinctions to bolster its own position at the expense of disadvantaged or marginal groups of people. So rich people may exploit poor people, men may exploit women, anglo-saxons may exploit native and ethnic groups, professors may exploit students – and often both parties willingly consent to the process. This usually happens because both parties are in the grip of an ideology that makes the process of exploitation seem legitimate.

The technique of deconstructing binary oppositions can be fruitful when applied to literature. If we look at Robertson Davies's work, for instance, it is clear that almost all the interesting characters are professionally successful and come from upper middle-class families. Most of them have strong connections to Europe, too. In Davies's world, if you are not successful, and if you stay in North America, you will probably live a dull and spiritually impoverished life. A deconstructionist would be quick to point out this implicit assumption about the world, and to question its validity.

The Prophet of Deconstruction: Jacques Derrida

The French thinker who was mainly responsible for developing deconstruction and popularizing it in North America in the late 1960s and the 1970s was Jacques Derrida. He published three important books in 1967; they had an immediate impact, and over the next ten years they were translated into English as *Writing and Difference, Speech and Phenomena,* and *Of Grammatology.*[2] Derrida is difficult to understand, for several reasons, and I cannot hope to give you a full introduction to his work in a few pages. But his influence as a critic in the English-speaking world since 1970 has been greater than anyone else's, in spite of the fact that many academics refuse to take him seriously at all. So it is important that you have some sense of his methods and his concerns, and if you want to understand him more fully, you can turn to Christopher Norris's helpful book on him.[3]

There are three aspects of his work which I will evoke briefly and relate to the central ideas of deconstruction:

(i) his critique of Western philosophy since Plato;

(ii) his sense of how words and languages embody assumptions and ideologies; and

(iii) his sense of how norms and standards (such as what constitutes a first-class essay) are not absolutes, but are constructed by groups of people for particular reasons.

Derrida's work is significant in part because it launches an attack on many kinds of instituted authority and received wisdom. This helps explain why many people refuse to read his books carefully: their positions are being challenged. It is worthwhile to begin with an explanation of why he wants to subvert authority.

Most people have, at some point in their lives, failed some test which other people have passed. This failure may be merited, but at times it may be the result of an arbitrary and irrelevant standard being applied, for example when a handicapped person is excluded from getting a position which she could do perfectly well, or a person with a degree is not considered because she has "too much education for the job." When this happens, you lose faith in the authority who is making these decisions, and you feel rewriting the rules is in order. Derrida was born in the suburbs of Algiers to a Jewish family; as a child he felt extremely isolated, being part of a tiny minority, during a time of racial discrimination and violence. Like Roland Barthes (who felt marginalized by the poverty of his family, and later by his homosexuality), Derrida grew up with a strong awareness that the norms of society were often unfair, and needed to be questioned. We can see this in some of his main concerns.

(i) The challenge to Western philosophy: Derrida has mounted a fundamental attack on the Western philosophical tradition since the time of Plato. It amounts to a criticism of how we have been thinking for the past 2500 years, and it suggests a radically different way of dealing with authority. Of course it is hard for most of us to understand, since it requires us to think in a new way. What he is criticizing is this: *that since Plato, philosophers have given direct communication through speech a higher status than communication through written texts. Speech is seen as primary, writing as secondary.* According to this tradition, to get at the fundamental meaning of writing, you would be best to talk directly to the author, and get his meaning orally, from him. Derrida would say that this shows that Western thought has a phonocentric bias: the voice (*phōnē*, in Greek) is at the centre, and writing is an inferior substitute for it.

This preference for speech over writing, Derrida would say, is not an accident; it is in fact the expression of an ideology, which was articulated by Plato in his dialogue *Phaedrus*.[4] The story is as follows: in Egypt the god of writing and geometry was called Thoth. One day Thoth came to the court of King Thamus, where writing was unknown. He offered Thamus the gift of writing, but after consideration Thamus declined it, for a number of reasons. He was afraid that once his subjects could write, their memories would atrophy through lack of use. Even worse, the bond between a student and his teacher, instead of passing through the living medium of the voice, might occur through the lifeless marks on the page. This might lead to error, since the teacher would not be there necessarily to explain the meaning of the words which were written down.

The ideology expressed by this story is essentially authoritarian and, in the West, it takes a patriarchal form. It implies that the job of the wise man is to explain the truth; and this truth exists prior to being expressed in language. The teacher can see error, and correct it, if the student does not grasp the truth correctly, because the teacher has access to that prior truth. The same ideology is at work in the idea that to really understand what an author means, we should ask that author – he knows what *his work* means. This puts the author in a God-like position.

What does Derrida want to contest in this model of the patriarchal transmission of the truth? One difficulty for him is the idea that a truth can exist prior to language, in some timeless form outside of history (as in Plato's doctrine of the eternal forms). Derrida would say that a statement can only exist *in language*; prior to its encoding in language, it has no existence. A second problem is the assumption of a phonocentric culture that "the truth" has its origin in some authority's personal consciousness. Since Nietzsche and Freud, at least, we have suspected that any individual's conscious mind will be riven by some divisions and contradictions, and cannot be relied on to deliver a pure truth.

Derrida's third, and most powerful objection, is that he feels that writing, not speech, is the primary condition of knowledge and culture. It is primarily in written form that information, knowledge, wisdom, and literature are handed down; and we cannot think of any of these realistically without the idea of writing being central. Philosophy is especially prone to deny this, because philosophers would like to think they have access to truths which are outside of time and language – truths which are prior to history – but essentially this just shows a desire for power on the part of philosophers, a desire not unlike that of theologians who feel they know about the nature of God.

Why does this matter? What difference does it make whether speech or writing is seen as primary? The main difference is whether authority is to be located within the person of the speaker, or within a written text. If we live in a community where *a person* has authority, our shared life will have certain characteristics – that person can change the meaning of his text, or revise it, because it is *his inner idea* which matters, not the words which express it. If, on the other hand, authority is vested in a text (such as a written code of laws), then it cannot be changed on the whim of a person, although it is open to different kinds of interpretation. To see and appreciate the centrality of writing in culture may limit a patriarch's authority, and may even dethrone him.

Derrida questions the hierarchy which makes speech superior to writing by pointing out that both are semiotic systems – that is, systems of signs which function in a social context. One feature of such systems is that words are repeatable – words could not convey a meaning if they were unique and could be used only once. So when someone says, "I love you," the fact that they are saying it does not guarantee its authenticity, especially if the person is an accomplished actor. (This problem is explored in John Fowles's *The Magus*, when the male protagonist tries to interpret the erotic actions of a woman, and makes the mistake of thinking she loves him. He eventually realizes that he is misinterpreting her actions – i.e. he does not understand the semiotic system she is using – and he finds this deeply upsetting.) So some of the limitations of the written word also apply to speech, or, to use a common phrase in deconstruction, "speech is always already written."

(ii) The second and third aspects of Derrida's thought can be treated more briefly. Derrida has a strong sense of how specific words and structures in language embody particular assumptions about life. For instance, he thinks that the assumptions of Western philosophy are built into our language, so that it is almost impossible to use the word "truth" without implying that you subscribe to Western phonocentric ideas of it. To indicate that a word is inadequate in this way, Derrida sometimes writes it with a line through it (like this: ~~truth~~); this is called writing the word *sous râture*, "under erasure." To see a paragraph with words written in this way can alter one's feeling about language, and the reliability of the meanings of words.

Derrida also has created a host of words and terms to express his revised vision of how culture works, terms such as "logocentric," "phonocentric," "*différance*," "aporia," and "the play of language." Using these words suggests that the writer is stepping into a Derridean universe. Derrida also uses a lot of puns, and games with words, to indicate that the materiality of words (i.e. the sounds of the words, or the letters we use to represent them) affects how we use and understand them. Derrida's habit of playing with words in this way causes some of his critics to refuse to take him seriously, and this is quite a simple way to reject his whole oeuvre; but it is short-sighted. He might reply that there is something fundamentally wrong with any philosophy which doesn't take account of the fact that the materiality of language affects the search for, or the expression of, truth.

If the significance of this point is not clear, an example may help. The proverb "haste makes waste" is easy to remember because it contains two rhyming words, and all three words have the same vowel sound. This fact is an accident; the similarity of the sounds has nothing to do with the truth or the relevance of the proverb. But this arbitrary feature of the proverb may cause us to remember it more easily than others. So language is not a transparent window; its materiality affects the way we use it in the same way that the material properties of a block of wood will affect what kind of sculpture we can make out of it.

(iii) The third aspect of Derrida's thought is related to the structuralist view of language, that words have an identity only because they are different from other words – they don't have an essence of their own. So the identity of the word "bat" depends on it being distinct from other words like it, such as "mat," "cat," "bad," and "bet." But none of these words is *better* than the others; they are just *different* from each other.

Derrida feels that sometimes norms and standards should work in a similar way. To have a social standard, you need to have an excluded group. Derrida, like Barthes, was sensitive to gestures of exclusion. To some extent the identity of the accepted group is created by the people who are excluded, by the fact of their exclusion. I once felt this quite strongly when I failed a group of exams which a number of my friends passed. What it meant to have passed the exams depended partly on my having failed, and I thought they owed me some thanks. I deserved to fail; but I might have felt very differently if I had been excluded for arbitrary or irrelevant reasons. Then I would have been excluded merely because I was different, not because I was less skilled than the others.

The crucial point here is that social norms, like fictional stories, are *constructed*. They are not absolute or natural. They may be constructed to deprive some people of power in an immoral way. On the other hand, norms may have a valid purpose, and be administered fairly, but they need to be watched carefully; and when they are unjust or unfairly applied they need to be changed. An example of deconstruction is realizing that a norm has been constructed, so it can be altered. If we see it as natural or eternal, the idea of changing it might not even occur to us. So deconstruction is an important strategy for advocates of social change.[5]

Some Practical Results of Deconstruction

What follows from this radical critique of the Western authoritarian idea of truth, and the reversing of the hierarchy which puts speech above writing? One main result is that when people speak or write, they are much less in control of what they are doing than was previously thought. What they can think and say is, in some important ways, structured by the language they speak, and the particular ways in which they speak it. This is sometimes expressed in the phrase, "We don't speak language; language speaks us." This is a striking formulation, but it gives an exaggerated impression of how passive we actually are when we articulate our thoughts and feelings. We are certainly constrained in interesting ways, but we are not the objects of a full linguistic determinism. We still have freedoms, although they may not be quite as great as we imagined they were.[6]

A second result is that we should pay more attention to hidden assumptions in our language and our culture, and especially in areas where people assume they are being neutral, factual, and objective. The creation and enforcement of norms deserve our careful scrutiny. We need to ask whose interests they serve, who is excluded, why, and whether this is what we really want. Another area which Derrida and others have investigated is the idea of reason itself. Most philosophers have assumed that reason is a reliable, neutral, universally valid tool for discovering the truth, but for Derrida it is a method which has a specific origin and serves particular interests. This issue is an important subject of debate in contemporary philosophy.

A third result which I have not discussed yet is the model Derrida provides for actually investigating situations and texts. You might easily conclude from my summary that Derrida ranges widely and wields a broad sword, dealing in generalities, and making sweeping assessments and critiques. In fact in his critical practice Derrida is careful and painstaking. He examines texts minutely, searching assiduously for details which are clues to hidden assumptions and predispositions of the author. One of his main criticisms of previous philosophers is that they have not paid close enough attention to the rhetorical nature of the major texts in the Western philosophic tradition. Derrida is a model of care and circumspection, and he resists generalities. This is a characteristic which he shares with Bakhtin and with postmodernism. So although Derrida has the status of a prophet in North American literary criticism, he does not declaim and decree. His manner of operation is much more modest, in keeping with his own feelings about the relativity of truth, standards, and norms.

Derrida is right to observe that cultures and languages operate partly through making binary distinctions, and some of those distinctions have one term that is privileged or valorized by the culture. If you think of the distinction "work/play," which is important in North American culture, you can see that in most instances work is given a higher value than play. This might be an error in some cases, and we need to be aware that the opposition between the two could itself be deconstructed – as in the case when you are able to find work that seems like play to you.

But there is a limitation in deconstruction. Try, for instance, to imagine a culture in which there are no valorized binary distinctions. What would such a society look like? If we cannot imagine such a society in practical terms, then we have to accept that societies *will* have valorized binary distinctions. We would want to be aware of them, to feel that they are worth supporting, to watch out for abuses of them, and above all to avoid claiming that they are eternal or natural. They are constructed, and provisional and practical in nature.

Deconstruction in Literature: *The Unbearable Lightness of Being*

Some works of literature have a strong deconstructive element in them, and often they help readers see that the assumptions of their society (embedded in its ideology) are not necessarily right. One striking example is Milan Kundera's *The Unbearable Lightness of Being*, which, in addition to being a moving and lyrical book, is thoroughly deconstructive, in an amusing but also serious way. It is the story of Tomas, a brain surgeon living in Prague around the time of the anti-Russian uprising of 1968, and it centers on his relationship with Tereza, a waitress whom he meets in a provincial town through "six fortuities," one of which is that Tomas has to peform an operation in that town because the chief surgeon at his hospital in Prague has had an attack of sciatica.[7] This questions the sentimental assumption that there is something inevitable about the greatest love in a person's life.

> We all reject out of hand the idea that the love of our life may be something light or weightless; we presume our love is what must be, that without it our life would no longer be the same; we feel that Beethoven himself, gloomy and awe-inspiring, is playing the *"Es muss sein!"* to our own great love.

> Tomas ... came to the conclusion that the love story of his life exemplified not *"Es muss sein!"* (It must be so), but rather *"Es könnte auch anders sein"* (It could just as well be otherwise).[8]

Many other norms and expectations are reversed in the course of the book. For example, Tomas maintains that what makes a relationship serious is not sex, but sleeping through the night with another person – sleeping and dreaming together. Another example is the reversal of progress in Tomas's career. Because he writes an article attacking the communist régime, he is dismissed from his job as a brain surgeon and assigned duties as a window-washer. Later on he and Tereza decide that he will give up that occupation so they can become farmers in the countryside:

> Her hands had started trembling again. She had aged. She was all that mattered to him. She, born of six fortuities, she, the blossom sprung from the chief surgeon's sciatica, she, the reverse side of all his *"Es muss sein!"* – she was the only thing he cared about.

> ... There was only one criterion for all his decisions: he must do nothing that could harm her.[9]

So the norm of personal progress is turned upside down, and both Tereza and Tomas become happier as they throw off the burdens of professional life and move to the country.

Another deconstructive feature of *The Unbearable Lightness of Being* is the fact that it has an extended section, entitled "Words Misunderstood," showing how words and images can have opposite meanings for different individuals, and so create disasterous confusions. At one point Franz, a male character, becomes inspired by the phrase "living in truth," and decides that he must make public his relation with the woman with whom he is having a secret affaire, and leave his wife and family. But for the woman, an artist who abhors publicity, "living in truth" can only be accomplished in utter secresy, away from the pressures of other people's opinions. So when Franz comes to live with her, she packs up and disappears forever from his life. This illustrates how uncertain the meaning of words can be, and how drastically this uncertainty can affect our lives.

The single image which, in my opinion, best conveys the feeling of deconstruction occurs in this book:

> Toilets in modern bathrooms rise up from the floor like white water
> lilies. The architect does all he can to make the body forget how paltry
> it is, and to make man ignore what happens to his intestinal wastes after
> the water from the tank flushes them down the drain. Even though the
> sewer pipes reach far into our houses with their tentacles, they are
> carefully hidden from view, and we are happily ignorant of the invisible
> Venice of shit underlying our bathrooms, bedrooms, dance halls, and
> parliaments.
>
> The bathroom in the old working–class flat on the outskirts of
> Prague was less hypocritical: the floor was covered with gray tile and the
> toilet rising up from it was broad, squat, and pitiful. It did not look like
> a white water lily; it looked like what it was: the enlarged end of a sewer
> pipe. And since it lacked even a wooden seat, Tereza had to perch on
> the cold enamel rim.[10]

The beautiful toilet bowl is a construction of society, a kind of collective work of art, and its function is to help us forget our bodily functions, our wastes and their smells. What deconstruction does is like "unbuilding" the toilet bowl: it reminds us of another aspect of reality which our polite conventions hide: the canals and conduits full of excrement and waste, to which the toilet is attached. This is a graphic and appropriate image for many euphemistic or sanitizing uses of language, such as calling torture "physical persuasion." A deconstructive critic might say that the toilet bowl is an accurate image for ordinary language as well: it looks clear, precise, elegant, and unproblematical; but in fact both the toilet and language are connected to hidden networks which are messy, imprecise, and always in flux. The system of language may not be such a pretty thing.

Kundera's image also makes clear the moral purpose behind deconstruction: to unmask our pretences, and destabilize the hierarchies on which a society relies. Here the binary distinction between beauty and ugliness is put into question in a forceful way. Normally we choose beauty over ugliness and mess, but what if beauty masks the truth, and ugliness helps us see reality more accurately?

So deconstruction can be extremely useful in certain situations, but it is a tool rather than a desirable philosophy in itself. It can alert you to the ideologies hidden in works of literature, and it can help you to liberate yourself from oppressive authorities, by questioning the accepted values and binary distinctions of society. But in the end it cannot *create* the structures which we want to operate in society or in literature. These problems will be dealt with more fully in the following chapter, in which the deconstructive frame of mind is related to three other mindsets which have a much greater constructive potential.

Notes

1.   *Fifth Business* (Toronto: Macmillan, 1970) is the first book in Robertson Davies's "Deptford Trilogy." The other two volumes are *The Manticore* and *World of Wonders*. The whole trilogy is steeped in Jung's ideas, which in part accounts for its great interest.

2.   The three books by Jacques Derrida published in 1967 are: *L'écriture et la différence* (Paris: Seuil, 1967), translated as *Writing and Difference* (Chicago: Chicago University Press, 1978); *De la grammatologie* (Paris: Minuit, 1967), translated as *Of Grammatology* (Baltimore: Johns Hopkins University Press, 1976); and *La voix et le phénomène* (Paris: Presses Universitaire de France, 1967), translated as *Speech and Phenomena* (Evanston: Northwestern University Press, 1973).

3.   Christopher Norris, *Derrida* (Cambridge, Mass.: Harvard University Press, 1987).

4.   Plato, *Phaedrus,* section 274 and following; *Collected Dialogues,* ed. Edith Hamilton and Huntington Cairns (Princeton University Press, 1961) 520.

5.   The link between deconstruction and social change is made clearly by Michael Ryan in *Marxism and Deconstruction.* He distinguishes between scientific Marxism, which he sees as rigid and metaphysical, and critical Marxism, which rejects authoritarian central state communism, and is opposed to both capitalism and patriarchy. In connecting Marxism and deconstruction he wants to show that "how we read or analyze, and how we organize political and social institutions, are related forms of practice" (xv).

6.   This point is made with great eloquence by Iris Murdoch in her book *Metaphysics as a Guide to Morals* (Harmondsworth: Penguin, 1993), Chapter 7, "Derrida and Structuralism," 185-216. She writes, "Because of the vast extent of language and the way in which meanings of words and concepts are determined by innumerable relationships with other words and concepts, no individual speaker can really 'know' what he means, we are *unconscious* of the immense linguistic beyond which we think we 'use' when it is really using us" (187). But she feels it is an error to exaggerate our helplessness in language. "Value, morality, is removed by the structuralist picture if taken seriously. This removal of value is, in a quiet way, characteristic of this age. ... [Heidegger's later concept of Being, and Derrida's theory of Language, as systems...] represent new forms of determinism. Determinism is always reappearing in new forms since it satisfies a deep human wish: to *give up*, to get rid of freedom, responsibility, remorse, all sorts of personal individual unease, and surrender to fate and the relief of 'it could not be otherwise'" (190).

7.   Milan Kundera, *The Unbearable Lightness of Being* (New York: Harper, 1984) 219.

8.   Kundera, 35.

9.   Kundera, 219.

10.   Kundera, 156.

Suggestions for Further Reading

Helen Crowley, *A Teacher's Introduction to Deconstruction* (Urbana, Illinois: National Council of Teachers of English, 1989).

Jonathan Culler, *On Deconstruction: Theory and Criticism after Structuralism* (Ithaca: Cornell University Press, 1982)

———- "In Pursuit of Signs," *The Pursuit of Signs* (Ithaca: Cornell University Press, 1981), 18-43.

Christopher Norris, *Deconstruction: Theory and Practice* (London and New York: Methuen, 1982). This book begins with structuralism and New Criticism, deals with Jacques Derrida, and has a chapter on the American deconstructive critics Geoffrey Hartman, J. Hillis Miller, and Paul de Man.

———- *Derrida* (Cambridge, Mass.: Harvard University Press, 1987).

Edward Said, *The World, the Text, and the Critic* (Cambridge, Mass.: Harvard University Press, 1983), especially "Criticism between Culture and System," 178-225.

Robert Scholes, *Protocols of Reading* (New Haven: Yale University Press, 1989).

CHAPTER NINE:

Vico and the Four Stages of Mental Life

ONE OF THE MOST POWERFUL THEORIES for understanding both literature and life was developed by an Italian historian of the 18th century, Giambattista Vico. He wanted to discover the reasons why civilizations seemed to have a cyclical pattern of development, passing through periods of growth, maturity, and decline. He identified four stages in this process, and they are very broadly relevant to a wide range of phenomena. This has been brilliantly demonstrated by Hayden White, who has used the four stages to analyze how historical accounts of events are written.[1]

In order to use Vico's four stages to understand literature, it is best to present them in terms of the growth of an individual mind – or, more exactly, in terms of the way in which an individual person relates to some institution that is important to him. For students of literature, the best example to use is the relation a student might have to "the institution of literature" – which includes the books he reads, the professors he encounters, the course-structure offered by his department, the critical works available in the library, and the reviews of new books in periodicals and newspapers.

Each stage in Vico's pattern of development is characterized by a dominant mental process, and each is directly related to a particular figure of speech (that is, a way of using language in a non-literal way, such as metaphor). A particular person might move through the four stages or stop permanently at any one of them. No stage is "better" than the others in a general way, although individuals may feel more comfortable with one stage than another. I will illustrate the stages by presenting them in terms of the development of a student of literature, but I hope the reader will be able to transpose them easily to other areas of life — such as relations with parents, or places of work.

Stage 1: Falling in Love

For my hypothetical university student — a young man of about eighteen starting out in a literature course — stage 1 is the period during which things are first discovered and named. The student is caught up in a numinous world, a new world he does not understand or control, a world that is exciting, inspiring, and perhaps terrifying at times. This is the stage of emotional identification, of falling in love, and of deep involvement. Stendhal is thinking of this stage when he says, of his time in Paris as a young man, "I lived exactly the life of a poet, except for the fact that I didn't write any poems." In Tolstoy's *War and Peace*, Nikolai Rostov is overwhelmed by a stage 1 feeling when the Tsar comes to inspect the troops before the battle of Austerlitz:

> Rostov did not remember and had no consciousness of how he ran to
> his place and mounted. Instantly his regret at not having taken part in
> the action [of the previous battle] and his humdrum mood among men
> he saw every day had gone — instantly every thought of himself had
> vanished. This nearness by itself, he felt, made up to him for the
> morning's disappointment. He was happy as a lover is happy when the
> moment arrives for the longed-for rendez-vous. Not daring to look
> down the line, and not glancing round, he was conscious by an ecstatic
> instinct of *his* [the Tsar's] approach. And he felt it not only from the
> sound of the tramping hooves of the approaching cavalcade, but because
> as *he* drew nearer everything around him grew brighter, more joyous
> and full of meaning, more festive. Nearer and nearer moved this sun, as
> he seemed to Rostov, shedding around him rays of blissful and majestic
> light, until Rostov felt himself enfolded in that radiance and heard *his*
> voice, caressing, serene, regal, and yet so simple.[2]

We can feel Rostov's excitement in this description. It is as though he has found heaven on earth, and he cannot believe that his life is suddenly so exciting and that all its miseries and tedium have miraculously disappeared.

Our hypothetical student, who is beginning a course of literary stud-

Vico's four stages of development: A Literature Student's Response

	STAGE 1: METAPHOR	STAGE 2: METONYMY
DOMINANT MENTAL PROCESS	Naming things, or learning the accepted names of things.	Connecting things with neighbors in time and space.
CHARACTERISTIC PSYCHOLOGICAL STATE	Numinous experience. Individual lost in an enormous new world. Implict faith in immediate experience. Hysteria, fetishism.	Desire to analyze things, to reduce things to a more basic level of organization; tendency toward positivism; ego very involved.
APPROPRIATE STAGE IN THE DEVELOPMENT OF A STUDENT OF LITERATURE	Discovering literature as field of interest. Great admiration for individual authors. Utter lack of understanding for other "major" authors. Little or no interest in criticism.	Establishing connections between authors, usually by locating them in their historical context. Accumulation of detailed knowledge without a strong sense of general pattern.
RELATED IDEOLOGY	Anarchist	Radical
STAGE IN THE DEVELOPMENT OF A CIVILIZATION, ACCORDING TO VICO	Age of the gods. Gods are projected on nature by man. Little social organization.	Age of heroes. Strong men dominate the institutions of a more complex society. Class divisions are established.

| STAGE 3: | STAGE 4: |
| SYNEDOCHE | IRONY |

Forming wholes by relating parts to each other. Idealizing and integrating.

Recognizing the inadequacies of the integration achieved in stage 3.

A complex reticulated structure present in the mind. Creation of a grand and panoptic vision (Blake, Coleridge).

Awareness of different viewpoints; uncertainty about things-in-themselves. Paralysis; mimicking as a way of taking action. Ego dissolved.

Development of a comprehensive pattern for literature-as-a-whole, in the manner of Frye, or a hierarchy based on merit (Leavis, Bloom), or a historical synthesis. Investigating the basis for this pattern can lead to structuralism and then to stage 4.

The discovery that the order in stage 3 is based on your own idiosyncratic conditions of development (class, education, place in the family constellation, your body, etc.). Everything depends on "what language you speak"; objectivity disappears. Deconstruction flourishes; attention focuses on criticism, because the "approach" determines what you see in a work of literature.

Conservative

Liberal (the benign stage 4). Nihilist (the malignant stage 4).

Age of humanity. Assertion of common humanity transcending class divisions. Development of written law; equal rights for all people.

Age of dissolution and *ricorso* or recycling. The human origin of institutions and standards is revealed; people no longer revere them, and seek their own private pleasures instead of the public good.

ies, is in a period of fascination with individual authors – the Gawain-poet, Shakespeare, Wordsworth, Yeats, Camus, Pasternak, for instance – who seem like shamans, because they appear to hold the secrets of life in their hands. There is a natural tendency in stage 1 to seek isolation, because others are unlikely to share the intensity of your feelings. As far as the study of literature is concerned, what you want to do most is to commune with your favorite authors and try to discover if there are any more who have a similar power and fascination for you.

A rich and continuing connection with an institution such as litera-ture seems to depend to some extent on beginning with a stage 1 in-volvement, which provides the drive and the enjoyment to nourish stages 2 and 3. Stage 1 also has a physical aspect to it, often – loving the feel of books, the different feelings associated with different typefaces, the atmosphere of the library, and on another level, the physical rhythms of English prose or verse.

Stage 2: The Search for Understanding

When you have become enthralled with an institution – take the Navy, as another example – it is natural at some point to want to understand how it works. In the middle of being excited to find yourself at sea in a destroyer, feeling the salt wind blowing in your face, you realize that you are a small piece of a large organization, which has its different parts, divisions, and hierarchies. Most likely your own future depends to some extent on how well you negotiate your passage through these various structures. This is the point at which you enter stage 2. In stage 2, the magical entities you have discovered in stage 1 are linked to one another and to the world through connections in time and space. You want to know who has power, and how people's influence alters the way things happen. Or you may simply want to know how certain mechanisms work. Feeling the shuddering might of the ship's engines is an emo-tional, stage 1 experience. Knowing exactly how they work, and why they were built the way they were, is a stage 2 matter.

In the study of literature, the passage from stage 1 to stage 2 usually occurs when you get interested in the causes of a literary work and in what was surrounding it when it was written. Since it is common to think that a literary work is the product of the author's "genius," our student of literature may want to read biographies and books about the historical background as he enters stage 2. He will start to consider questions such as, "Was Shakespeare concerned with the psychology of twins in *The Comedy of Errors* because his own twins, Hamnet and Judith, were beginning to cause interesting confusions?" Or, "When Wordsworth wrote his famous 'Lucy' poems, was he in fact writing about his sister Dorothy? What was the nature of his relationship with her, and how did that affect the poems?" Stage 2 often has a reductive element in it, because one level of experience (the text, the experience of reading) is tied to, and supposedly explained by, another level of reality (the author's life).

Stage 3: Integrating and Idealizing

Stage 2 is dispersive, because in it you connect a work of literature with other things – your interest flows outward from the work to biography and history, which have no clear boundaries. In stage 3 you shift to an integrative and idealizing mode of thought: you are interested in discovering the essence of a thing, institution, or person. You try to move from the outward appearances to the inner reality that generates them. In stage 3 you might decide that the core of *Hamlet* is the oedipal struggle between Hamlet and Claudius, and that Hamlet's bitter love for Gertrude is at the heart of all his problems. In stage 2 you often have the feeling that you are wading through a mass of detail (and stage 2 people are often good at dealing with a great deal of detail); in stage 3 you make a firm distinction between those things that are central and essential, and those that are peripheral and non-essential. There is a Platonic tendency in stage 3 thinking – you feel as though you ought to be able to discover to the central essence or core of anything you encounter. If stage 1 produces the poet, and stage 2 the administrator, stage 3 seems to hold the promise of wisdom: a thorough immersion might qualify you to become a philosopher-king.

In order to be in charge of an institution (or a branch of an institution, such as a course in a literature program), it is valuable to have the stage 3 perspective on what you are doing. When you are embedded in stage 3, you know how things run (you have learned that in stage 2); you retain your love for the whole process (which marked the stage 1 experience); and you understand the goals or aims of the entire operation. That makes it possible for you to understand the rules "from above" (instead of just enforcing them mechanically). You can see what the rules are *for*, and so you can tell when they ought to be broken or modified, because they are hindering the real purposes of the institution. Our stage 2 student is likely to run his operation "by the book," because he isn't aware of the goals which the rules serve. In stage 3 the student knows that the rules are only an approximation to what is desired, and that they have to be modified in special circumstances.

If we think of the institution of literature as a whole, then it is clear that you have to be very ambitious to develop your own stage 3 understanding of the field. This would involve a huge amount of knowledge, and a remarkable ability to find patterns and interrelations in that knowledge. Fortunately there are others who can help us into stage 3 – critics such as Samuel Taylor Coleridge, F.R. Leavis, and Northrop Frye, who have developed large syntheses to express their feelings and intuitions about literature-as-a-whole. In a more humble way, there are people whose natural and characteristic movement of mind is from details to wholes and back to details again. Often such minds have a religious quality, because, as Coleridge observed in one of his poems, thinking about wholes leads you to think about God. The Stage 3 experience is very exciting, because it makes you feel that you are on the verge of understanding the world, and your place in it.

The Figures of Speech Related to Stages 1, 2, and 3

So far we have dealt with how the mind characteristically works in stages 1, 2, and 3. Before going on to stage 4, we need to consider the relationship of these stages to three figures of speech. The first two of them were introduced in the chapter on paradigmatic and syntagmatic relations:

Stage 1	Metaphor
Stage 2	Metonymy
Stage 3	Synecdoche

Metaphor is appropriate to a stage 1 consciousness because it is a way of relating new experience to old experience, through discovering appropriate parallels. There is a kind of vertical movement back and forth between the new and the old. In stage 1, you are plunged into a new world. How are you to talk about what is in it? One method is to take images from the rest of your experience and apply them in a metaphorical way. When Macbeth is talking about his own death, he says, "Out, out brief candle!" He is using what we all know about candles to express his feelings about what we know very little about – our own deaths. Metaphor is appropriate in stage 1 because it is an effective way of expressing emotions, and stage 1 is drenched in emotions.

Metonymy is the figure of speech which indicates things by naming something near them in time or space. This is appropriate to stage 2, which is a matter of exploring how things are laid out in time and space. If you say, "Ottawa has decided to proceed with sanctions against South Africa," this use of metonymy is based on your knowledge that the seat of the Canadian federal government is in Ottawa – something a stranger to Canada might not know. Metonymy often depends on a common knowledge of the external world for its meaning to be understood.

Metonymy usually carries less emotional intensity than metaphor. This is partly because metonymy depends on how things are located in the real world, and often their location is arbitrary or accidental. The fact that the federal government is located in Ottawa does not tell you much about the government's essential nature. One of the frustrations of moving around the word in a stage 2 way is that a lot of what you find *is* arbitrary and accidental, and learning about it does not always reveal meaningful or useful patterns. Sometimes narratives that have a strong stage 2 feeling take on a senseless or absurd quality, overwhelming us with information from a chaotic world.

The literary figure of speech associated with stage 3 is synecdoche, in which a part is made to stand for the whole (as in "All hands on deck!") or the whole is made to stand for a part ("Canada goes to the Olympics"). The characteristic mental operation in stage 3 is creating (or identifying) the wholes that unify a set of disparate parts or appearances; this shows why synecdoche provides an appropriate verbal parallel. But synecdoche is not a common literary device, and it does not carry any identifiable emotional overtones.

There is something necessarily abstract about our stage 3 student, which distinguishes him from his stage 1 counterpart. The idea of the whole is not immediately given to consciousness – it is constructed out of the component parts, and a person looking after a whole institution (whether large or small) has his attention moving from part to part, although he may have a very strong feeling for the complete institution and what it is doing. A similar observation can be made about the integration of a work of literature. It is obvious that with a long novel, such as Tolstoy's *Anna Karenina*, you have to make a considerable effort to unify it, and to see how the various parts contribute to its whole effect.

How, for instance, do the three main marriages fit together – Oblonsky's conventional, flawed marriage to Dolly, Anna's passionate and doomed relation to Vronsky, and Levin's relation to his wife Kitty? Once you do manage to unify the novel in your perception, the whole may have a much greater effect than any of the parts on its own. This is part of the attraction of the stage 3 experience.

Stage 4: Liberalism and Disillusionment

We are now prepared to deal with stage 4, which is of a different order than any of the first three stages. They all involve connecting yourself with an institution; stage 4 is a matter of freeing yourself from an institution, which usually involves a process of deconstruction. If stage 3 develops the philosopher-king – that wise individual who understands the world, the person we trust to direct important institutions – stage 4 turns the philosopher-king into a nihilist, who is alienated, sterile, and unproductive. Although this may not sound like progress, there are some attractive features to this transition, which, in its more benign form, tends to produce liberalism rather than disillusionment.

Stage 4 develops out of stage 3, and is dependent on it. You can't have a stage 4 experience without getting into stage 3 first. In stage 3 you have a great deal of confidence in your understanding of the world, and this assurance helps you handle power. You feel that you know what your are doing. You begin to slip into stage 4 when you realize that your understanding is based on certain assumptions, or certain arbitrary features of your own life, which you thought were universal. Now you suspect, or know, that they are not universal, and so your understanding is fundamentally flawed and incomplete.

As an example of the transition from stage 3 to stage 4, we could consider Charles Smithson in *The French Lieutenant's Woman*. Smithson is typical of 19th-century intellectuals in that he lives almost exclusively in a male-dominated world. Men control his schooling, his university, and much of his social life. Women are simply excluded from a lot of his activities. One of Charles's projects in life is to gain a general understanding of human experience, and he tends to see this project in universal terms. He thinks that once he finds out *the truth* about the world he will have knowledge that is applicable everywhere. He confidently anticipates a stage 3 understanding of how the world operates. But to be catapulted into stage 4 he has only to realize that his "truth" is fundamentally built on his condition as a white upper-class male, and that what he thinks of as "true" is in fact fundamentally wrong or unacceptable for almost everyone who is *not* an upper-class male.

A similar process of disillusionment can be seen in a vivid way in some Marxists and Christians, who have gone through a period of utter commitment and then become disillusioned by discovering a radical fault in their ideology. The result for such people is far worse than simply being returned to a neutral, agnostic attitude: it is felt as an acute loss. A committed partner in a marriage can feel a similar loss when the union breaks down. The person feels bereft of something that he or she depended on for a identity and for a means of taking action in the world. Hence the bitterness of the acute stage 4 experience.

The passage from stage 3 to stage 4 is greatly assisted by structuralism, which suggests that "reality," as we apprehend it, is encoded in a particular language (such as English, or Hindi), and so the reality which you see depends in part on the language which you speak. This perception is at first satisfying and liberating, because it allows you to understand the variety in the world and the conflict between individuals. Critics may not agree about the meaning of a novel because they "speak different languages" – that is, they have been nurtured in different cultural traditions and, in effect, they live in different worlds. This is a benign form of the stage 4 experience, which produces a liberal attitude toward the world.

Stages 1, 2, and 3 all provide a basis for action; stage 4 provides a way of attacking any rationale for action that claims to be certain. The verbal devices associated with the first three stages all provide ways of saying things, of presenting a vision of the world. The verbal device that corresponds to stage 4 is irony, which is a means of conveying two or more ideas at once, and leaving the reader uncertain about what you really mean. Some professors have a way of saying, "That is an interesting idea," which leaves you uncertain as to whether they want to hear more about it or whether, indeed, they never want to hear you mention it again. In much ironic language (as in sarcasm), the implied meaning is the opposite of the literal meaning. The lack of certainty that irony expresses is appropriate to stage 4, because our student in stage 4 never really knows what he thinks is true.

Stages 1 and 3 are attractive because of the sense of wonder that characterizes them; it is hard to imagine a person immersed in either of these stages who is untouched by awe and reverence. A person in stage 2 can be nastily self-assertive, and one in stage 4 has all the problems associated with the death of God and the birth of the absurd. Most productive literary scholars operate in a stage 2 mode, compiling information and doing historical research, an activity based on connections in time and space. The characteristic modern situation has the nature of stage 4, in which there are many ideologies in conflict with one another, and no overarching sense of truth.

This quality of stage 4 is evident in the broken, ironic quality of T.S. Eliot's early poetry, and blatant in his long poem *The Waste Land*. The rise of interest in literary theory, and the importance of theoretical conflicts in literary discussions, indicates that stage 4 is important to students of literature now. It seems clear to many people that there are various ways of viewing the world of literature, and that we cannot settle the most important disputes simply by appealing to "the facts." We need to classify the various ways of looking at literature (or of speaking about it). Only then can we see what the main paradigms are, and work out some way of dealing with paradigm conflicts. This problem faces most university English departments, although few of them manage to address it directly.[3]

Vico's Ricorso: The Process of Recycling

It is not hard to imagine someone going through the four stages in her relation to an institution such as literary studies or Chrisitanity, although she might just as well stop permanently at any one of the four stages. But what comes after stage 4? Vico suggested that civilizations in stage 4 tend to be invaded and taken over by more vigorous outsiders (often seen as barbarians) who are in stage 1 or 2. What this suggests is that the individual who has reached stage 4 may then go through a *ricorso* which leads her to stage 1 in another field of activity. For example, a person who had arrived at stage 4 in literary studies might well feel that there was such radical disagreement between critics that the whole field was impossibly chaotic. But in her progress through the stages she might have come to feel that the most important meanings in literature for her were those related to the functioning of the unconscious mind in authors and readers. This might turn her in the direction of psychoanalysis, which to a large extent studies the workings of the unconscious mind. In the attempt to recognize and come to terms with her own unconscious, she might enter analysis herself – and feel some of the reverence for trained analysts which she once felt for her professors of literature. This would be a sign that she was starting off again in stage 1, and a *ricorso* would have taken place.

How to Use the Paradigm of the Four Stages

Vico's paradigm is a useful one because most people seem to be able to relate the stages to their own experience, in a variety of ways. They can usually think of different areas of their lives in which they are operating in one or another of the stages. So a university student might be in stage 4 with respect to his high school experience, in stage 3 with a small business he is operating, in stage 2 with his university career, and in stage 1 with a woman he is in love with. It would probably be clear from his actions that he is behaving quite differently in each of the four areas – which might seem inconsistent to him if he didn't know about Vico's paradigm.

People viewed from the outside, by others, sometimes seem to be predominantly fixed in one or another of the stages in most of their activities. A person who was regularly in stage 1 would have an emotionally charged life and probably would lead a chaotic existence. A person who was always struggling through a jungle of detail and trying to work out how to master it would be a stage 2 person. A stage 3 person might find her natural niche in life as a chief executive officer in whatever she did, and a stage 4 person would be permanently disillusioned and cynical (or – in the benign stage 4 – a liberal).

The four stages can help you understand certain works of literature, either through offering a classification system for the characters in the work, or through allowing you to see the progress of one character through several stages of development. Examples can be seen in the chart on pages 142-143. Some readers may object that Vico's four stages are like a straight-jacket, and that imposing them on works of literature (or on people) is distorting. Of course this may be true in individual cases, and I am not claiming universality or absolute "rightness" or "completeness" for Vico's paradigm. It is valuable when it allows you to see a pattern in a work of literature, and when that pattern helps you understand your own emotional response to the work. If you find this happening, then the use of the four-stage paradigm will seem amply justified. If you find that it isn't useful in this way, you will probably forget about it, and that will be for the best. There is no point in hanging on to theories that aren't useful.

I will provide two brief examples of how Vico's paradigm can be used to illuminate poems by Wordsworth. The first is "She was a Phantom of Delight," the moving short poem about Wordsworth's wife Mary. In the first stanza he falls in love with her image: she "gleams upon his sight," and he finds her

> A dancing shape, an image gay,
> To haunt, to startle, and way-lay.

This is stage 1 material; and it is striking that Wordsworth recognizes the ambiguity of stage 1 – it is at one and the same time delightful, enthralling, and threatening. Mary seems to him to be a "phantom" that could "haunt" and "way-lay" him. In the second stanza, Wordsworth sees Mary more closely: "a spirit, yet a woman too" –

> A creature not too bright or good
> For human nature's daily food.

This stanza has a more down-to-earth feeling and seems more like stage 2 experience: Wordsworth is concerned with working out the details of day-to-day living.

The third stanza represents stage 3, with its broad perspective and the tranquillity which accompanies it. (Twentieth-century readers may be put off by the word "machine" in this stanza, because we see machines as inhuman; but there were very few machines in Wordsworth's life, and the word was often used to describe the human body.)

> And now I see with eye serene
> The very pulse of the machine;
> A being breathing thoughtful breath,
> A traveller between life and death;
> The reason firm, the temperate will,
> Endurance, foresight, strength, and skill;
> A perfect woman, nobly planned,
> To warn, to comfort, and command;
> And yet a spirit still, and bright
> With something of angelic light.

The steadiness of stage 3 may seem a little oppressive in the first eight lines of this stanza (could life ever be that controlled?), but it is alleviated by the continuing presence of stage 1 in the last two lines.

In Wordsworth's long autobiographical masterpiece, *The Prelude*, different parts of the poem show the process of him moving through the first three stages of Vico's paradigm. In the early (and best known) part of the poem Wordsworth is a child, discovering the power of nature. He seems clearly to be living in stage 1: he is possessed with the beauty, the majesty, and the terror of being isolated in a natural setting. In the middle of the poem he describes the period he spent in France in his twenties, just after the French Revolution, when he became concerned with the significant political issues of the day, especially how to organize a just society to replace the monarchy which had been overthrown. Here he seems to be viewing life in a stage 2, metonymical way; he is concerned with practical questions about how people can live together. In the final section of *The Prelude*, Wordsworth consciously uses synecdoche – that is, he uses a part of his life to illuminate the whole. He describes climbing Mount Snowdon, passing through a layer of clouds, and emerging above them on the mountain-top to gain a grand panorama of the surrounding landscape. He compares this experience to having toiled through bewildering events in his own life and then reaching a stage in which the whole of his life makes sense to him.

It is an interesting feature of Wordsworth's development that he does not seem to have arrived at stage 4 in his relation to nature. At the end of *The Prelude* he sees himself as a "prophet of nature," teaching his readers about the joys of having a nourishing relation with the natural world. The passage makes him seem conservative and somewhat pompous in his relations with others, and shows some of the disadvantages of becoming too identified with stage 3. But Vico's paradigm is illuminating about Wordsworth's development up to that point.

Another useful function of the four-stage model is that it can help explain the kind of reception certain texts receive from different kinds of readers. If a stage 4 professor presents a stage 4 text (such as Joseph Conrad's *Heart of Darkness*) to a group of students who are mostly in stage 1, predictable difficulties – such as boredom and lack of comprehension – will result. Many of the students simply will not be able to appreciate the intricacies and subtleties of stage 4 experience and they may not want to encounter it.

Vico's model can also help you understand your relations with other people. Students in stages 1 and 2 often seem to be operating in entirely different worlds. A stage 1 student usually doesn't want to talk very

The application of Vico's four stages to some works of literature

	STAGE 1: METAPHOR	STAGE 2: METONYMY
THE TEMPEST **(WILLIAM SHAKESPEARE)**	Miranda, being initiated into society.	Caliban, trying to understand and usurp Prospero's power.
THE FRENCH LIEUTENANT'S **WOMAN (JOHN FOWLES)**	Charles's first encounter with Sarah.	Dr Grogan's explanation of Sarah's behavior as hysteria and masochism.
THE PRELUDE **(WILLIAM WORDSWORTH)**	Childhood encounters with nature.	Radical theorizing about society in France. Breakdown because of lack of integration.
HEART OF DARKNESS **(JOSEPH CONRAD)**	Marlow the innocent; the harlequin.	The pilgrims at the Central Station.
THE WHITE HOTEL **(D.M. THOMAS)**	Pornographic sections	Freud's discourse
ZEN AND THE ART OF **MOTORCYCLE MAINTENANCE** **(ROBERT PIRSIG)**	Chris, the child tempted by devils, as in Goethe's "Erlkönig."	Phaedrus as a student of science; he is not satisfied because he needs stage 3.
THE MAGIC MOUNTAIN[3] **(THOMAS MANN)**	Hans learning the routine of the ill in the Berghof, up to "Walpurgisnacht."	Hans receives Clavdia's X-ray. The Naphta-Settembrini debate.

STAGE 3: SYNECDOCHE	STAGE 4: IRONY
Prospero, organizing society and preparing for his return to Milan.	Antonio, cynical and power-hungry.
Charles in the church, after being seduced by Sarah, trying to understand his world.	Confrontation at the end between Charles and Sarah: two possible modes of life for Sarah; two possible endings for the novel.
Climbing Mt Snowdon; conscious symbolism, using the part to represent the whole.	Wordsworth doesn't reach this stage. This contributes to his self-centeredness and his tendency to be pompous at times.
The idealization of Kurtz by Marlow and others; his success seems to indicate a superior understanding of the operation.	Marlow returns to Brussels, feels revulsion for modern civilization, and lies to Kurtz's fiancée about Kurtz's last word.
The Promised Land	Babi Yar
Phaedrus wants to place things in the context of "quality." The narrator's integrated attitude toward technology.	Phaedrus's mental breakdown and catatonia. A *ricorso* is attempted through shock treatment. The effect seems to be to return him to stages 2 and 3.
"Snow": Hans, caught in the blizzard, sees the meaning of his stay in the Berghof.	The deaths of Joachim and Naphta. Hans's sense that he can't return to an earlier stage.

much about literature at all, since his experience of it is personal and intense, and he probably doesn't want to negotiate with other students
about the meaning of a novel which is important to him. Stage 2 students often work very hard but they sometimes give the impression that
they don't know where they are going. It is usually the professor's role
to be in stage 3, and to point out the view from that perspective — but
sometimes the value of this view is incomprehensible to students who
are in the first two stages, although it can still be dazzling or impressive
in some way. ("How could anyone know that much, and be able to pick
out just the right technique of analysis for that particular text?" I used to
ask myself about some of my professors.) Often stage 4 people (whether
they are professors or students) are hard to get along with, because they
are full of cynicism and denial. They can show what is wrong, selfish, or
self-centered about almost any point of view, but they don't know what
they believe themselves.

A final advantage of Vico's paradigm is that it shows how important
the humanities can be in our present cultural context. If we accept the
structuralist position, then we admit that we see the world *through* the
language we use (that is, the world is "coded" in a particular language).
If there is a choice to be made between four fundamentally different
ways of viewing the world, then the disciplines that explore that choice
will be very important. In English literature it is possible to study how an
author's choice of a particular stage creates a particular kind of personal
or social reality. It is necessary to admit, however, that there may be
more than four stages; and it is almost certainly true that Vico's paradigm
can be further developed.

One disadvantage of the four-stage model is that some of the stages
may seem unreal to those who have not experienced them. Someone
who has little experience of stage 3 or 4 may simply not know what
these stages feel like. Also, some students may resist the "relativizing"
effect of the whole paradigm. Vico does away with the possibility of absolute knowledge. These are real difficulties, but identifying them and
working on them can have considerable educational value. Studying a
novel such as Boris Pasternak's *Dr Zhivago*, which contains characters in
the various stages, can help to break the ice. In any case, this is a difficulty frequently encountered in the study of literature: readers are required to respond to, and discuss, experiences that they meet in books
but that they have not encountered in their own lives.

Notes

1. Hayden White, *Metahistory: The Historical Imagination in Nineteenth-Century Europe* (Baltimore and London: Johns Hopkins University Press, 1973); *Tropics of Discourse* (Baltimore and London: Johns Hopkins University Press, 1978); *The Content of the Form: Narrative Discourse and Historical Representation* (Baltimore and London: Johns Hopkins University Press, 1987).

2. Leo Tolstoy, *War and Peace*, trans. Rosemary Edmonds (London: Dent, 1950) 300.

3. In *Professing Literature: An Institutional History* (University of Chicago Press, 1987), Gerald Graff suggests that the best way to deal with conflicts between different views of literary study is to make them part of the curriculum, so that the differences are openly debated, and the vitality which often emerges in the discussion of curriculum reform can actually be transferred to students via the curriculum itself.

4. This analysis of *The Magic Mountain* is taken from an article by Hans Kellner, "The Inflatable Trope as Narrative Theory," *Diacritics*, Spring 1991.

Suggestions for Further Reading

Hayden White, *Metahistory: The Historical Imagination in Nineteenth-Century Europe* (Baltimore and London: Johns Hopkins University Press, 1973), especially the Introduction, 1-42, which acknowledges White's debt to Northrop Frye.

—— *Tropics of Discourse* (Baltimore and London: Johns Hopkins University Press, 1978).

CHAPTER TEN:

Myths and Demystification

IN LITERARY CRITICISM THE WORD "myth" is used in two very different ways: it can refer either to a story that provides you with a fundamental truth, or to one that is designed to delude, mystify, and perhaps exploit you. When the word is used in its honorific sense, it is often linked to religion or religious experience:

> What human beings have in common is revealed in myths. Myths are stories of our search through the ages for truth, for meaning, for significance. We all need to tell our story and to understand our story. We all need to understand death and to cope with death, and we all need help in our passages from birth to life and then to death. We need for life to signify, to touch the eternal, to understand the mysterious, to find out who we are.[1]

> [Myth] is a condensed account of man's Being and attempts to represent reality with structural fidelity, to indicate at a stroke the salient and fundamental relations which for a man constitute reality. A myth in this sense is primitive, communal, and religious in origin.... Myth is not make-believe but the most direct and positive assertion of belief that man can discover. Myth is an indispensable principle of unity in individual lives and in the life of society.[2]

The common elements in these two descriptions of myth are striking: they both assert that myths present what is sacred, eternal, or vitally important for an individual person, and they imply that myths fulfill a need that is shared generally in society. So the myth of Sisyphus, who was condemned in Hades to roll a boulder to the top of a hill only to see it roll to the bottom again, may take on a sacred or primordial meaning for someone who begins to see her life as a struggle that involves beginning things over and over again. W.B. Yeats's mythic image of the ancient Celtic tower, which he had reconstructed as his workplace for writing poetry, can seem like a shared image for the contemplative mind that needs to stand firm and strong in the midst of adversity.

Literature that moves us deeply often does so by gaining access to a deep level of our being, and articulating a pattern that we feel is crucial for us. Hermann Hesse's *Siddhartha* can provide a powerful image for a young man searching in the secular and religious worlds for his spiritual home, and finding it in an unexpected and unusual place. Margaret Laurence's *The Diviners* can provide a moving pattern of a woman's search for meaning in life. A Jungian psychologist has said that you get the true meaning of a myth when you feel its force within you.[3] He argues that myths live in our unconscious minds and that powerful literature can draw on what we know unconsciously, even though we may not have articulated this knowledge.

It is useful to have a word such as "myth" to designate those works of literature which are most meaningful for the individual. A problem arises, however, when myths are said to be "eternal" or "universal." People who maintain this are generalizing in a very broad way, and often they seem to assert more than is intended, or indeed knowable. If you say that James Joyce's *Portrait of the Artist as a Young Man* attains the status of myth because it presents the universal quest of a young man beset with restricting influences to find his own, lonely way forward in life, another reader may think that the experience is not universal. He may feel that Joyce's novel presents a limited and particular experience, and that the protagonist's solution to his problems – escape from family, religion, and country – is facile.

When you see myths from the opposite side – from the side of the person on whom they are imposed (and for whom they falsify experience) – you may find yourself using the word in its pejorative sense. Myths then become misleading or incorrect stories, which are especially annoying when they are presented as "the truth" to an audience which is unable to assess them critically. Roland Barthes explores this aspect of myths in his witty and iconoclastic book *Mythologies*.

Barthes was particularly sensitive to the imposition of myths because he grew up as an outsider to the middle-class culture of France in the 1930s. Because he was a Protestant amid a Catholic majority, because he was poor, because he suffered from tuberculosis and had to spend long periods in sanatoriums, perhaps above all because he was gay, Barthes could tell that many of the values enshrined in middle-class life were not appropriate for him. He knew that these values were not universal or eternal, and he became interested in how they had been created and disseminated throughout France in advertising, television, and popular literature.

Barthes defined the central feature of the deceptive kind of myth as being the substitution of an "eternal status" for history. What he meant by this is that a historical event (such as the Russian Revolution) may be presented not in terms of what actually happened (an outcome of a conflict between groups in society, the result of which was uncertain at the time), but as an event that *had* to happen, as though some omnipotent force (or god) had decreed it would happen. Using this approach, it would be possible to write an account of the Russian Revolution that would make it appear *inevitable*. The author would have to leave out a lot of information, and in this process he would be creating a myth. The myth would express an ideology: it would bolster the set of values promoted by the Revolution.

It is easy for Westerners to scoff at the idea that Russian historians could rewrite their history in a falsifying way. It is more alarming to think that a similar process could occur in one's own society – and Barthes's book was forceful because he pointed out how this falsification occurs in everyday life. It happens, for instance, when politicians and journalists call an event that has just occurred "historic," even though in ten years it may seem insignificant. They are, in part, trying to make the event seem historic by describing it in this way. A example in the area of literary studies is the belief that great works of literature (such as *The Odyssey* or Shakespeare's plays) are eternally and permanently great. This is the myth about "great" literature. The *historical* account of "great" literature is that certain texts, such as *King Lear*, achieve the status of greatness because they are widely read and performed, and that this happens because of the decisions of readers, teachers, and directors. If (for some historical reason) the work starts receiving much less attention, it will no longer belong to the canon of great literature.

Another myth that has some currency in universities is the idea that it is possible to read everything. Of course no one is able to do this, but sometimes students assume that professors have an infinite amount of knowledge at their disposal, simply because the professors have *more* knowledge than students. Scholarly books often seem to assume that there are no limits to the amount of information the reader wants about that particular subject – which can be very oppressive for readers, who may feel inferior because they can't imagine absorbing all that material.

Barthes's idea of myth is based on the notion that those who accept a myth are being deceived in some way. This may imply that somebody or some group of people are doing the deceiving, but it may not. To take a very simple example, it often happens that when we are asked to give an account of some aspect of our life (why we went to a certain university, for instance) we make that choice seem more intelligent than it actually was. We are then presenting a myth about our own lives – either consciously or unconsciously. Similarly a company, when advertising its product, will want to promote a myth about how wonderful that product is. Often the tone of voice in television advertising is enough to make it clear that a myth is being promoted.

It is easy to accept that an individual or a group might consciously try to deceive an audience, but there is a more complex idea behind Barthes's *Mythologies*. It is possible for elites or dominant groups in a society to spontaneously generate myths about their own superiority, and to use those myths to maintain and further bolster their position. Barthes feels that this is what happens in capitalist bourgeois society – that through the mass media capitalist bourgeois values and norms are programmed into the minds of almost everyone, with the underlying assumption that these values and norms are "naturally right." This promotes striving for material goods and competition between people, which ensures the continuance of a capitalist economy, with its key distinction between the wealthy and the poor.

Myth Analysis and Literature

To analyze a myth in Barthes's sense means to move from accepting it uncritically (as the truth) to being aware of its implications and perhaps to rejecting it. How is this useful for students of literature?

In the first place, myth analysis is useful in reading many aspects of popular culture that can be thought of as "texts," even if they are not entirely presented in words. Advertising, political speeches, sermons, and packaging, for example, can be based on implicit myths. If we are aware of this possibility, we are in less danger of swallowing the hook or accepting a meaning that it is not in our own interest to accept. It can also be exciting to see the overlap between literary studies and more general cultural analysis.

In the second place, myth analysis allows us to understand at a new level certain forms of literature that are themselves based on powerful and widely accepted myths. The standard Harlequin romance is based on the idea that a woman can find happiness through romantic love, and very often this happiness involves marrying a man from a higher social or professional group. So in these novels nurses marry doctors, and thereby enter a "higher" level of life that they think will be wonderful, even though what actually goes on in their husbands' lives may be either unknown or very unattractive to them. We tend to "romanticize" areas of life that are inaccessible to us, and Harlequin romances are built on this tendency. When we demythologize stories like these, they will probably have much less power for us.

Thirdly, a good deal of literature is about the process of demythologization, which often clears the way for a more satisfying kind of myth. Bertolt Brecht's *The Life of Galileo*, for instance, presents a famous scientist *not* as a great man but as someone who, at a crucial moment in the development of science, gave in to fear and his own sensuality – and so prevented science from entering a period of rapid development. One of the themes of the play, which Galileo articulates at the end, is that "great men" oppress those around them. Another example of demythologization occurs in *Zen and the Art of Motorcycle Maintenance*, by Robert Pirsig. The protagonist is an English teacher at a college in the Midwest who comes to question the value of the very teaching he and his colleagues are doing. This teaching, he finds, is based on a myth about the value of following the rules of grammar and rhetoric, and he wants to develop a mode of instruction that will allow students to consult their own intuition a great deal more. This leads him to undermine one of the central myths of Western civilization, a myth that splits the world into two fields – the technological and the humanistic. In the process of demystifying this binary opposition, the protagonist comes into conflict with the academic authorities at the University of Chicago, who do not want to have the myth challenged.

So literature is often about demystification, and the idea of myth is helpful in analyzing the ways in which mystification takes place. But literature frequently promotes myths, also, and we need to be aware of this process as well.

The Awkward Position of the Myth Analyst

Barthes notes that mythologists put themselves at risk, because every myth they uncover distances them from the social group that accepts the myth. If myth analysts continued their activity indefinitely, they could end up in complete isolation. Since their work is closely related to deconstruction, they might well find themselves in a virulent stage 4 world, with all their structures collapsing around them. There are two answers to this problem. The first is that there is a great difference between the myths promulgated by the dominant group in society and those put forward by minority groups. The dominant group's myths have power on their side. They are repeated from every corner of the world, or so it seems, and they may become especially immune to criticism. This makes it all the more important to examine these myths critically, to determine what they imply about human life and social organization, and what processes of exploitation they endorse. Otherwise the myths of the dominant group in society can be extremely oppressive. The myths of minority groups are less dangerous, because they are constantly under attack by the dominant group, and their shortcomings will usually be made evident. So an analyst of myths is likely to be most useful when she looks at the sacred cows in her society – although these have so much backing that they are unlikely to collapse easily.

The second answer to the problem of myth analysis leading to a meaningless stage 4 world is that some myths can survive the analysis and emerge stronger because of it. For instance, most religions are built on myths, and those myths cause certain social practices to be followed in particular religious groups. (The parable of the Good Samaritan might be a case in point.) But if those social practices (such as helping people in distress) are in fact the ones desired by the group, they can be examined critically and accepted consciously – not accepted because the myths on which they are based are "absolutely" or "literally" true, but because the people in the group find it is best to behave in a particular way.

The value of analyzing myths is related to the fact that social groups create paradigms and so (in part) create "reality," and literature itself can be an effective way of both creating social realities, and of uncovering how this process works. Life seems to be a process of growing up with a set of myths, criticizing them, and discovering new myths when the old ones fail. This is the process outlined in Vico's four stages. Recognizing myths and analyzing them are powerful tools for understanding literature.

Notes

1.   Joseph Campbell and Bill Moyers, *The Power of Myth* (New York: Doubleday, 1988) 5.

2.   George Whalley, *Poetic Process* (London: Routledge and Kegan Paul, 1953) 178. An excellent description of myth is given by C.S. Lewis in *An Experiment in Criticism* (Cambridge: Cambridge University Press, 1961) 40-50. Lewis says, "The experience [of myth] may be sad or joyful but it is always grave.... We feel it to be numinous" (44).

3.   Robert A. Johnson, *He: Understanding Masculine Psychology*, 2nd ed. (New York: Harper Row, 1989) x.

Suggestions for Further Reading

Roland Barthes, *Mythologies* (Frogmore, Herts.: Paladin, 1973).

George Whalley, "Symbol and Myth," *Poetic Process* (London: Routledge and Kegan Paul, 1953) 164-189. This book presents a view of the art of literature from the artist's point of view, making large claims for the "reality" which artists intuit and create. It is difficult to read, and immensely rewarding.

CHAPTER ELEVEN:

Structuralism (iii): Narratology

Narratives exist everywhere in the world, as Roland Barthes pointed out in a famous article.[1] We encounter them in books, movies, myths, comic strips, and confessions. They exist in every known society, and the ability to enjoy them is common at a very early age. Most people have a good sense of both when a narrative is satisfying and when it is not. In the second case they say, "What's the point of that story?" or "You haven't finished your story." In the first case they read or listen with close attention, and when the story is over they feel as though an important human issue has been brought to a conclusion.

Narratology is the study of how stories work and how readers understand them. It asks questions such as: "What are the elements of a narrative? Are there rules that tell us how to combine those elements to form a good story? What other formal properties are there in narratives? What unacknowledged agreements are there between authors and readers, so readers can have expectations that authors can fulfill?" It is tempting to say that narratology is the *science* of how stories work, but like most interesting literary investigations it cannot pretend to be entirely objective. It achieves its purposes best when it helps us understand our subjective responses to literature, or the shared response of a community that sets a high value on a particular story.

Narratology seems very general and ambitious, concerned as it is with the rules that might apply to *all* narratives. This can be off-putting to a person who has read widely but is just beginning to think about narrative. Some of the ideas developed by narratologists, however, *can* be helpful and stimulating. They can highlight elements of texts that are often overlooked. They can help explain why some endings are satisfying while others are not. They can also help us discover similarities between texts that at first seem very different.

The Elements of a Narrative

What are the elements of a narrative? The answer to this question depends on the way in which we approach the text, and this involves an arbitrary choice. There is no single "right" way, and an analysis needs to justify itself by producing interesting insights about the texts we care about. In this chapter I will deal with four different kinds of analysis, which focus on different elements in the text. The first method begins with the act of narration itself; the second focuses on how "discourse" mediates events; the third deals with speed of action; and the last explores patterns of plot structures and the role of "actants."

The Act of Narration

A good place to begin is the act of telling a story, and how it is presented in the text. At this level there is someone telling the story, the story itself, and someone listening to it or reading it. The teller and the listener are often present in the story, but usually we can distinguish them from what is being narrated. In Hugh MacLennan's *The Watch that Ends the Night*, the narrator tells the story of his life, and, as we hear about it, we learn a good deal about his consciousness.[2] He is, for instance, interested in Freudian psychology and well versed in world politics. In the course of his life he has acquired a kind of wisdom which is present in his narrating voice from the start of the novel. What we hear about in the novel is what *he* thinks is important.

The novel begins with the sentence, "There are some stories into which the reader should be led gently, and I think this may be one of them." The author has in mind a reader whom he wants to take care of in some way. The person or audience that is present in the text is called the "narratee," and that audience is often different from the actual reader. Nevertheless it may be an important aspect of the narrative that it defines a particular audience. In Coleridge's "The Rime of the Ancient Mariner," the response of the narratee (the Wedding-Guest) suggests the spellbinding power of the Mariner, and a person reading the poem almost two centuries after it was written may also feel this same power.

In Joseph Conrad's "Youth," Marlow talks to a group of successful people who began their working lives in the merchant marine. His subject is the enthusiasm for life that he felt as a youth and how it has disappeared – a theme directly related to the experience of his middle-aged listeners.

Some texts say a lot about the narrator and the narratee, and others say nothing explicit at all. Many novels are written from an "omniscient" point of view: the identity of the narrator is not specified, although he or she has access to the minds of all the characters. Even in these novels it is sometimes possible to detect limitations in the understanding of the speaker. Similarly, the fact that a narratee is not specified does not mean that the audience is not characterized. In reading a text you may get the feeling that it is written for someone who isn't paying attention (because things you remember are repeated from time to time) – or, at the other extreme, you may feel that the story goes over your head, and is intended for someone much more knowledgeable than you. The status of the narrator and narratee may be important elements in the text, and greatly influence our response to it.

"Fabula" vs Discourse: The "events-as-they-happened" vs the story that presents them

The Watch that Ends the Night is about a series of events that we can imagine as actually having happened. Here are some of the key events, in the order in which they would have occurred:

1. George Stewart, the protagonist and narrator, grows up in Montreal and, as a teenager, falls in love with Catherine Carey, who has a rheumatic heart.

2. Catherine goes to McGill University and marries Jerome Martell, a successful surgeon. They have a child.

3. Jerome leaves his family to fight in the Spanish Civil War, and he is reported dead.

4. Some years later, George and Catherine marry.

5. Jerome returns and wants to take up his relation with Catherine.

6. Catherine has an embolism and nearly dies because of the strain of having Jerome come back; George as a result comes close to a nervous breakdown.

7. Jerome manages to save both Catherine and George from their plights.

8. Jerome leaves Montreal and is not heard from again.

We could *imagine* being fully informed about all of these events, as though we had an omniscient or God's-eye view of them, or as if we had videotapes of everything that had happened. But as soon as we consider this possibility, we realize that (a) a huge number of tapes would be needed, (b) the tapes would not show us what was going on in the minds of the characters, and (c) each character would have a somewhat different view of what had happened.

The purpose of imagining a complete account of the events-as-they-happened (the technical term for this, invented by the Russian formalists, is *fabula*) is to make us realize that a novel cannot begin to give a *complete* account of anything. Any narrative condenses most events greatly, skips long periods completely, and often provides only one character's view of what is happening. What we are given is not the events-in-themselves, but a *discourse* about the events. (The word "discourse" simply means "something which is put into language." But this will involve certain choices about *how* the events will be put into language.) If we want to describe the novel, we need to talk about how the discourse modifies the events in presenting them, that is, how it *mediates* the events.

The most dramatic way in which the discourse of *The Watch that Ends the Night* alters "reality" is that it doesn't give the events in the order in which they occurred. The story begins with Jerome's return to Montreal after his long absence and his presumed death. We feel the tension of the situation and the bizarre quality of Catherine's being married simultaneously to two men. Then the author goes back in time to explain what led up to it. Much later, the book concludes with what happens after Jerome's return. The terms of narratology can help us describe these structures, so we can understand better how the text works. (The technical term for a flashback is *analepsis*; a jump forward in time is called a *prolepsis*.) One purpose in having the novel begin in the middle and not at the beginning is to hook the reader with an intensely dramatic situation: Jerome has returned from the dead, so to speak, to find his wife married to another man. The reader wants to know how this situation came about, and how it will be resolved.

Changing the order of events is only one way in which the discourse can modify the "fabula"; there are many others, which are catalogued in Gérard Genette's *Narrative Discourse*.[3] The prolepsis or flash-forward, although rarer in literature than the analepsis, can be extremely powerful. It is often used in autobiography to stress the importance of an event, by saying how strong and clear the narrator's present memory of it is. Genette gives an example from Proust:

> Of late I have been increasingly able to catch, if I listen attentively, the sound of the sobs which I had the strength to control in my father's presence, and which broke out only when I found myself alone with Mama. Actually, their echo has never ceased: it is only because life is now growing more and more quiet round about me that I hear them afresh, like those convent bells which are so effectively drowned out during the day by the noises of the streets that one would have supposed them to have been stopped for ever, until they sound out again through the silent evening air.[4]

Another device which allows the discourse of a novel to affect its fabula is *focalization*. This occurs when the narration passes through the mind of a particular person. In Henry James's *The Ambassadors*, Strether provides all the information, and so nothing can be included in the novel that Strether would not know. Also, the way in which things are seen will depend on the ideology of the person through whom the narrative is focalized; for instance, people in different stages of consciousness (see Chapter 9) will conceive of things in different ways.

Speed of Action and Catalytic Material

When approached in another way, the material in a text can be divided into two categories: hinge events and catalytic material. Roland Barthes was the first to propose this distinction.[5] The hinge events are those in which there is a turn in the story: they mark a significant new stage in the narrative, and, taken together, they form a structure in which each of them is necessary. If you leave any one out, the structure doesn't make sense, or becomes very different. In the first two parts of Coleridge's "The Rime of the Ancient Mariner," these are the first four hinge events:

1. The mariner goes to sea as a member of a ship's crew.

2. He shoots the albatross.

3. The weather improves, and the sailors approve of the shooting.

4. The ship is becalmed; the sailors curse the mariner and hang the albatross around his neck.

The third event is a hinge event, because, as Coleridge tells us in the marginal gloss, the sailors make themselves accomplices in the crime by approving of it, and so they deserve their punishment later on.

In between the hinge events the author can put as much catalytic material as he wants, without changing the plot of the story. (It is called "catalytic material" because, like a negative catalyst or "inhibitor" in a chemical reaction, it slows down the rate at which the action occurs.) This catalytic material can consist of other non-essential, non-hinge actions, such as the sun rising or an iceberg floating by; or of "information" – description, or philosophical reflection.

What is the value of knowing that narratives are made up of hinge events and catalytic material? This distinction allows us to account for the difference in feel between a story made up of a lot of hinge events and relatively little catalytic material (a thriller, for instance, in which there are continual threats to the life of the hero, and so a lot of suspense), and a very different kind of story in which there are relatively fewer hinge events, but a lot of description and reflection. Poems by William Wordsworth (such as "The Thorn") often have very little action, and stress instead the quality of the feelings people experience. Novels by Honoré de Balzac and Thomas Hardy often have long descriptive passages, which usually set the mood of the story or tell us something about the characters. A novel by Virginia Woolf can seem to be composed almost entirely of catalytic material – which may make it frustrating to a reader looking for action, and satisfying to someone willing to read it at a much slower pace.

What is most significant in the distinction between hinge events and catalytic material is the *relative* presence of each in a particular text. A text in which hinge events predominate often has a syntagmatic feel (see Chapter 7): we ask, what is going to happen next? How is this going to end? The events form a long chain, and we want to reach the conclusion. In a story which contains more catalytic material, often we ask questions of a paradigmatic nature, such as "What does this mean?" Often the reader sorts out the structure of the hinge events on the first reading, and the second provides an opportunity to pay attention to the catalytic material. So some stories can be grasped quite fully on a first reading, while others are worth several readings.

"Actants" and Plot-Grammars

A fourth way to approach narrative structures is to focus on general (and perhaps universal) patterns in the structure of plots. According to a system developed by the French structuralist A.J. Greimas, narratives contain six roles that form three pairs:

- *the subject* (the hero), who searches for *the object* (which may be a person – for example, a loved one – or a state of being);

- *the sender* (the person or institution that gives the subject a sense of values and sends the subject in search of the object), and *the receiver* (who receives the object looked for by the subject); and

- *the helper* (who aids the subject in the quest), and *the opponent* (who tries to hinder the subject).[6]

Greimas calls these entities "actants," and he thinks of them as existing on a "deep" or hidden level in the text; they *may* appear on the surface level in *several* actual characters or other elements. So Hamlet is the subject in Shakespeare's play; his father is the sender, and Horatio is the helper; but the opponent is split up into several characters, including Claudius, Polonius, Rosencrantz, and Guildenstern.

When characters are split up into these six categories of actants, three basic patterns of action emerge:

- desire (the subject's desire for the object);

- communication (from the sender to the receiver);

- help and hindrance (from the helper and the opponent).

The general structure of a work of literature, analyzed in this way, takes one of two forms. It can be a progression from disorder to order, as in the case of *Henry IV, Part One*: King Henry has to put down the rebellion in the north and enlist the wayward Prince Hal as a participating member of his entourage. The second form moves from the existence of a contract, through a breaking of that contract, to punishment. This form can be seen in *Hamlet* and *Macbeth*.

What is the value of being aware of these very abstract patterns in fiction? The first thing to say is that they are not absolute facts, and they are not *necessarily* valuable at all. Their value to us as readers lies in their usefulness. When they shed light and make us feel we understand something, then they are valuable. Here are some examples where they do this.

One of the strongest and most satisfying feelings in reading literature is the sense that an engaging story has come to a conclusion, and that the problems which it has raised have been dealt with in a satisfying way. This occurs in *The Watch that Ends the Night*, when George Stewart avoids succumbing to a breakdown, and returns to life with his wife Catherine, not with the panic-laden feeling that she may at any time be taken from him by her illness, but with the confidence that he is secure enough in himself to go on after her death. We could say that the ending is satisfying because the subject has finally attained his object, which has not been professional success or marriage, but the sense of his own security in the world. Attaining this object makes him feel as though he is living in harmony with a divine plan.

The categories of actants can be helpful, too, when you map a work of literature onto them. At the begining of *The Prelude*, Wordsworth's long autobiographical poem, the poet is quite unclear about what he wants to do and at the end he is embarrassed by the fact that he has concentrated so much on himself. But if we see the story in Greimas's terms, it becomes clear that Wordsworth's object is to reach a stage in which he considers himself qualified to write a long, important poem; and an essential part of that process is his recognition that for him the sender – the agent that instructs him in his true values and sends him on his quest – is Nature itself. His ultimate object is to achieve a role as a poet-prophet, offering redemption through nature to a society being transformed by the industrial revolution and the growth of cities.

Conclusion

This chapter has presented a brief survey of four areas in narratology, which is a field of literary criticism which became important only in the 1960s as an aspect of structuralism, and which is evolving rapidly. The new terms I have introduced – narrator, narratee, analepsis, prolepsis, fabula, discourse, hinge events, catalytic material, and the six actants – all allow us to talk about features present in narratives. They may be significant or not in any particular narrative, and may or may not help explain its importance or effect.

One final source of interest of narratology concerns the stories that we tell rather than those we read. In both John Fowles's *The French Lieutenant's Woman* and Margaret Laurence's *The Diviners*, the authors suggest that all of us are continually making movies about our lives in our heads, thinking about the past and the future. When we create those narratives, to what extent are we constrained by the formal features and rules of narrative? To understand our own lives, do we need to know who is the sender and who is the opponent? To tell our stories, do we need to discover the hinge events in our lives? When we speak and wish to be understood, we usually follow the rules of grammar – but this only guarantees the coherence of our sentences. Narratology can help us understand the larger stories we construct in our lives, both those that explain the past and those that reach into the future.

Notes

1. Roland Barthes, "Introduction to the Structural Analysis of Narratives," *A Barthes Reader*, ed. Susan Sontag (New York: Hill and Wang, 1982) 251–296.

2. Hugh MacLennan, *The Watch that Ends the Night* (Toronto: Macmillan, [1958] 1975).

3. Gérard Genette, *Narrative Discourse*, trans. Jane E. Lewin (Ithica: Cornell University Press, 1980).

4. Marcel Proust, *A la recherche du temps perdu*, quoted by Gérard Genette in *Narrative Discourse* (Ithaca: Cornell University Press, 1980) 70.

5. This distinction was made by Roland Barthes in the article in note 1,

pages 265 and following.

6.   A.J. Greimas, *Sémantique structurale* (Paris: Larousse, 1966) 155 and
following.

Suggestions for Further Reading

Roland Barthes, "Introduction to the Structural Analysis of Narratives,"
A Barthes Reader, ed. Susan Sontag (New York: Hill and Wang, 1982)
251-296. This essay was first published in 1966 in *Communications* 8
(Paris: Seuil), which contains a number of seminal articles on
narratology, by A.J. Greimas, Umberto Eco, Tzvetan Todorov, and
Gérard Genette.

———- *S/Z*, trans. Richard Miller (New York: Hill and Wang, 1974),
first published by Seuil in 1970. In this rich and innovative book Barthes
breaks up a short story by Balzac into units of a sentence or two, and
shows how readers make sense of narratives.

Gerald Prince, *A Dictionary of Narratology* (Lincoln: University of
Nebraska Press, 1987). This provides useful definitions of many of the
technical terms in narratology.

Didier Coste, *Narrative as Communication* (Minneapolis: University of
Nebraska Press, 1989).

Gérard Genette, *Narrative Discourse: An Essay in Method*, trans. Jane E.
Lewin (Ithaca: Cornell University Press, 1980). Originally this was
published as *Le discours du récit*, in *Figures III* (Paris: Seuil, 1972). This
study is focused on five "elements" of narrative as they appear in
Proust's *A la recherche du temps perdu*: order, duration, frequency, mood,
and voice.

CHAPTER 12:
New Historicism

NEW HISTORICISM IS INTERESTING because it takes the lessons of structuralism and deconstruction seriously, and applies them in the search for a fuller meaning in works of literature. It has attracted a lot of attention in the last ten years, and some of its practitioners are brilliant. Many avant-garde professors are using it, and a serious student of literature is almost certain to encounter it. As I explained in Chapter 5, historicism is the belief that past events can best be understood not in universal terms but in terms of the particular contexts in which they occurred. New historicism characteristically finds meanings in texts by looking in detail at some aspect of the period in which they were created, such as attitudes to sex. What is new about this process is that the past is imagined in a new and complex way, which is derived partly from the thought of Michel Foucault, an influential French post-structuralist philosopher and historian.

A simplified account of Foucault's view of the past would begin with the idea that what counts as knowledge differs from one era to the next. For example, data about the movement of the Earth simply did not count as knowledge for the Catholic Church prior to 1600, because of the firm belief that the Earth was fixed at the centre of God's creation. Similarly what might be taken as a divine revelation in one era might be considered evidence of psychosis at another time. Foucault's conclusion was that what counts as *knowledge* at a particular moment in history depends crucially on certain key institutions in society, such as the church, the university, and the political system, and on the ideology which they promulgate.

Furthermore, Foucault points out that if you look carefully at any one period in history, such as the era of Shakespeare in England, you can usually see that there is a struggle for supremacy between the supporters of different ideologies. The winning party is in a position to define what "knowledge" or "justice" or "normality" is, and often they can put those who disagree in jail. Such a struggle went on in Shakespeare's time between the Protestants and the Catholics, and, to some extent, between the nobility and the businessmen of the rising middle class. In addition there were marginal or suppressed groups with quite different beliefs about what was important in life – the Wyccans would be one example. The witches in *Macbeth* owe something to this group of marginalized people.

A belief of the "old" historicism was that it was possible to define, quite objectively, a "spirit of the age," and that the major works of literature in that age expressed that spirit more or less clearly. The new historicism maintains, in contrast, that any period in the past will contain a struggle between a number of different ideologies, carried out mostly in the institutions which allocate power, such as (in Shakespeare's time) the monarchy, the church, the system of patronage, the schools and the universities. There will probably be a dominant ideology, and its proponents will almost certainly be trying to maintain and extend their control of society. But new historicists feel it is very important to look for other, non-dominating elements of the culture. These may be "residual" (and dying out slowly), "emergent" (just being developed), "repressed" (by the authorities), or "marginal" (flourishing far away from the centres of power).

So when a new historicist looks at a work of literature, she is careful to watch out for the voices of the non-dominant cultures or ideologies, and the conflicts which they might cause. Sometimes these are quite evident. In *The Merchant of Venice,* there is an obvious conflict between the members of the Christian bourgeoisie (Antonio, Bassanio, and Portia) and the marginalized Jew Shylock, whose financial code of conduct is very different from that of the people he is lending his money to.

Why does this matter? One reason is that some new historicists believe that the "great art" of the past has often been used to help the dominant class maintain their hegemony, partly by presenting the culture or ideology of the rulers as though it were the *only* culture. So art can function, in effect, as propaganda, and help repress dissident elements in the culture. The work of art may well go on doing similar work today. By highlighting the social struggles of the past, some new historicists can shed light on the conflicts in our own times. This seems to me to be a worthy object, and we can be grateful to have a more complex and fuller view of ideological struggles in the past.

A second assumption of new historicism is that we will be able to see the meaning of a work of art more fully if we see it in relation to other forms of discourse created at the same time, such as political speeches, religious pamphlets, and medical treatises. This is an application of the structuralist idea that an utterance has its meaning because it is part of a system, and you will lose something if you lift the utterance out of that system and put it on a separate plane. A typical procedure in new historicist criticism is to discuss some other aspect of culture, and the documents which relate to it, and then show how this material illuminates what is happening in the play. In one well-known article a pamphlet promoting investment in the colony of Virginia is used to illuminate the character of Hal in the two parts of *Henry IV*. [1]

The underlying idea here seems to be that society is very complex, and that to see one of its products clearly you need to see it as part of that original complexity. This is a standard historical argument, but it raises two problems when it is applied to literature. One is that we are always lifting things out of their contexts to some degree – it is impossible to deal *fully* with the original complexity of the embedding of a Shakespearean play in its social context. Literature (by one definition of literature) is distinguished from other verbal records by the very fact that it still has lively and interesting meanings *even when it is taken out of its context of origin*. By tying a play to its context of origin you in fact make it function less well as literature and more like ordinary discourse. This can substantially *reduce* its interest. [2]

My second objection to this manoeuvre has to do with the teaching of literature to undergraduates. Putting a play in its original context demands a lot of knowledge, more than even many professors are able to acquire. An individual may devote a lot of time to acquiring this knowledge, and may be able to illuminate a work of art as a result, in his role as an "expert on the period"; but it is not reasonable to expect undergraduates to take on this exercise. They may be dazzled by the professor's erudition; they may be inspired to emulate it; but they will almost certainly not be able to do this in an undergraduate course.

The heart of this objection, coming as it does in this book, is that new historicism does not help an undergraduate group have a good discussion about literature, which usually depends on the members of the group having an approximately equal knowledge of the book. New historicism basically allows an expert to hold forth, and perhaps be challenged by a rival expert. This may produce interesting achievements by capable and competitive people, but it is not a good model for a university class.

A third and final assumption of new historicism rests on the insights of narratology. New historicists are narratologists in believing that the past is essentially available to us in narratives which have been formed by others, and those narratives are not transparent; they do not simply give access, like a window, to a reality which exists beyond them. History is based on stories, and is told in the form of stories, and so it is mediated by narrative. So there can be no simple grasping of the facts of the past. Two people, or a community of people, may agree on certain facts about the past; but linking them to form a narrative will impress on them a structure and an ideology. I agree fully with this position, and it leads me to think that new historicists should look more carefully at the motives for their own narrations. I will return to this subject to complete this chapter, after giving an example of new historicism in action, performed by the man who invented the term.

Stephen Greenblatt and Othello's Self-Narration

Stephen Greenblatt is a scholar and interpreter of the Renaissance who has written two fascinating and influential books which represent this school of criticism well. He has said that an openness to recent theoretical discussions, and especially to the work of Michel Foucault, is characteristic of work in this mode, but he denies that there is any central doctrine:

> My own work has always been done with a sense of just having to go about and do it, without establishing first exactly what my theoretical position is. [3]

He opens *Shakespearean Negotiations* with the statement, "I began with the desire to speak with the dead. This desire is a familiar, if unvoiced, motive in literary studies...."[4] This desire leads him to engage not only with a vast range of Renaissance literature, but with many of the texts of deconstruction and post-structuralism. An essay on *Othello* entitled "The Improvisation of Power" illustrates well how he makes use of this wide and unusual kind of expertise. [5]

The main question Greenblatt addresses is one which has challenged many critics. How is Iago able to arouse Othello's jealousy of Desdemona to such a pitch of certainty that Othello is willing to murder his loving and faithful wife? The argument passes through three main stages. The first is to show that Othello constructs his identity around the story of his life as a heroic soldier. He likes telling this story; he uses it to win Desdemona's love; and he defends himself to the Venetian senate with another account of his life when Desdemona's father objects to their marriage. So Othello seems a good supporting example for twentieth-century psychoanalysis: his felt identity is a product of his ability to narrate an arresting story.

The second stage is for Greenblatt to show that a common way for one person to achieve power over another is to enter into another person's narrative of identity, to see it and understand it as a fiction, and to subvert it to his own ends. To illustrate this, he describes an incident from a text written in 1525 by Peter Martyr, in which the Spanish in Hispaniola (the island of which Haiti now forms a part) were searching for slaves to work in their gold mines. They found a tribe in what are now the Bahamas whose religion told them they would be transported to a heavenly island after death, where they would be joyfully reunited with their loved ones. The Spanish managed to insert themselves in this narrative, by persuading the natives that the Spanish ships had been provided by their god to take them to this paradise. The natives were profoundly moved by this prospect, and joyfully left their homes to board the Spanish vessels. Upon arrival in Hispaniola the fiction came to an end, and they were enslaved.

Greenblatt says that Iago is brilliant at precisely this technique of understanding another's story well enough to improvise an entry into it, with the aim of achieving control over it. He can see the importance of Othello's account of himself, and he finds a crucial point of access. To understand this, Greenblatt introduces us to another set of documents relating to the issue of whether a married couple in Shakespeare's time could enjoy sex with a clear conscience. It seems clear from these documents that adultery was viewed as one of the most terrible sins (worse, even, than homicide), but that also some theologians considered adultery to include loving your own spouse too ardently, or taking too much pleasure in intercourse. The play itself makes clear that Desdemona and Othello have experienced powerful sexual joy in their marriage, and one conclusion (I am leaving out a lot of the subtlety and the detail of the argument) is that Othello feels compelled to kill Desdemona *because he accepts that her enjoyment of sex is sinful and punishable by death*: "he must destroy Desdemona both for her excessive experience of pleasure and for awakening such sensations in himself."[6] This turns a crucial item in Othello's self-narration against himself, and causes him to act on a religious doctrine which he has subconsciously accepted.

The conclusion, then, is that Othello kills Desdemona not just because he suspects she has had sexual relations with Cassio, but essentially because she openly admits her sexual joy *with her husband,* Othello. When Iago's villainy is revealed, Othello is then driven to kill himself for much the same reason – for loving not wisely, but too well.

This argument needs to be enjoyed with all the details of its original presentation, but I have summarized it here to give a concrete example of how new historicism tilts texts so we see them in a new light – a light which comes largely from other texts in circulation in the culture, texts which most of us have not read. This article also shows clearly two other features of new historicism: its inclination to see both authors and characters as enjoying very little freedom, imprisoned, as it were, in their social surroundings; and a tendency to see authors almost in terms of comparative anthropology, so they seem very different from us. Many critics have presented an Othello who suffers from a comprehensible form of sexual jealousy; it will be harder for most of us to empathize with him if he is acting not out of jealousy but because of an obscure and outmoded theological doctrine about sexual pleasure. Greenblatt wanted to speak to the dead, but in the end his Shakespeare seems to be signaling to us from an alien culture.

The Ideology of New Historicism

In the new historicists' approach to texts, we find that works are tied in a thousand ways to the context which produced them. This context is characterized by competition between the dominant ideology and subversive rivals; and freedom seems to disappear both for characters and for authors. In the epilogue to *Renaissance Self-Fashioning* Greenblatt says that he began his study wanting to confirm his feeling that a strong individual in the Renaissance was free to construct his own identity. But, he says,

> as my work progressed I perceived that fashioning oneself and being fashioned by cultural institutions – family, religion, state – were inseparably intertwined. In all my texts and documents, there were, so

far as I could tell, no moments of pure, unfettered subjectivity; indeed, the human subject itself began to seem remarkably unfree, the ideological product of the relations of power in a particular society.[7]

Another critic introduces new historicism in the following, more abstract, way:

> The writing and reading of texts, as well as the processes by which they are circulated and categorized, analyzed and taught, are now being construed as historically determined and determining modes of work. What have often been taken to be self-contained aesthetic and academic issues are now seen as inextricably linked to other social discourses, practices, and institutions; and such overdetermined and unstable linkages are apprehended as constitutive of the ideological field where people and collective structures are mutually shaped.[8]

The feeling of this atmosphere should be familiar from our discussion of Vico in Chapter 9. This is stage 2 thinking – metonymical, horizontal, and deterministic. The individual is shaped by the forces which impinge upon him or her; there is little freedom and no chance of escape. This is the scholarly equivalent of the constraining social world which Balzac describes in *La comédie humaine*. In it people are defined by the discourses which surround them.

Perhaps the clearest indicator of this ideology is the belief that *nothing is transcendent*. At the beginning of *Shakespearean Negotiations* Greenblatt establishes seven basic assumptions. Among them are the following:

> There can be no appeals to genius as the sole origin of the energies of
>   great art.
> There can be no transcendent or timeless or unchanging representation.
> There can be no autonomous artifacts.[9]

Here Greenblatt is reacting to his education in the New Criticism, with its emphasis on genius, timeless truths, and autonomous works of art, and what he says sounds reasonable: works of art do not appear from nowhere, or rule the world autonomously. But in another sense he is, I believe, wrong. The root meaning of "transcendent" is "something which has climbed above the rest" or "something which is outstanding." Certainly there *are* some texts, and some moments in our lives, which are transcendent in this sense: they are outstanding. Why are they outstanding? *Because they feel that way, and we allow them to take on a special existence.* There seems clear evidence that our lives can be enriched by allowing certain moments, and certain texts, to have this unusual status.

In our lives, transcendent moments are often those when we make important choices or have unusual insights which alter our lives. We feel free or morally engaged or wise or privileged. I see no value in erasing such moments, or denying that they exist. And in my experience of literature there are transcendent texts — texts which stand out. When a group of people largely agree that a certain text is transcendent, it becomes part of that group's canon. This does not mean that it emerges from nowhere, or that it has no relation to other texts of the period. But these factors seem to matter less, often because the text in question seems to point toward the future.

An analogy may make my argument clearer. Imagine we come across a mature maple tree in a forest near where we are building a house to live in. The new historicist is like a botanist-ecologist who has been watching the tree develop over a forty-year span. He can tell us (because he knows a lot about this ecological system, as well as about trees) why the tree is the shape and height it is; he can explain how it grew slowly at first because it was in the shadow of other trees, but when they were blown down it suddenly had much better access to the sun. He can even explain how the weather patterns over the years will have affected the tree's inner strucure.

We listen with interest and respect. But we want to harvest the tree and take it to the local sawmill so that we can use the wood for our flooring material. We are glad to know that it is a healthy maple — it will make beautiful, durable floors, with attractive patterns in the grain. But there is a limit to the amount we want to know, or can absorb, about the tree's history; and we need to get on with our own life rather than observe and understand the life of the tree.

It is possible to use literature in a similar way. I am sure that *King Lear* has helped many thousands of people to understand their relations with an aging parent and to come to terms with that situation.[10] I am sure that for some of these people certain parts of the play seem to contain a transcendent wisdom, and that they are better off because they allow the play to have this role in their lives. So in a sense the play *does* contain a transcendent element, and Greenblatt would be wrong to deny the experience of these people.

To conclude: we can be grateful to the new historicists for pointing out the complexity of the social networks in which works of literature have their origins, and for their skill in recovering voices in texts which have been obscured or suppressed. We can acknowledge that their investigations may alert us to ways in which we ourselves are not free, living our lives as we do in languages and societies not of our own making. But we do not need to accept their ideology, or allow it to diminish our freedom or our moral sense when we make choices of our own. Above all we should not allow new historicism to undermine the exaltation and *feeling* of transcendence which some works of art give us. We need to be aware of the consequences of those feelings. They may annoy or even oppress some people. But there is no reason to deny they exist. They too are a link to the past, and in them we may be able to hear, it seems to me, the voice of the dead.

Notes:

1. Stephen Greenblatt, "Invisible Bullets," in *Shakespearean Negotiations: The Circulation of Social Energy in Renaissance England* (Berkeley and Los Angeles: University of California Press, 1988) 21-65.

2. John M. Ellis makes this point with great clarity and force in *The Theory of Literary Criticism: A Logical Analysis* (Berkeley and Los Angeles: University of California Press, 1974).

3. Stephen Greenblatt, "Towards a Poetics of Culture," in H. Aram Veeser, ed. *The New Historicism* (New York: Routledge, 1898) 1.

4. Greenblatt, *Shakespearean Negotiations*, 1.

5. Stephen Greenblatt, *Renaissance Self-Fashioning: From More to Shakespeare* (Chicago and London: University of Chicago Press, 1980), 222-254.

6. Greenblatt, *Renaissance Self-Fashioning*, 250.

7. Greenblatt, *Renaissance Self-Fashioning*, 256.

8. Louis Montrose, "New Historicisms," in Redrawing the Boundaries: The Transformation of English and American Literary Studies, ed. Stephen Greenblatt and Giles Gunn (New York: Modern Language Association, 1992), 392.

9.   Greenblatt, *Shakespearean Negotiations*, 12.

10.   A fictional example of someone using *King Lear* in this way is *Scar Tissue*, by Michael Ignatieff (Toronto: Viking, 1993). When his mother is afflicted with Alzheimer's disease, the protagonist, a professor of philosophy, explores the meaning of her behaviour, partly by re-reading and giving lectures on *King Lear*.

Suggestions for further reading:

The books listed in the notes above, and particularly those by Stephen Greenblatt. Many critics doing new historicism seem very self-effacing, and some retreat into a style which is extremely abstract and turgid (using phrases such as "negotiated transactions between discursive formations" and "the refiguration of the sociocultural field"). Greenblatt does this rarely, and he has a refreshing directness and concern with his own motivations and desires as a reader and – suprising as this may seem for a new historicist – a person making choices in the world. He obviously enjoys telling anecdotes about himself, and he does it well. See, for instance, the three-page epilogue to *Renaissance Self-Fashioning*, which captures neatly a central irony of new historicism. Chapter 1 of *Shakespearean Negotiations* ("The Circulation of Social Energy") depicts the ideology and program of new historicism in a lively way. He is modest about the importance of new historicism, and thinks that literary pedagogy will remain focused primarily on goals which the new critics would have agreed with: "sustained, scrupulous attention to the formal and linguistic design" of literary works. But at other moments he seems wildly ambitious: "We need to analyze the collective dynamic circulation of pleasures, anxieties, and interests." He is referring to Shakespeare's England.

Jonathan Dollimore and Alan Sinfield, *Political Shakespeare: Essays in Cultural Materialism,* 2nd ed. (Manchester University Press, 1994). Cultural materialism, which has developed in Britain under the influence of Raymond Williams and Marxism, is quite similar to new historicism in many ways. Some of these are outlined in the introduction by Jonathan Dollimore ("Shakespeare, cultural materialism, and the new historicism"). Two differences, traceable to the Marxist roots of cultural materialism, are (i) a greater concern with how Shakespeare is used in the present – how his works are situated in our own cultural field; and (ii) a clear political commitment:

> Cultural materialism does not, like much established literary criticism, attempt to mystify its perspective as the natural, obvious, or right interpretation of an allegedly given textual fact. On the contrary, it registers its commitment to the transformation of a social order which exploits people on the grounds of race, gender, and class. (viii)

This volume contains a concluding afterword by Raymond Williams.

H. Aram Veeser, ed., *The New Historicism* (New York: Routledge, 1989) is an anthology which represents the variety of new historicism well. It concludes with an assessment of the volume, and of new historicism, by Stanley Fish, who feels that it is not really "new" at all.

CHAPTER THIRTEEN:

Reader-Response Criticism

Il dépend de celui qui passe
que je sois tombe ou trésor
que je parle ou me taise
ceci ne tient qu'à toi
ami n'entre pas sans désir

Paul Valéry[1]

INTEREST IN READER-RESPONSE criticism has increased greatly in the past fifteen years, partly as a result of the attempt to connect literary theory to what actually occurs in the classroom. The central idea behind reader-response criticism is that a work of literature does not exist as "words on the page." It has no objective existence: it only exists when it has entered the mind of a particular reader. When it enters your mind, it is accommodated to what is already in your mind – for example, to the particular meanings that individual words have for you. We all have slightly different associations with the word "river," for instance, and when we encounter this word in a poem, those associations are activated. On a larger scale, there are different methods of interpretation, and the way in which a work is understood by a particular person will depend on what method is being used (even if the person is not *aware* of there being different methods). Finally, our own personal histories influence how we respond to different works of literature and which themes have the most meaning for us. Reader-response critics argue that it is important to take all of this into account; they say that any pretense that literary criticism can be "objective" is a grave distortion of the realities of how literature is experienced.

When reader-response critics stress the experience of the subjective individual, a danger seems to loom: if each of us only pays attention to individual experience, the communal basis for the discipline will disappear and literature classes will have nothing to hold them together. One of the main challenges that reader-response critics have to face is to provide a satisfactory solution to this problem. The answer generally takes one of two forms. The first is that although we all read differently, we can classify reading procedures into a small number of types, and then talk generally (and profitably) about these types. The second answer is that we are not free to simply read any way we want *and* be part of a community of readers – that communities impose ways of reading in the same manner that tennis clubs impose the rules of tennis. If you want to be part of a particular community, you have to play according to the rules.

Roland Barthes and Four Pleasures of Reading

As an introduction to different types of reading, I would like to mention briefly four kinds of reading which Roland Barthes outlines in *The Pleasure of the Text*.[2] He bases them on Freudian psychoanalysis, and gives them names which many people will find unattractive, but the differences between them are striking, and to some extent they correspond with the four stages outlined by Vico.

In the first kind of reading, the reader takes the world described in the text as reality, and experiences a kind of hallucination, often through identifying with a particular character. Adolescents who are enthusiastic readers often read in this mode; they lose all sense of the world around them, and they disappear into the story with energy and delight. To this kind of reader, literary criticism is an impertinence, and to reach the end of the book is a small disaster, because it leaves the reader bereft of an imaginative world. This kind of reading seems to correspond to Vico's stage 1, in which the person is lost in a numinous world.

The second kind of reading demands a good deal of intellectual activity, and usually involves certain rituals which are repeated as you read. One of these rituals might be constantly searching for the theme of what you read. Both analysis and synthesis are needed for this activity, and it can be very demanding. This kind of reading is often highly valued in university courses, because it can lead to a stage 3 understanding of the work of literature as a whole. Other interpretive rituals which would fit in this category are constantly looking for the significance of symbols in the work of literature and working out allegorical meanings. The goal of both of these processes is to achieve a global understanding of the work in question.

The third kind of reading mentioned by Barthes is appropriate to detective stories: here the satisfaction lies in seeing how all the details and clues fit together to form the main structure of the story. The general shape of this structure is known in advance, because there are generic rules about detective fiction that are clearly understood by both writer and reader.

The fourth kind of reading pleasure is the opposite of the second and the third in that the focus is not on the text as a whole, but rather on fragments of the text: sentences or even phrases. Barthes calls this the fetishistic manner of reading, because a few small parts of the text are chosen as somehow containing the essence of the work or the author's world view, just as in some indigenous African religions the forces of nature are thought to be controlled by gods who reside in particular objects, such as the claw of an animal. People who get this kind of pleasure in reading tend to underline or copy out certain sentences or formulas and often memorize them. Anyone who has learned a foreign language while living in a strange country must have felt this way about certain words and expressions that seem to promise some control over the transactions of everyday life.

A fifth kind of reading (not mentioned by Barthes) finds pleasure in the information the book contains about the author's life or his times. This pleasure seems to be primarily available to people who already know a good deal about a particular period, and so it is common among professors. Undergraduate students do not usually have the same enthusiasm for it, because they are often beginning from scratch, and don't have the structure in their minds to fit the knowledge into. To many students this kind of knowledge seems like a collection of unrelated facts which are hard to remember.

These five kinds of pleasure – taking the text as reality, looking for themes, savoring complex structures, collecting fragments, and assembling historical information – could all be experienced by a single person, although it is unlikely that anyone would enjoy all five equally. But trying to extend the kinds of pleasure availiable to us through mastering different kinds of reading is a worthwhile goal for anyone studying literature.

The Individual Approach to Reader-Response Criticism: Norman Holland

I will now examine three different focuses in reader-response criticism, beginning with the most individual one, which has been developed by Norman Holland in *Five Readers Reading*.[3] Holland's basic thesis is that each person has a central structure to his or her personality (which he calls an "identity theme"), and that when we read a book, essentially we try to reproduce the main elements of that structure. If we can't, we get frustrated and probably don't like the story. A person's identity theme establishes the crucial issues in his or her life: the attitude toward parents, toward authorities, toward friends and lovers, and what expectations the individual characteristically harbours about the greater world in which he or she moves. The identity theme expresses what a person wants in life, and what he or she fears – and it indicates what defences will be established against those things which seem dangerous.

An example may make clearer what Holland means by the term "identity theme." He describes the poet Robert Frost as a man who lived in permanent fear of large, dangerous, and chaotic elements in the world (and in himself), but who felt that he could use small things, such as words, as magical symbols which could help him control his life. Holland describes Frost's identity theme in this way:

> To be in touch with, to create, and to restrain huge unknown forces of sex and aggression by smaller symbols: words or familiar objects. Or, more briefly, to manage great, unmanageable unknowns by means of smaller knowns.[4]

Using this formulation to explain and unify bizarre elements in Frost's life, Holland calls on the support of some of the poet's well-known sayings, such as "Every poem is an epitome of the great predicament; a figure of the will braving alien entanglements"; and "I started calling myself a Synecdochist when others called themselves Imagists or Vorticists. Always, always, a larger significance. A little thing touches a larger thing."

Holland sees three basic stages in the process of reading a narrative. First of all the work of art has to get past your network of defenses, which are there to protect you from things which you fear, either consciously or unconsciously. If the work doesn't make it through these defenses, you stop reading in any meaningful sense. As an example of defences coming into play, Holland cites the case of a rigid, obsessional man who went to see a film about a sea captain who had to endure mutiny on his ship, and the loss of his authority. This viewer could not bear to see such a process take place, and left the theatre half-way through the film. Something similar can occur when we read, and often the response we are aware of is boredom.

Once the work of art has come through the gates of your personality, so to speak – once it has been allowed admittance, and perhaps been welcomed, your mind takes its contents and starts building fantasies. The materials for these fantasies are supplied by the narrative, but the kind of fantasy you like to build will depend on your own mind. Your fantasies may or may not reflect the "main theme" of the narrative, but they will certainly reflect your identity theme.

Because he is a Freudian, Holland sees these fantasies as falling into three groups. (1) The first has to do with the feeling of being unified with the greater world around you, and losing yourself in it – the oceanic feeling, as Freud put it. These fantasies are related to the earliest bond that the infant feels with her mother, in which the infant is not even aware of the distinction between herself and the rest of the world. (2) The next group has to do with the feelings we have about the things we make or create – we may feel proud and possessive about them; we may want other people to admire them; we may work out ways of preventing others (especially authorities such as parents and teachers) from forcing them out of us. (3) The final group of fantasies involves the themes of competing with other people for success and of accepting limits to our sexual and social ambitions.

As an example of how Holland's categories might work, I will suggest three fantasies a student might have about writing an honours thesis on Boswell's *Life of Johnson*. A fantasy of the first type might focus on Johnson as someone who has a deep and valid understanding of the nature of life. The student might feel that his main goal is to extract from the *Life of Johnson* its essential teachings and to identify with them as closely as possible. He might believe that this would allow him to repose securely in these truths and live in harmony with the world. A fantasy of the second type might be that the student's supervisor is trying to make him organize his thesis in a way that the student feels is not right for him. So a lot of effort might go into resisting the supervisor and holding onto the thesis until it is exactly what the student wants it to be. The third type of fantasy is that the student might think of his thesis primarily in terms of how it might advance his career, by putting him ahead of his peers and getting him into graduate school. Holland's point is that in a particular individual one of these three fantasies might be more likely to occur than the others. This would be a significant reflection of the student's personality and would in turn influence how the student reads.

These three categories – based on Freud's conception of human sexual development – may be off-putting to many people, and they could seem inadequate or simply wrong. It could be that another classification of fantasies would be more appropriate for a particular reader. The key element in this part of the theory, however, is whether or not there is an important element of fantasizing in your response to literature that deeply involves you.

The first two stages of the reading process (according to Holland) include the work of getting past the defenses and of fantasy-building. The third stage is the drive toward public meaning. This is more social and rule-bound than the second stage. You take your fantasies about the story, and you take the psychological processes that are natural to you, and you put them together in a way that helps you discover the meaning or the theme of the story. You might do this in response to a teacher's demand for an essay on the story. You might try to work out a theme to help you talk with someone else about the story. If "unity" is an important characteristic of the things you like, then you will want your expression of the theme to be well unified and to cover the story well.

Holland tests his theory by looking at how five students find meaning in a short story by William Faulkner. He describes their identity themes (which he has worked out by using a number of psychological tests) and shows how each of them finds a reflection of his or her own identity theme in the story.

What is the point of this for students of literature? It seems to really be applicable only in tutorial situations, where a professor can investigate in detail the response of a particular student to a particular work. It would appear very solipsistic, as though each reader created the meaning of the work on his or her own. The whole idea of a person having an "identity theme" may seem much too restrictive (not to say Freudian) for many people. Holland compares finding the identity theme of a person to finding the theme of a novel, and in both cases there is a reduction of variety to unity. This can certainly be overdone, and we need to be careful that the search for themes (in books and in people) does not become oppressive and reductive.

But there are three main points of general interest. The first is that Holland's theory allows us to look carefully at why we respond very powerfully to certain books. Is it because they are "great?" Or is it because they reflect our identity themes? Or some combination of the two? Are "great books" those that touch on elements of identity themes which are very widely shared? A second point is that many students of literature *are* interested in self-knowledge, and this theory provides one way of obtaining it. A third point is that Holland's theory allows us to understand other readers better. Once we become familiar with some of the variety of identity themes, we realize that an interpretation of a novel which seems bizarre to us may be perfectly plausible for someone with a different identity theme.

Reader-Response Criticism and the Creation of Knowledge in the Classroom: David Bleich

One of the main themes of David Bleich's work is that knowledge in the humanities has its roots in subjective experience, and that this is especially so in the study of literature. It is simply not possible to give anyone objective knowledge of a work of literature; it has to be experienced subjectively, and then that experience has to be negotiated into knowledge through discussion in a group. In *Subjective Criticism* Bleich says, "To know anything at all is to have assigned a part of one's self to a group of others who claim to know the same thing."[5] What counts as knowledge depends on how individuals form groups and how these groups circumscribe the existence of other groups. It is a consequence of this that the classroom is a place in which knowledge is *created*, because the group is able to form a consensus about what a work of literature means. This knowledge is limited to the existence of the group, and if it is submitted to a larger group (through the publication of an essay reporting the conclusions of the group, for instance), the knowledge may not produce a consensus there. But the main point is that the process that occurs in this larger group (made up of professors of literature, let us say) *is very similar to* the process in the small group. Knowledge is created by groups; and the groups need to take responsibility for what counts as knowledge. Bleich puts this eloquently:

> Subjective criticism is a way of reaching knowledge of language and literature, of bearing responsibility for it, and of assembling collective interests in the pursuit of such knowledge. In practice (as opposed to in imagination) none of these purposes are separable from one another. Once you and I enter either a conversation or a classroom, we are proposing knowledge, bearing responsibility, and defining a community of common interests. There is no way to reduce the scope of these simple activities; when taken seriously, they become difficult and

complex. The only recourse is to increase awareness of them and to establish a vocabulary of subjective initiatives that can command our thoughts and regulate our relationships. Beyond these thoughts and relationships there is no way to authorize knowledge.[6]

This leads directly into the area known as the sociology of knowledge. We want to know how interrelated groups *create* knowledge, and how the classroom fits into that network.

Bleich describes a number of possible classroom activities. He points out that while students are often good at expressing ideas they tend have difficulty expressing feelings, and so the first item on his agenda is to get them to talk about their feelings. Usually a complex set of feelings lies behind ideas and thoughts, and usually these feelings are not discussed. They are assumed to be "subjective," while the ideas are thought to be "objective." Bleich will use an inflammatory statement such as "Women are smarter than men" simply to cause a feeling-reaction in students, which can then be discussed publicly.

Bleich argues that readers recreate works of literature in their own minds according to the dominant needs of their personalities at the time of reading. A particular reading of a text is an expression of the reader's own style and concern. He encourages students to ask themselves why they produced a particular reading of a work – to see what they added in their imaginations and what they suppressed, and why. When powerful feelings are aroused by a book, usually there are other situations in the student's life which have produced similar feelings – often involving an important personal relationship. Exploring these issues can lead to valuable self-knowledge.

An obvious objection to this method is that the exploration of one student's feelings and associations can be fascinating to the student, but boring for the rest of the class. This is especially likely to happen when other students have either not read the text or not responded to it very strongly. If this is the case, then *the story does not exist for them* in a real sense, and they will not want to be part of the group discussion.

At a later stage of Bleich's work with a class, he will ask the students to develop a community consensus about some significant issue. For instance, when studying Thackeray's *Vanity Fair*, Bleich asked his students first to write down their emotional responses to the novel and then to develop an idea of what is Victorian about it. The collective definition of the term "Victorian" that results from such a process can turn out to have less to do with the facts of social history in the nineteenth century, than with the main concerns of the people in the group. One group of students wrote a good deal about the experience of sexuality and how it is repressed in the novel – offering a confirmation of the observations of some historians that history is just as much about the historian as about the past.

Bleich points out that in any class there will be individuals who are simply unable or unwilling to a full and detailed report on their own experiences. He argues that these people should not be penalized for their apparent lack of cooperation, and that there are undoubtedly good reasons for it in their own past history. Bleich says that many students who are not good at expressing their feelings will have a talent for more traditional literary criticism, in the objective mold, and that they should be allowed to work in that way if they want to.

An important question for any student to answer when she enters a class is, "How much do I want to be involved in what is going on here? Do I want to bring my subjective experiences and make them public in this forum? Do I want to negotiate about them, in the hope of seeing them take on the added authority of communal assent, and become knowledge?" Perhaps many students just want to watch. Perhaps some mainly want to establish a relationship with an authority – either the teacher or the authors on the reading list. Some students seem to want to engage in a kind of ritual in which personal feelings are not significant at all. It is unlikely that one class could cater to all of these needs at once.

Bleich says that the most difficult task in the practice of subjective criticism is for a group to define itself as an interpretive community. Success in this area involves aligning the activities of the group with the motives of the participants for being members of the group. To some extent this means getting the members to speak roughly the same language. Bleich points out that taking over another person's language is one way of entering into a new kind of community with that person. Just as students are expected to articulate why they are involved with the class, Bleich feels that teachers should be willing to examine and make public to the class why they are concerned about literature. If Jesuits and psychoanalysts are required to examine their motivations before they are allowed to practice in the world, teachers of literature (or at least their classes) might benefit from a similar requirement.

The method and ideology of subjective criticism are based on the idea that the study of literature is a powerful avenue to self-knowledge. Bleich thinks that the desire for self-knowledge is the main motivation for students in literature programs. "Public" knowledge arises from agreements reached in communities through negotiation, and *for most of us the first and most important of these communities is the classroom*. This explains why Bleich is so concerned with what happens in the classroom, in contrast to most scholars, for whom the location of knowledge is much more objective – perhaps for them it resides primarily on the shelves of a library. The excitement of what Bleich is doing comes from the fact that he is showing us how to reappropriate knowledge and to make every interested person an active participant in the creation of knowledge. Certainly he introduces difficulties that providers of objective knowledge can avoid, but these difficulties are necessary if we want to link knowledge with subjectivity.

Objectivity and the Community: Stanley Fish

Norman Holland deals with reading as an individual activity; David Bleich is concerned with what happens in the classroom. The questions explored by Stanley Fish in *Is There a Text in This Class?*[7] relate to the functioning of the institution of literature as a whole. There seems to be a fundamental conflict, Fish says, between the objectivists in literary studies who think there is *one* correct meaning to a literary text, and the subjectivists, who think that meaning is entirely dependent on the idiosyncrasies of the individual. To put the question another way, who controls what? Does the text dominate readers and impose its meaning on them, or do readers dominate the text and impose their meanings on it?

Fish's answer is an interesting and useful one. He says that there is a basic error in thinking of reading as a battle between text and reader for power, because they are not two independent entities. The texts that are widely read in universities are "chosen" by the community of reviewers, scholars, professors, and students. They would not be on the bookshelves at all unless they were perceived as having broad support within the community. Also, students have been taught to read by members of a similar community. So there is probably a certain harmony between readers and the texts they are likely to read in a university course.

In theory, when we sit down to read a book, there is nothing to prevent us from reading it in any way we please – forwards, backwards, in fragments, or skipping the boring parts. But for your reading to make sense to others, or be significant within the literary community, you have to either work by the rules currently in force, or persuade a lot of people to change over to new ways of reading. So there are severe restraints imposed on your freedom, but they come neither from the text, nor from yourself, but from the literary community of which you want to be a part.

We could rephrase these observations using Thomas Kuhn's idea of how paradigms unite communities: to participate in a community, you have to use its paradigm, and the important texts in the community will be ones that fit in (to some extent) with that paradigm. The paradigm holds the community together and provides the standard of "objectivity" – which is not absolute objectivity, but objectivity defined by, and relative to, the paradigm in force in the community.

An important element in this argument is the idea that *symbolic objects cannot be perceived on their own, objectively*. They are always perceived within a paradigm or an institutional framework that gives them meaning. To illustrate this, Fish uses the example of a student raising his hand and shaking it vigorously during a discussion in a university classroom. The members of the class will see this as an urgent request to add a point to the discussion. But that is not the "objective meaning" of the gesture; in other contexts the same gesture might mean something entirely different. In a primary school, for instance, it would be a sign that the pupil wanted to go to the bathroom.

The fact that poems and gestures do not have *objective* meanings does not mean that they do not have *shared* meanings for certain cultural groups. As long as university classes continue to exist in their present format, the raised hand will have a clear, accepted meaning. It is the survival of cultural institutions such as universities, and schools of literary criticism, that allows meanings to be stable, and that provides definitions for what will be acceptable interpretations. We are not able to think "anything we like" – we are not radically free in this sense – because we are encouraged to think things that our cultural institutions find acceptable. This does not mean that we cannot have new ideas. This sometimes does happen. But these ideas do not become socially significant until the community or the institution is persuaded to accept them, and people who insist on pursuing their own ideas, and who don't get community validation for them, will be isolating themselves culturally. They will in effect cease to be members of the community that nurtured them.

Why does this matter? It matters because it shows the importance of traditions (and the communities that sustain them) in the study of literature. Students find that different professors emphasize very different aspects of literary study. Professors find exactly the same problem at conferences – there are different traditions or methods operating side by side. So what looks from the outside like an integrated field of English studies is in fact seriously fragmented. This poses two problems for each of us: (1) Which tradition speaks most forcefully to me, and demands my allegiance? And (2) how can I relate my work in that paradigm to the other – neighbouring but very different – traditions?

Reader-response criticism is unusual among the paradigms for literary study because it leaves much more room than most traditions for the development of groups on their own. Some of the standard practices are set out in advance, such as the need for members to report on their responses, and be willing to listen to others. But what will turn out to be acceptable to the group as a whole cannot be determined in advance. That makes the whole enterprise of reader-response criticism challenging and exciting.

Notes

1. "The person who passes here determines whether I am a tomb or a treasure, whether I speak or am silent. This concerns only you; friend, do not enter this building without desire." This inscription was one of four compsed by Valéry for the *Palais de Chaillot*, which was built in Paris in 1937 to house museums and a theater. It is an eloquent statement of one of the principles of reader-response criticism.

2. Roland Barthes, *The Pleasure of the Text*, trans. Richard Miller (New York: Hill and Wang, 1975) 63.

3. Norman Holland, *5 Readers Reading* (New Haven: Yale University Press, 1975).

4. Holland, 189.

5. David Bleich, *Subjective Criticism* (Baltimore: Johns Hopkins University Press, 1978) 296.

6. Bleich, 294.

7. Stanley Fish, *Is There a Text in This Class? The Authority of Interpretive Communities* (Cambridge, Mass.: Harvard University Press, 1980).

Suggestions for Further Reading

The texts mentioned in the notes above.

David Bleich, *Readings and Feelings: An Introduction to Subjective Criticism* (Urbana, Illinois: National Council of Teachers of English, 1975). This is a very short, useful book.

Joseph Gold, *Read for Your Life: Literature as a Life Support System* (Toronto: Fitzhenry and Whiteside, 1990). This is a book about how readers can use reading to enrich their lives, to help resolve difficult issues, and to realize the importance of story in their understanding of themselves and those they are close to. Gold is critical of much academic writing on literature because it ignores the feeling-responses of readers; his book is based on such responses – his own and others'.

Robert Scholes, *Semiotics and Interpretation* (New Haven and London: Yale University Press, 1982). This is lucid application of semiotic theories to individual texts, with a glossary and a good annotated select bibliography.

Susan Suleiman and Inge Cross (eds), *The Reader in the Text: Essays on Audience and Interpretation* (Princeton: Princeton University Press, 1980). An anthology with articles by Jonathan Culler, Tzvetan Todorov, Gerald Prince, and Norman Holland, and a good bibliography.

Jane Tomkins (ed.), *Reader-Response Criticism: From Formalism to Post-Structuralism* (Baltimore and London: Johns Hopkins University Press, 1980). An anthology containing a good introduction to reader-response criticism by the editor, articles by Gerald Prince, Stanley Fish, Jonathan Culler, Norman Holland, and David Bleich, and a good bibliography.

CHAPTER FOURTEEN:
Feminist Literary Criticism

IF YOU WERE A FLY ON THE WALL at a small, middle-class dinner party in a North American city, you might find the men speaking about 70 percent of the time, and the women 30 percent of the time. You might also find that 80 percent of the questions are asked by women, and only 20 percent by men. Why does this happen?[1] Is it fair? Does it bear any relation to the study of literature?

In a typical undergraduate English program in Canada, roughly 80 percent of the authors studied are male, and about 70 percent of the students are women. Once again men seem to be doing most of the "talking" and women most of the listening. Why does this situation occur? What do we want to do about it?

The Central Problem

These statistics strongly suggest that there is a system in place in our society that encourages men and women to take on different roles in mixed company. Men are more likely to be active, productive, and assertive, while women tend to be passive, receptive, and inquiring. Although we are all aware of exceptions to these rules, and it is possible for any person, by force of will or determination, to become an exception, that does not change the fact that if you are born a woman you are more likely to be listening than talking in most situations where men and women interact.

The system, sometimes known as "the patriarchal order," that causes men and women to take on these different roles is hidden, like the rules of grammar in a language. Children learn to speak in complete sentences long before they know what a complete sentence is, and men and

women often fulfill their assigned roles in social groups without knowing that an assignment has taken place. One way of perceiving these
roles is to make a list of what is seen as "masculine" and "feminine" in
North American culture.

MASCULINE	FEMININE
thinking	feeling
aggressive	compliant
liking a hierarchy that estab-lishes authority	liking a network that dis-perses authority
oriented to sight	oriented to touch
attack and penetration	receiving, holding, nourishing
closed	open
rational	transrational
fixed	fluid
going out into the world to work	maintaining a home, nurturing
seeking the truth	allowing for different truths
wanting to enter a new place	wanting to contain
speaking	listening
taking strong action	being passive or taking weak action
liking sciences	liking the arts
mathematics	clinical psychology
economics, thrift	abundance, giving
the conscious mind	the unconscious, dreams, fantasies

This list is far from complete, but something like it is operating in North
America today. We need to ask why. One simple answer often given by
conservative thinkers is that "life is like that," that it is "natural" for men
to have some characteristics and women to have others. People who
take this attitude sometimes ascribe the differences to biological distinctions between the sexes, such as women's ability to breast-feed an infant,
or the differences in the shapes of the male and female sexual organs
(convex vs. concave, penetrating vs. receptive). It might seem likely that
these differences would be reproduced in the roles typically taken on by
men and women, although there are no clear rules for extrapolating
from anatomical differences to patterns of behavior.

The influence of physical sexual differences on psychological sexual
differences is a subject of intense and continuing debate. One way of distinguishing the two spheres is to use the word "sex" to refer to physical

differences and the word "gender" to indicate differences that are culturally created and passed on. In her influential and fascinating study, *In a
Different Voice*, Carol Gilligan provides some examples of how boys and
girls are encouraged to develop in different ways because of systematic
social processes.[2] Both male and female infants usually have their primary
bond with their mothers, and many psychologists would say that this
bond is the strongest and most important relation which the individual
will ever know. But in order to develop to maturity, a boy has to switch
his primary relation from his mother to his father, which is not the case
for a girl. So maturing for a boy means separating from the mother and
moving into a more masculine world, the focus of which is usually outside the parental home. A maturing girl usually has to distance herself
from her mother too, but the same sharp break is not necessary.

Gilligan also discusses the differences in how groups of boys and girls
play. Girls, it seems, tend to play in small groups, often in pairs, and the
emotional bond between the members is much more important than
any set of "rules of play"; often there are not any articulated rules. Boys,
on the other hand, usually play in larger groups, often at semi-organized
games like pick-up baseball or hockey. There is usually a complex set of
rules in effect in these games, and it seems typical for boys (when not su-
pervised by adults) to spend about as much time discussing the rules of
the game and arguing about their application as they do actually playing
the game. Also the existence of a larger and formalized social structure
(for example, the "team") makes it natural for a hierarchy to develop (at
its top we find "the best player on the team"), and some of a boy's self-
knowledge will consist of his awareness of how he fits into the structure
of the team. At the same time a boy playing on a team may feel no need
for intimacy or emotional bonding, whereas that bonding is often essential in a girl's friendships.

We do not need to assume that these distinctions are always in effect
to conclude that differences *like* these may often be operating, with far-
reaching effects on how men and women see themselves when they are
mature. If boys do spend a lot of time at games, it makes sense that as men
they will know a lot about working within power-structures, systems of
rules, and hierarchies, and that the demands of big organizations may
well be relatively familiar and congenial to them. On the other hand they
may be poor at, and indeed frightened of, intimate relations, and may not
be at home with feelings in general. Women, in contrast, may have a lot
of experience with friendship and the various feelings that arise in inti-

mate relations, but feel incompetent, threatened, or repelled by the negotiations and competition that occur in big organizations.

From these differences it might be possible to generate many of the distinctions in the list of masculine and feminine characteristics on page 188. It is important to realize that, while biology may play a part in the construction of the two categories, "cultural" factors also have a strong influence. Sometimes the cultural factors can be altered. For example, when schools encourage girls to play hockey, and boys to study home economics, there may be some impact on the development of masculine and feminine stereotypes in our culture.

In the past twenty years there have been significant changes in the way in which gender stereotypes are imposed. In some professions there is much less discrimination based on sex than there used to be, although other professions (such as civil engineering, for instance) seem to have changed very little. Each person, probably each day, faces situations in which it is possible to make protests or changes, large or small. Is it better to support a woman than a man for public office just because she is a woman? Is arousing the prejudices of a narrow-minded man (or woman) in authority worth the penalties that might follow?

To some men the feminist program in any form seems like a threat of loss – men have to give up their "advantage" so that women can get closer to "equality." Real sacrifices can be involved, but often there are significant gains for men as well, because the whole feeling of a social unit changes when both sexes feel they are being treated fairly. In *The French Lieutenant's Woman*, a whole new vista of human relations opens up for Charles Smithson when Sarah Woodruff insists on certain kinds of equality, such as the right to contradict him when she feels he is wrong.

A final dimension to the central problem is that it has ramifications far beyond the conflict of the sexes. Women are a marginalized group and as such there is systematic discrimination against women in patriarchal society; but their situation is similar to that of many other marginalized groups, such as people of colour and gays.

How the Central Problem Arises in Language, Literature, and Criticism

The patriarchal order can leave its imprint on almost any area of social life. Many feminists feel that the English language itself is sexist, and conveys the implication that men are central and women marginal, particularly through the use of "man" and male pronouns to refer to "people" in general. (In Mandarin the character meaning "goodness" is a combination of those for "woman" and "child"; and "peace" is composed of "woman" under a roof. Although English does not contain exactly this kind of ideological assumption in its orthography, we should be on the watch for similar "meanings" hidden in our language.) Grammar itself, because it is a system of rules, may have a masculine feel, and some feminists assert that subversion of those rules has a feminine quality – as in Molly Bloom's long monologue at the end of *Ulysses*, in which punctuation is eliminated and the stream of consciousness flows freely.

Can figures of speech be sexist? Since all figures of speech involve a logical contradiction, figurative language (compared to literal or scientific language) can convey a feminine atmosphere. But some critics go further than this, and assert that the contrast between metaphor and metonymy can be (partly) mapped onto a masculine-feminine axis. Because metonymy is based on contiguity (in time or space) and so conveys attention to a *particular* time and place, it might be seen as "feminine" for this reason. Metaphor leaps through time and space in search of similarities, which can be dramatic and forceful. Metonymy rarely has these qualities.

"Literature" as an institution seems to bear a heavy imprint of patriarchal culture. Most of the canonized authors are male, as are most of the professors, critics, and editors who keep the canon in place and maintain its authority. Many of the dominant themes of great literature (for example, adventure, heroism, political struggle, ambition, and conquest) are closely related to the masculine qualities in the list on page 188, and some important genres (such as the epic and the picaresque novel) seem suited to the masculine and antithetical to the feminine. But the important judgments in deciding this issue are of a more subtle and less categorical nature, and the most we can do is to raise pertinent questions without trying to settle them in a definitive way. Think of the ten most important works of literature that you have read. Do they (as a group) focus more on masculine or feminine experience? Are women usually relegated to a subordinate position? Are the dominant fantasies in the works typically masculine or feminine? Is the feminine seen as "the other," and therefore that which is hard to understand? Do you see yourself reflected?

Finally, we can consider sexism in criticism. It seems logical and inevitable that commentary by men on a dominantly male canon will reflect patriarchal concerns, and that is often true with author-centered criticism. When commentary is concerned with the *meanings of works* (as opposed to the biography of the author) it is revealing to note the value given to the "legitimate" or "correct" meaning, which is usually the "author's meaning," and the hierarchy of authority this meaning establishes. (You have to know a lot about the author's life to be certain about what this meaning is.) A parallel can be drawn here between determining the "legitimate" meaning of a text and the legitimate children of a man.[3] In each case you need a complex intellectual and social apparatus (with a lot of repression, rules, rule-enforcers, and experts) in order to determine what (or who) is legitimate. But it is perfectly obvious to everyone assisting at a birth who the child's *mother* is; and, similarly, in reader-response criticism, it is obvious what the *reader's* meaning is. So we might feel justified in suspecting that author-centered criticism has many connections with the masculine, or patriarchal, paradigm.

Criticism centered on individual works of literature is also dominantly masculine, especially when the work is seen as a complex mechanism that requires analysis. (The romantic analogy between a work of literature and an organism softens this view.) Reader-centered criticism involves more feminine qualities – a dispersal of authority, a plurality of "valid" meanings for a work, and a concern with community rather than authority.

Dealing with Gender Issues in Individual Works of Literature

We now turn to several questions that can be applied to almost any work of literature, to investigate how a work presents the masculine and feminine aspects of experience.

Perhaps the most important general question to ask is, "Whose experience is rendered most fully and faithfully?" Is this a novel that presents men's experience from the inside, sympathetically, with the sense of the man as someone evolving with some inner freedom and choice? At the same time, are women presented as stereotypes (the alluring mistress, the dominating bitch, the all-providing earth-mother)? Are women seen as locked into those patterns, with no significant freedoms or flexibility? Is there hidden misogyny – or, indeed, overt misogyny? Are masculine and feminine activities and values presented differently? Is adventure valued more than cherishing and nourishing? Do men dominate women or vice-versa? From whose point of view is this process seen?

Another set of questions has to do with how the author presents the society she or he is setting the work in, and the ideology of that society.

If you are writing about Montreal society in the 1930s, as Hugh MacLennan does in *The Watch that Ends the Night*, the desire to be realistic entails showing that in public life men occupy more positions of authority than women. But what attitude does the book take toward that fact? Is it critical, or in favor of it, or neutral?

A third set of questions, complementing the first, is concerned with "gaps" in the work. Of course not even a long novel can provide a complete view of social life, although "epic novels," such as *War and Peace*, provide a great deal of information. But there may be systematic exclusions. Most of Joseph Conrad's works accord a very minor place to women. The men in Margaret Atwood's novels are often viewed from the outside and are also often stupid. Specific exclusions or gaps can indicate a lot about an author's ideology.

We can also ask questions about how the reader or the narratee (see Chapter 11) is "constructed" in the text. Many novels give explicit specifications about what kind of readers they are soliciting, and the actual readers may fit in with those specifications, or resist them, and find themselves reading against the grain of the novel. Some novels encourage masculine rather than feminine readers.

We should also be on the watch for large generalizations about life made by the author. *Anna Karenina* begins with the statement that "Happy families are all alike; but every unhappy family is unhappy in its own way." Jane Austen begins *Pride and Prejudice* with "It is a truth universally acknowledged, that a single man in possession of a good fortune, must be in want of a wife." Austen has her tongue in her cheek and Tolstoy is serious, but in both cases it is useful to ask whether these statements reflect the experience of men or of women. Is any social group being privileged or marginalized?

A final set of questions is: "Whose desires and fantasies are driving the novel? When it comes to an end, does the feeling of completion come from the fact that someone's desires have been achieved or assuaged?" In *War and Peace*, Pierre's search for a wife is a principal theme in the book; and after an unsuccessful marriage with Hélène, he finally marries Natasha. This is also a terminus for Natasha. In D.H. Lawrence's *Women in Love*, Ursula and Birkin, although they end up with each other, have some of their desires frustrated – Birkin wanted to have a committed tie to Gerald Crich, who is dead, and Ursula hoped that Birkin would be completely satisfied by having his main human contact only with her – and he wants more than that.

All these questions raise issues about how our culture divides qualities into sex-based categories, and how particular works of art reinforce or contest habits of mind and speech that we deplore. Feminist literary criticism has a political and moral dimension. It doesn't need to be revolutionary, but, like Marxism, it does aim at changing the world and the consciousness of people in the world.

Beyond Masculine and Feminine

Carl Jung's view was that just as we all contain male and female genes, we also house within our psyches both masculine and feminine characteristics. Most girls growing up in North American society are encouraged to repress their masculine traits and develop those that show them to be "attractively feminine." Similarly, most boys are urged (by their parents, their peers, and advertising) to leave their feminine attributes hidden or undeveloped, and to become aggressive and ambitious. (The table on page 188 is one result of these processes.) Jung, however, maintained that ignoring one side of human nature leads to incompleteness, and that one penalty we pay for mistreating members of the opposite sex is that we do violence to the inner contra-sexual element in ourselves. Some of Jung's followers have maintained that the tradition of Western philosophy and science has drastically impoverished itself by largely ignoring the reality of women's experience.[4]

So one possible consequence of feminism is political – righting the wrongs that are evident almost everywhere. Another is deconstructive – we need to take apart the powerful opposition between the masculine and feminine, recognize how it is passed on socially as part of our ideology, and subvert it when possible. This is an important theme for the French feminists Julia Kristeva and Hélène Cixous. Kristeva stresses the contrast between closed "rational" systems and more open, playful, "irrational" fields of expression. These are associated with the experience of the infant in the earliest stages of life, in the womb and at the mother's breast, before the age at which sexual differentiation becomes significant for the infant.

In her essay "The Laugh of the Medusa," Hélène Cixous is eloquent about the need for women to break out of patriarchal modes of thought, and one method for achieving this is to concentrate on the body:

Women must write through their bodies, they must invent the impregnable language that will wreck partitions, classes, and rhetorics, regulations and codes, they must submerge, cut through, get beyond the ultimate reserve-discourse.[5]

There is a strong utopian element in this essay, most clearly shown by Cixous's assumption that we can live on the basis of our desires, without rules, and that the love and giving of women and women's writing can overcome the scarcity engendered by a masculine economy of the mind and spirit. There is a concomitant sense that paradigms are unnecessary – that they can always be changed, or replaced, when that is needed. This is an inspiring element in feminist criticism, because there is no doubt – in literary criticism and in university education – that some paradigms are in need of change.

Notes

1. It is of course hard to find reliable statistics in this area, and so readers need to test these figures against their own experience. Dale Spender and Sally Cline report that their field research shows that "in conversation with men it is almost unheard of for any woman to talk for more than one third of the time...women consistently report that they have had a fair share of the conversation, even if that 'share' was less than 20%." *Reflecting Men at Twice their Normal Size* (London: André Deutsch, 1987) 8-9.

2. Carol Gilligan, *In a Different Voice: Psychological Theory and Women's Development* (Cambridge, Mass.: Harvard University Press, 1982).

3. This subject is discussed in Jonathan Culler's *On Deconstruction* (Ithaca: Cornell University Press, 1982) 58-61.

4   A Freudian psychiatrist who has written on this theme is Karl Stern, in *The Flight from Woman* (1965; New York: Paragon House, 1985).

5. Hélène Cixous, "The Laugh of the Medusa," *Signs* 1 (1976) 875-93.

Suggestions for Further Reading

Catherine Belsey and Jane Moore (eds), *The Feminist Reader: Essays in Gender and the Politics of Literary Criticism* (London: Macmillan, 1989). A collection of essays by Dale Spender, Mary Jacobus, Sandra M. Gilbert and Susan Gubar, Hélène Cixous, Julia Kristeva, and others, with a glossary and a short, selective bibliography.

Carol Gilligan, *In a Different Voice: Psychological Theory and Women's Development* (Cambridge, Mass.: Harvard University Press, 1982).

Mary Eagleton (ed.), *Feminist Literary Theory: A Reader* (Oxford: Blackwell, 1986). This book provides short statements (some as short as a page) by writers and critics, grouped into five chapters: "Finding a Female Tradition," "Women and Literary Production," "Gender and Genre," "Toward Definitions of Feminist Writing," and "Do Women Write Differently?" The introductions to the chapters, written by the editor, are especially helpful.

Sandra M. Gilbert and Susan Gubar, "Introduction" to *The Madwoman in the Attic: The Woman Writer and the Nineteenth-Century Literary Imagination* (New Haven: Yale University Press, 1979).

Toril Moi, *Sexual/Textual Politics: Feminist Literary Theory* (London: Methuen, 1985).

CHAPTER FIFTEEN:

Marxist Criticism

MARXIST CRITICISM, LIKE FEMINIST criticism, is essentially political. Karl Marx was keenly interested in how certain groups or classes in society acquire and keep power, and Marxist criticism pays a lot of attention to the social structures that allocate power to different groups in society. Marxist critics often judge literature by how it represents the main struggles for power going on at the time it was written, and by how it may influence those struggles, through changing readers' minds about key issues. Marxists often applaud works of literature that seem likely to have the social or political results they desire.

Marxism: The Basic Theory

Marxism is fundamentally concerned with human freedom and solidarity; its main theme can be expressed as "how we can wrest a realm of freedom from a realm of necessity."[1] Marx said that the achievement of freedom is "a restoration of the human world to man himself." The meaning of these statements is that in most social and economic situations the majority of people find themselves oppressed, and forced to behave in ways that they don't like, for not very good reasons. Some of these oppressing "necessities" (such as the need to work at alienating jobs) can, through honesty, reasonableness, and cooperation, be transformed into freedoms (for example, the opportunity to work at satisfying jobs), and groups of people can choose to make their communal life as rewarding and productive as possible. Marx's hope for a good society can be seen in the famous formula about how to decide how much individuals will work and how much they will be "paid": "From each according to his abilities, to each according to his needs."

Marxism is built on a theory about progress in history. Marx believed that economic factors determine the important values and practices in a culture, and that most economic systems divert huge amounts of wealth from an exploited class to a privileged group of people. In the feudal system of the Middle Ages, the aristocracy owned the land that was the basis for agricultural production, and that class was thus able to take and use much of the wealth produced by the work of the farm laborers. During the industrial revolution, the new class of town- and city-based (or "bourgeois") capitalists became able – though was a slow process – to dominate the aristocracy because the main basis for creating wealth was no longer land, but industrial production. Bourgeois capitalists caused a new exploited class to come into being: the industrial laborers, or proletariat. Marx predicted in the 19th century that, because of inexorable economic processes, the capitalists would become fewer and fewer, while the proletariat became larger and larger. Eventually, he said, this would lead to open conflict between the two classes, which the proletariat, because of their overwhelming numbers, would win. Following their victory, the proletariat would take control of the means of production, and use those means to create a good society, in which justice and fairness would replace privilege and exploitation. In this society, which looks quite like the Christian idea of the new Jerusalem or the "just city," there would be economic and social cooperation, and, as much as possible, individuals would feel free and fulfilled – not only in their work, but also in their families and friendships.

With the spread of socialism after Marx's death, a split developed between those who believed that socialism could be achieved through peaceful, evolutionary means, and those who thought that violent revolution was essential to creating the new society. The latter group triumphed in Russia in 1917 and established communism as one form of Marxist socialism; but Marxist influence is also clear and strong in the creation of the welfare state (with socialized medicine and unemployment insurance, for instance) and in the trade union movement.

Although Marx's aspirations have borne valuable fruit in actual social changes, a number of his key theories have been disconfirmed or discredited by historical developments. In the West, capitalists have not become fewer and fewer, and driven more and more of their competitors into the proletariat, thus paving the way to revolution. Instead, a substantial and materially well-rewarded middle class has prospered, and the actual living conditions of workers in many capitalist countries have improved over the last fifty years. In the 1980s the centrally planned economies of the Soviet Union and the communist east-bloc countries in Europe have done poorly at meeting the real needs of their peoples, and rule by one-party systems has been massively rejected. Finally, Marxist revolutionary socialism has not led to the abolishment of privilege or the "withering away of the state," as Marx predicted; on the contrary, most communist countries have fostered privileged elites and sprawling, inefficient government bureaucracies.

In the West, most people familiar with Marxism are critial of it because (1) in the past forty years, communist countries have been seen as "the enemy"; (2) the results of Marxism in Russia, China, and elsewhere do not look attractive (although it is difficult to make reliable comparisons between "life" in the East and the West), and (3) the unfulfilled predictions mentioned in the previous paragraph make Marxism seem flawed. Still, if we want to discover what is best in Marxist literary criticism, we do need to appreciate Marx's fundamental devotion to humane values and to the development of community life.

Why Marxist Literary Criticism Is Worth Our Attention

For Marxists a work of literature does not have its meaning "on its own." The work is seen as an expression of existing ideologies and class conflicts, and those conflicts form part of an enormous historical process emerging in feudal times and reaching far into the future. So to understand *Hamlet* in Marxist terms, you have to know about Shakespeare's times, the class conflicts present then, and how that period fits into the slow process of cultural and economic development over the past thousand years. While these questions are too big for most people, they are also intriguing and, in their scale, awe-inspiring. They are an example of the stage 3 mind (see Chapter 9) tackling a vast expanse of human experience.

Another aspect of the large scale of Marxist literary criticism is that it places the study of literature in the context of important social questions. The feeling of this context may be suggested by some of the following issues: "What do you think of a world in which some people become rich by manufacturing hydrogen bombs and other instruments of war, while one-fifth of the world's population (one billion people) have no proper access to clean water and have a life expectancy of less than 45 years?" Or, "Every work of culture is also a work of barbarism" – meaning that for every person who is able to spend five hours a day reading literature there are another ten who are illiterate and twenty more who never read anything more complicated than a comic book or a newspaper article.[2] Given the existence of pressing social issues as well as class systems that tend to restrict the availability of "high culture" to members of the upper-middle class, we need to ask hard questions about why we should pay attention to literature at all. Any particular individual might conclude that he or she did not feel justified in spending a lot of time on literature; or, on the other hand, it might seem a socially responsible activity because it makes us more aware of how our actual social practices contribute to creating the kind of society we live in. How, we might ask, does giving grades for literature courses create a class system within the university?

There is an unconscious hostility to some marxist ideas in most students, especially if they are conscious of trying to "improve themselves." One way to measure how much you are improving is to see how you are rising on the social scale; and if you feel you have moved yourself up to a new level, that is a clear indication of success. But this measuring stick entails a class system, with many of the unattractive features inherent in such a system, such as competition, and the victory of the winner being paid for by the suffering of the loser.

Marxism and Ideology

One of the valuable aspects of Marxist criticism is that it accords great importance to ideology, and it places ideological questions at the center of its literary enquiries. Michael Ryan provides a good definition of ideology:

> The term ideology describes the beliefs, attitudes, and habits of feeling which a society inculcates in order to generate an automatic reproduction of its structuring premisses. Ideology is what preserves social power in the absence of direct coercion.[3]

Ideology preserves the character of a society by maintaining these "structuring premisses," for example the class system that is in effect and which establishes what someone has to do to move from the lower class to the middle class. So ideology is necessary to the ongoing culture. At the same time, however, it diminishes an individual's freedom, because (while it is in force) it blocks a person off from even *having* certain thoughts. So it is extremely liberating to be able to discover the ideology we have been living by (sometimes by seeing it portrayed in a novel) and to find we can step outside of that ideology.

James Joyce gives an example of this process in *Portrait of the Artist as a Young Man*. Stephen Dedalus is raised in institutions that support the Catholic Church, and for a brief period he lives by its ideology. But when the question is put to him whether or not he wants to become a priest, he realizes he is repelled by the dryness of the lives of the priests he knows. In a similar way he escapes the nets that Ireland and the Irish nationalists are trying to throw over him. The novel ends with him leaving Ireland and the church, and going to Europe to become an artist. This poses a question about what ideology he is now adopting – it might be called "pan-European aestheticism."

Most students, consciously or unconsciously, live by an ideology that is often called liberal humanism. It is an ideology that accords great importance to the freedom of the individual, and sanctions big differences in wealth or income, because to insist on economic equality would restrict individual freedoms greatly. "Humanism" implies that the important values in this ideology are derived from the experience of humanity, rather than from a source of dogma such as the Bible, the Pope, or Chairman Mao. One aspect of Marxist criticism is that it throws these assumptions into question. North Americans tend to value the freedom of the individual over the well-being of the group, whereas one of Mao's main aims in the Cultural Revolution in China in the 1960s was to prevent intellectuals from passing on to their students their liberal beliefs and subverting the Marxist insistence on the primacy of the group. So we might draw a parallel between a North American student reading *Portrait of the Artist as a Young Man* and going on a trip to China: both provide the experience of immersing oneself in an alien ideology.

Joyce's novel consciously criticizes an existing ideology, presenting it first from the inside and then viewing it from outside. But artists do not have to be conscious about their relation to ideology. Many of the most powerful presentations of ideology occur when a novel seems ideologically naive, and reflects in an honest way how fundamental conflicts in society are being worked out (usually unconsciously) by its members. In Balzac's *Père Goriot*, Rastignac, the protagonist, comes from the middle class, and at one point in the novel he hopes to rise in the world through his own merit; but he soon sees that he can advance himself much more effectively by winning the protection of an aristocratic woman. The aristocracy itself is being undermined by the financial power of the bourgeoisie. Goriot's two daughters can gain access to the world of the aristocracy because of their father's wealth, even though he made it by manufacturing pasta. So although superficially *Père Goriot* seems to be about the adventures of Rastignac, it can also be seen to be fundamentally about the struggle for power between the landed aristocracy and the bourgeoisie.

The English critic Terry Eagleton says that the true value of a work of art lies in the way it presents (consciously or unconsciously) the reigning ideology or offers a criticism of that ideology.[4] The main function of the high modernism of the 1920s, he argues, was to offer a criticism of, and to fight against, the hegemony of capitalism. T.S. Eliot's *The Waste Land*, then, would be seen as a depiction of the sterility of European bourgeois capitalism in the early twentieth century.

Texts may be more than simply a direct criticism of the reigning ideology or a positive statement about it. They may be sites of struggle themselves, where different views of the world fight with one another. This is clearly the case with *Dr Zhivago*, in which the protagonist starts out as an adherent of the revolution and then devotes much of his energy to presenting an alternative to the platitudinous conformism demanded by the communists – the alternative being the life of the artist who pays attention to language, feelings, and nature.

Another depiction of conflict in ideologies can sometimes be seen in the literature of colonial and postcolonial countries, where the values of the colonist are in conflict with those of the indigenous population. This struggle may be universal in colonial situations, but it receives an interesting twist when people in a colonized country instinctively put the values of the dominating culture above their own. This occurs in Paul Scott's novel *The Jewel in the Crown*, which is set in pre-independence India. One character, Duleep Kumar, wants to acquire a British way of speaking and thinking so he can then acquire the power and prestige that he sees the British in India possess. Wanting "the best" for his son Hari, he educates him in England and tries to prevent any Indian influence from reaching him; but after his father's death Hari is forced to return to India alone and in great poverty. Except for the color of his skin, Hari is an educated, upper-middle class Englishman; but in India he is rejected by everyone – by the English because he is not white and by the Indians because he has no Indian culture or language. In this novel, the ideological conflict between the colonizer and the colonized is focused in the fate of a single, tragic character.

Works of literature that are more ideologically naive can be analyzed in yet another way, which involves seeing them from a "superior" position and pointing out where they are inconsistent or self-contradictory – pointing out the "gaps" or "fissures" or "blindnesses" that they contain. For instance, a critic might describe a popular television show as constructed out of "one-liners," usually humorous but at some moments serious. This kind of program may seem blind to the fact that many issues in life cannot be dealt with in such a staccato manner. This condescending *de haut en bas* approach is not likely to be useful for students of literature, especially if they are reading canonical works, although it may help the cause of demystification to suggest that even great works have some limitations.

A further role of Marxist criticism is that of pointing out and documenting the way in which literature and "the literary" function as a part of ideology. In Tolstoy's *Anna Karenina*, Karenin, Anna's dull but eminent husband, makes a concerted effort to keep abreast of the latest developments in literature and in the artistic world generally. He does this because he feels it is an essential part of his role in life to be able to discuss contemporary art intelligently at social gatherings, in spite of the fact that he has little feeling for it. Here "literature" is functioning, or being used, as a way of separating people into different social groups.

A final important way in which ideology can be involved in the study of literature occurs in the phenomenon known as "aestheticism." This is an ideology that places supreme value on the experience of art – the reading of great works of literature, for instance – and maintains that this activity will provide us with the highest and most intense experiences in our lives. Some critics take this view, and it also attracts some students of literature because it makes what they are doing seem very important. But many intellectuals outside the field of literature find aestheticism a narrow-minded and unattractive ideology.

An element in aestheticism is the belief in something that might be called "the rich inwardness of the private life." Studying the canon of Western literature tends to promote a feeling that there are certain powers of mind that are inherent, indestructible, and eternally valuable (the qualities of "man's unconquerable mind," as Wordsworth puts it); and that these powers can be attained through the essentially private activity of reading. Marxism, on the contrary, insists that nothing in human experience is eternal and that private activities only take on real significance when they have social consequences.

William Blake wrote that "Bless relaxes; damn braces." One of the invigorating elements of Marxist literary criticism for us is that it braces us by approaching us with a true and lively spirit of opposition.

Conclusion: The Bourgeois Uses of Marxist Criticism

Roland Barthes says that one function of literature in the West is to give people the belief that they are individuals, as though this were a healthy fiction for them to embrace (in the way that Kant thought it was valuable to believe in the immortality of the soul). The teaching and study of literature are often bound up with fostering a belief in the importance of individuals. Marxists tend to reject this belief as an opiate that distracts people from paying attention to questions of overriding importance, such as the state of the class struggle. But teachers and learners often work best at the "local" level, even when they have large aims in mind. This was put eloquently by Robert Pirsig in *Zen and the Art of Motorcycle Maintenance*:

> I think that if we are going to reform the world, and make it a better place to live in, the way to do it is not with talk about relationships of a political nature, which are inevitably dualistic, full of subjects and objects and their relationship to one another; or with programs full of things for other people to do. I think that kind of approach starts at the end and presumes the end is the beginning. Programs of a political nature are important *end products* of social quality that can be effective only if the underlying structure of social values is right. The social values are right only if the individual values are right. The place to improve the world is first in one's own heart and head and hands, and then move outward from there. Other people can talk about how to expand the destiny of mankind. I just want to talk about how to fix a motorcycle. I think that what I have to say has more lasting value.[5]

This attitude seems appropriate for students and teachers. It is important to be aware of the big problems that affect the world as a whole, but concentrating exclusively on them can lead to a frustrating feeling of powerlessness.

One reason that ideology is a compelling area for attention in literary studies is that it is not limited to the political sphere. Although we all have assumptions about how we slot into the existing class system and how we would like to see that system evolve, we also have assumptions (many of them unconscious) about much more local matters, such as what the good life is, how rewarding friendships work, and how children should be raised. We have ideas (often inherited from our parents) about the role of emotions in ordering our lives, about the relative claims of work and of family life, and about whether good fences make good neighbors. Many of the books studied in the undergraduate curriculum deal with these matters. That is one reason why they can be fascinating.

Marxism encourages us to look at big questions, and it has developed impressive tools for doing that. The main use of Marxism in literary studies rests in adapting those methods, especially those dealing with ideology, to help us talk about and resolve the smaller problems, which occupy most of us most of the time.

Notes

1. This phrase is taken from Fredric Jameson, *The Political Unconscious: Narrative as a Socially Symbolic Act* (Ithaca, New York: Cornell University Press, 1981) 19.

2. Walter Benjamin, quoted by Terry Eagleton in *Walter Benjamin, or Towards a Revolutionary Criticism* (London: Verso, 1981).

3. Michael Ryan, "Political Criticism," in G. Douglas Atkins and Laura Morrow (eds), *Contemporary Literary Theory* (Amherst: The University of Massachusetts Press, 1989) 203.

4. Terry Eagleton, *Marxism and Literary Criticism* (London: Methuen, 1976) 19 .

5. Robert Pirsig, *Zen and the Art of Motorcycle Maintenance* (New York: Bantam, 1988) 267.

Suggestions for Further Reading

Terry Eagleton, *Criticism and Ideology* (London: New Left Books, 1976).

Terry Eagleton, *Marxism and Literary Criticism* (London: Methuen, 1976). This book is short (86 pages), clear, and has a select bibliography with seventeen entries.

Fredric Jameson, *The Political Unconscious: Narrative as a Socially Symbolic Act* (Ithaca, New York: Cornell University Press, 1981). This is a dense and demanding book, and shows a committed Marxist's insistence on historicizing the work of literature, by showing how the work presents the contradictions in society, the struggle between the classes, and the "cultural revolution."

Raymond Williams, *Marxism and Literature* (Oxford: Oxford University Press, 1977).

CHAPTER SIXTEEN:

Postcolonial Criticism and Multiculturalism

POSTCOLONIAL LITERATURE IS LITERATURE written in the shadow of the great European empires which, by one estimate, held eighty-five percent of the rest of the world in their sway by 1914. This means that the vast majority of non-European peoples have been affected by the fact that they were colonized by a foreign power. Some eminent critics would insist that the culture of Europe itself is fundamentally marked by its leading role in colonizing the world. It was a project energized in part by high ideals: the desire to bring the benefits of European culture, science, technology and medicine to millions of natives leading lives which were viewed as primitive and impoverished. However in the second half of the twentieth century it has been seen more often in its less attractive aspect:

> The conquest of the earth, which mostly means taking it away from those who have a different complexion or slightly flatter noses than ourselves, is not a pretty thing when you look into it too much.

This is Marlow, the narrator of Conrad's *Heart of Darkness* (which was written in 1899). He considers the possibility that empires are fundamentally "just robbery with violence, aggravated by murder on a grand scale."

The widespread interest now in postcolonial criticism is a natural result of the vast extent of the world's colonial systems, and the efforts of many of the colonized to gain their independence, both economically and culturally. Here are some of the issues raised in postcolonial criticism: How did the culture of the colonizer affect that of the natives? How did exploitation occur, and what reparations are in order? How open were the people in power to the experience of the natives? How does a person form a solid identity when he or she is part of a group which is consistently viewed as vicious, irrational or subhuman by the dominant forces in society? When there are vast cultural differences between two peoples (for instance, between the British and the Hindus in India), can a common form of reasoning, of rationality, be found? Is science ideologically neutral? What effect does the canon of "great literature in English" have on native writers, and on English-speaking settlers in the new world who are writing about an experience different from that of the canonical authors? And, finally, the "multicultural questions": When a country contains several cultures, should some have precedence over others? How should state support be allocated to the various cultural groups? What languages should be spoken in the schools? What literature should be read?

It is hard, and perhaps impossible, to be impartial about these questions. Anyone approaching them will have assumptions and commitments already established. In particular your attitude will depend on two issues. Are you predominantly a victim of colonialism, or a beneficiary of it – perhaps an unwitting beneficiary? And, secondly, is the culture you currently live in one which basically empowers you, by presenting you with images of people you can identify with who are successful and happy in life (to put it crudely), or is your culture one which regularly suggests that people like you are likely to be exploited, harassed, or denied a hearing, or fair wages?

People from "subaltern" groups, which have suffered widely from discrimination (such as blacks in the United States, or Hindus and Moslems in British India), are often aware of the need to deal with an alien, but dominant, culture, or speak a language other than their own. People from dominant, or colonizing groups, however, often are much less aware of the system of oppression which is in place. The group you belong to will affect the way you see issues of postcolonialism and multiculturalism. We will begin by considering one of the early and most eloquent advocates of the colonized peoples of Africa, Frantz Fanon.

Frantz Fanon's *The Wretched of the Earth*

Frantz Fanon, who was born in 1925 in the French West Indies, was the psychiatrist in charge of a hospital outside Algiers in the 1950s, where he could see the evidence of the extreme suffering of the Algerians during their war of independence, which lasted from 1954 to 1962. During that time approximately 100,000 Algerian soldiers died. The French, who had up to 500,000 soldiers stationed in Algeria, made fierce attempts to control the country with counter-terrorist operations. Torture was widely used. Fanon gave up his hospital work in 1956 to become one of the leaders of the Algerian National Front, and the editor of its newspaper.

In *The Wretched of the Earth,* Fanon says that not only was the French colonial policy in Algeria one of economic exploitation, but also that it included an attempt on the part of the French to create "a systematic negation of the other person, and a furious determination to deny the other person all attributes of humanity." [1] The aim of the colonizers was not only to dominate, but to eliminate everything in the lives of the natives which might have given them a sense of identity or dignity. Their language, history, culture, and achievements were devalued or erased, and they were seen as a species of subhuman animal.

Why would the French colonizers engage in this kind of systematic abuse of the native population? (There is a lot of evidence, in more moderate books, that abuse in colonies is very widespread.) Fanon's answer would be that the essential goal of the French in Algeria was extreme exploitation, and that to engage in this successfully, the colonizers needed to see the native peoples as subhuman. He says,

Europe is literally the creation of the Third World. The wealth which smothers her is that which was stolen from the under-developed peoples. The ports of Holland, the docks of Bordeaux and Liverpool, were specialized in the Negro slave-trade, and owe their renown to millions of deported slaves. [2]

Colonialism and imperialism have not paid their score when they withdraw their flags and their police forces from our territories. For centuries the capitalists have behaved in the underdeveloped world like nothing more than war criminals. Deportations, massacres, forced labour, and slavery have been the main methods used by capitalism to increase its wealth, its gold and diamond reserves, and to establish its power. [3]

He goes on to compare the Algerians' demand for compensation from France to the demands made by Europeans of the Germans, after their effective colonization of Europe during the Second World War.

Fanon says that the confrontation between the colonizers and the colonized generates a kind of Manichaeism, an extreme polarization into good and evil. The colonizers need to see the natives as depraved human beings, or not human beings at all – somewhat in the way that Shakespeare portrays Caliban in *The Tempest*. When the natives realize this, Fanon says, their only effective response will need to be equally extreme. They cannot negotiate with their oppressors, or take partial measures. They need to resort to violence.

At this point in his argument Fanon articulates many themes which re-appear in subsequent postcolonial literature and criticism. One is the process by which, before the struggle for independence takes place, some natives cooperate with, and assimilate themselves to, the foreign dominators, partly because this gives them some access to power, but also because it allows them to constitute themselves as *selves*. (Fanon felt that one important result of colonial subjection was that most indigenous people could not imagine having a "self" in the Western sense.) Westernized natives may then may be unwilling to support a revolution which will throw out the colonizing power, because this will take away the basis for their own favoured position. Those who do become revolutionaries face further challenges. One is to rouse the mass of the natives to action; another is to recover the original native culture which has been largely obliterated by the colonizer. But inevitably this culture, even if it can be brought to life, will be archaic. A later task for workers for independence will be to create a *living* culture which responds to the current reality facing the native population.

Fanon is a genuine idealist, envisaging the possibility that Africans can create a new, communal, compassionate society which renounces violence and exploitation. Although he admires the success of European civilization in subduing the world, he sees it as cruel, harsh, and self-centred. He says,

> Europe undertook the leadership of the world with ardour, cynicism and violence. Look at how the shadow of her palaces stretches out ever further! Every one of her movements has burst the bounds of space and thought. ... [But, he adds,] let us waste no time in sterile litanies and nauseating mimicry. Leave this Europe where they are never done talking of Man, yet murder men wherever they find them, at the corner of every one of their own streets, in all the corners of the globe. For

centuries they have stifled almost the whole of humanity in the name of a so-called spiritual experience. [4]

As opposed to the hierarchies set up by European colonists, Fanon sees the independent Algerian republic working on the principles of extreme decentralization, contact and interchange between the leaders and the rank-and-file, and a clear understanding that the government is at the service of the masses. "Women will have exactly the same place as men, not only in the clauses of the constitution but in the life of every day: in the factory, at school, and in the parliament." The living expression of the nation will be found not in the leaders, the palaces, or rituals of politics, but in "the moving consciousness of the whole of the people: it is the coherent, enlightened action of men and women." [5]

One of Fanon's greatest admirers, and a leader in the postcolonial movement in literature, is the Palestinian-American professor of literature Edward Said. In his book *Orientalism*, written in 1978, he expands Fanon's view of how the French denigrate the Algerians, to give an account of how Europeans in general have seen Moslems and other peoples from the Middle East and the East in a stereotyped way, lumping them together as a single class of people who are lazy, unreliable, and unreasonable. Said points out that the category of "the oriental" is culturally constructed, often with the help of established scholars, and it seems in the West to have the status of a fact, whereas it misrepresents and misunderstands the variety of Eastern peoples and civilizations, and is really a myth generated in the West for Western purposes. Like Fanon, Said is concerned with practical politics, and in lifting the burden placed on indigenous people in countries like Palestine. (He has been a member of the Palestinian National Council.) In the academic world, one of his goals is to produce a kind of knowledge which does not oppress or coerce minority groups in society. He wants to take apart systems of domination which are constructed by colonialism and, he would say, by culture itself.

Encountering "the Other"

One of the principal elements in colonial and postcolonial literature is the encounter with "the Other" – either the indigenous nations encountering European culture, with its panoply of hierarchy, weaponry, Christianity, and disease, or, on the other hand, the European settlers encountering what seems to them the mystery, the darkness, and the threat of a native culture. How does the mind react when it encounters something new and strange? I would like to illustrate this process with a visual analogy.

Recently I showed forty slides of paintings by van Gogh to a class of 11-year-olds, and spoke about his life, the development of his style, and the meteoric growth in his popularity in the 20th century. I spoke about his early attempts to work as an assistant in an art dealer's store, as a teacher, and as a minister of religion; about his failure in love, and his loneliness and poverty at many periods of his life. I mentioned that in 1987 his painting of irises brought the highest price ever paid for a single painting, $53.9 million. I then asked them to do a drawing which would be an imitation of something van Gogh might have painted. I suggested (jokingly) that it might command a high price if it looked like an authentic work, and I put a "Vincent" signature in the bottom left-hand corner of the paper I gave them to draw on.

The drawings which the children produced seemed very revealing to me of the ways in which they dealt with the otherness of van Gogh's life and works. The results fell into three basic categories. Several children drew cartoon characters which they clearly knew how to draw before seeing the van Gogh paintings. The one I have reproduced on the next page is of "An Average Teacher." The subject was perhaps suggested by our discussion of Vincent's life, but visually the drawing owes nothing to the paintings we saw. At the other extreme, two or three children tried to reproduce, almost exactly, a picture by van Gogh which they had in front of them. "The Sunflowers" illustrates this. Here there was a lot of van Gogh, and relatively little of the child.

"The Baseball Glove" and "Three Lonely Flowers" fall between these two extremes. The first was inspired directly by van Gogh's early painting of a pair of peasant's boots. This child took an ordinary object which was sitting on his desk, and tried to do for it what van Gogh had done in "The Boots." This produces a mixing of the child's life and van Gogh's painting. "Three Lonely Flowers" is a more complicated combination because it works on an emotional as well as a visual level. I had shown them a painting of a vase of flowers, and we had talked about the rhythmic use of lines, or swirls, in van Gogh's paintings; these are present on the vase. But the "loneliness" – and the flowers do seem disconnected and lonely – I am sure comes from my brief narrative of the painter's life.

A: The Average Teacher, by Bill Cruess

B: The Sunflowers, by Sandra Henderson

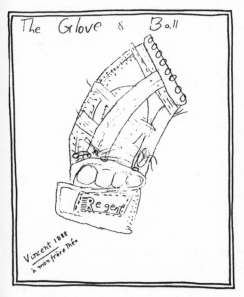

C: The Glove & Ball, by Lloyd Elliott

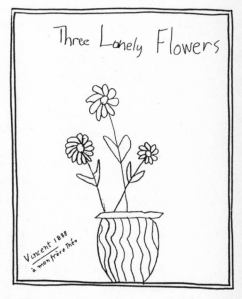

D: Three Lonely Flowers, by Will Bonnycastle

Three modes of interacting between the self and the other:
A: The self dominates; B: the other dominates; C and D: a balance between the self and the
other produces hybridization, a blending of two sensibilities which is similar to dialogue.

What this suggests is that when you encounter "the other," you may

(i) stick with your own experience, and be relatively uninfluenced (this is what happens for most of the English settlers in *A Passage to India*, who cannot imagine sharing anything important with a native Indian);

(ii) you can abandon your own culture and adopt that of the other (this is what happens to the figure played by Kevin Costner in the film *Dances with Wolves*, when he abandons his own people and takes up life with the Sioux); or

(iii) you can develop a response which mixes elements of yourself with elements of the other (Fielding and Mrs Moore do this in *A Passage to India*; they make a genuine attempt to interact, and learn from, the Indians).

The third response is probably the most common of the three, because few people can be entirely unaffected by encountering another culture (though there will be a range of how much different people are affected). In postcolonial criticism this response is sometimes referred to as "hybridization" – a new, hybrid form is produced, which contains elements of different cultures or languages. Some critics feel that a culture can exist in a pure form, and that to be authentic you need to preserve that purity. An example of this would be the attempt on the part of the *Académie Française* to eliminate many words imported into French from other languages, particularly English. It seems more likely that the purest manifestation of culture, however, will have diverse roots, just as Shakespeare's English is a combination of the Germanic Anglo-Saxon and the French brought by William and his Norman conquerors.

What happens when we encounter "the other" in the literature that we read? One of the biggest difficulties in reading a novel about a culture very different from your own is that many of the details of what happens will not have clear meanings, simply because you cannot supply an appropriate background for them. This was certainly true when I first read *Arrow of God* by the Nigerian novelist Chinua Achebe. It is focused on the chief priest of an alliance of six villages of the Igbo tribe, who tries to lead his people effectively while they establish relations with the British colonial administration. One struggle he undergoes is to maintain his position of authority within the alliance, where there is a good deal of formal consultation between the elders of the villages. He also endeavours to learn about the local Christian mission, by sending one of his four sons to "be his eyes" there.

Much of the first part of this moving novel is a description of events which take place in the social and religious life in the chief priest's village. This is given without much explanatory material, and a lot of what happens is hard to understand at first if you are unfamiliar with the culture. This task is made more difficult by the fact that the characters' names are hard to remember, and Achebe uses Igbo words for some objects, presumably because no English equivalents exist. I found that the novel first became very involving during a section in the middle which narrates the attempt by the British district manager to set up a "clan chief" (he wants to choose the chief priest, whom he admires), because this is the policy which his superiors have decided to impose. (The manager himself disagrees with it.) He sends a black messenger to command the chief priest to come to see him; and the messenger wants to impose *his* authority on the priest and his village. One reason I found this section compelling is the fact that the subject of conflict between rival authorities, and the problems of having a centralized administrative system, are very familiar to me from reading English literature, and living in the Western world. *This* subject does not feel like "the other"; it feels like an aspect of my own culture. But interpreting this section of the novel is difficult because it is hard to know what the normal role of the priest is in Igbo society, and what is liable to offend his dignity.

My point here is that encountering "the other" is difficult in itself, and often we deal with it by seeing parallels with our own familiar experience. Perhaps the most we can hope for in perceiving "the other" is a hybrid mixture of two cultures, rather than direct insight into the unfamiliar one. "Encountering the other" is, of course, a subject which occurs in many areas of literary study: the incomprehensible other in a work of literature may be another character in the protagonist's own culture, or an aspect of himself which is repressed. Comparative literature raises the possible gaps between the self and the other to the level of cultures and languages, and postcolonial criticism adds to this the dimension of a hierarchical relation between cultures: at first the culture of the colonist will probably be fiercely dominant, and the task of the indigenous culture is to reassert its own claim to authority and dignity.

The category of postcolonial literature also includes the work produced by *settler cultures*, which find themselves placed between the indigenous peoples (for whom they represent the colonizing power) and the mother country (for whom they may represent a marginal and uncivilized group). Settler cultures have to find their own identity in the new conditions of the new country, and their own authentic voice in literature, which will inevitably be different in form and style from the models available in the mother country. American literature seems to have gone through this process of self-definition in the nineteenth century, and Canadian literature in the twentieth century. The major works in these traditions can then be reabsorbed into the canon of "literature in English," and the canon of "English literature" may be transformed as a result.

This is particularly striking in the case of the literature of Ireland, which has a long history of suffering from English colonization, although this fact is often forgotten. From the twelfth to the twentieth century Ireland was brutally treated by England, her land expropriated, and her citizens disenfranchised. Edward Said points out that

> In Ireland ... the idea of murdering Gaels was from the start "as part of a royal army or with royal approval, [considered] patriotic, heroic, and just." The idea of English racial superiority became ingrained; so humane a poet and gentleman as Edmund Spenser in his *View of the Present State of Ireland* (1596) was boldly proposing that since the Irish were barbarian Scythians, most of them should be exterminated. [6]

Approximately one-quarter of Ireland's population died or was driven abroad during the potato famine of the 1840s (1.6 million Irish men and women emigrated to the United States alone), and the process of gaining independence from England dominated Irish politics in the early part of the twentieth century. It seems ironic now that the works of Yeats and Joyce, both of whom were strongly affected by the liberation movement, are seen as two of the outstanding authors of twentieth-century *English* literature.

A similar process of merging two opposed cultures can be seen at the level of language in nations which have emerged from colonial rule. If English became the language of administration during the colonial period, then indigenous authors may have a strong incentive to use English rather than their native language, so their works can reach a wider audience. But in whose English should they write? The idiomatic language of London and Oxford will carry overtones reminiscent of the former rulers and their condescension. Another possibility is to write in idioms of the native users of English in their particular nation, which has its own authenticity. This language is sometimes referred to as "english" with a small letter e. Some authors achieve wonderfully subtle effects by combining and contrasting these two forms of the English language.

What conclusion can we reach about these encounters with "the other" in postcolonial literature? One relevant warning must be the difficulty caused by dipping into a series of unfamiliar cultures in a course on postcolonial literature. The temptation on the part of the teacher may be to *explain* a lot of details, to make the novels more accessible, but in some ways this disempowers the reader and insults the novel. *Arrow of God* is comprehensible without any footnotes, and supplying them in class may be an error. Another caveat might be that what is radically "other" may well be simply inaccessible – this is the case with the Hindu parts of *A Passage to India* for many readers. Then the challenge for both the reader and the teacher is to allow that gap to remain empty, rather than fill it with familiar ideas from Western religion. But drawing the line between these cases, and those in which some form of blending (or hybridization) is appropriate, must be a sensitive and important issue in teaching postcolonial literature.

Mono- and Multi-Culturalism

The study of postcolonial literature focuses on nations emerging from hegemonic domination and discovering their own identities. The pressing questions posed by multiculturalism arise in countries where there is more than one culture alive and struggling for recognition, such as the native, French, and English cultures in Canada, or the Black, Hispanic, and European cultural groups in the United States. (In both of these countries there are other cultural groups seeking recognition as well.) Until perhaps twenty years ago many countries like these adopted a mono-cultural attitude, symbolized by the idea of the melting pot: that there was one dominant culture, and groups with different cultural backgrounds needed to assimilate themselves to that standard, to "the way we do things here." Increasingly in recent years groups from different cultures have demanded, and received, better treatment, which has usually caused bitter resentment in the dominant, hegemonic culture.

There are two main arguments for adopting a multicultural viewpoint in a country like Canada or the United States. The first is that to stick with mono-culturalism – one language, one central tradition, and one ideology – is far too limiting, and that everyone misses out on a lot that is valuable in other cultures. This argument is often put forward to justify opening up, for instance, the canon of "great books" to include works by Asian and African-American authors.

An even more compelling argument depends on a view of human development which places strong emphasis on the importance for a young person growing up to be part of a recognized and valued group. This view is closely related to some of Frantz Fanon's arguments, and he is a principal influence in its development. The main contention is that if you grow up as part of a group which is not recognized, or which is actually publicly considered inferior or subhuman, then you are likely to internalize those attitudes toward yourself, and have, as it were, an agency within yourself which devalues and criticizes you. This is such a disadvantage to members of the subaltern group, that a democratic society will want to take action to mitigate that disadvantage and to give its members equality of opportunity. One way to do this is to publicly recognize and value the cultural works of members of these groups. (The overlap with feminist issues is worth pointing out here. A similar argument can be made for including more works by women authors in university literature courses.)

An extreme multiculturalist might want to say that all human cultures are of equal value, or equally interesting, and that we should revise our canons of important literature in a much more inclusive way. Perhaps in a school with equal numbers of students of Asian, black, Slavic, and Anglo-Saxon descent, the compulsory literature courses should contain an equal concentration on authors from these four ethnic groups. But it is hard to know what the statement, "All human cultures are of equal value," really means. Within the corpus of Canadian novels we generally make complicated collective judgments about literary merit, and our contribution to a multicultural canon would be based on those judgments. The Canadian philosopher Charles Taylor has recently pointed out that minority groups in Canada which would like to have more presence in the canon would (and *should*) be insulted by an automatic judgment that their novels are as good as Canadian novels. Such a judgment should only come after careful study of the other culture; and presumably the standard for evaluating works of literature written in Mandarin (for instance) would be quite different from those in operation in English-Canadian culture. A lot of work would be necessary before we could approach judgments of this sort. [7]

Taylor's proposal, with which I agree, is that we should set out to study other cultures with the *assumption* that we may find works which are as interesting, or more interesting, than those we love from our own culture. What we discover when we have done the necessary work will almost certainly be that our ways of judging what is interesting or good literature will have changed, as will our personal lists of the books we esteem most. As Taylor says, there may be a moral issue here, which is to recognize that "we are very far away from that ultimate horizon from which the relative worth of different cultures might be evident." "What [is required] of us is not peremptory and inauthentic judgments of equal value, but a willingness to be open to comparative cultural study ...." [8]

But where does this leave us in deciding what should be taught in a compulsory first-year university literature course, for instance? I have no answer to this difficult question. I agree that it is important to recognize the various cultures present in our social makeup, and represent them in our canons. I feel we also need to take account of the difficulty of entering other cultures, and the limited ability of most people between the ages of 15 and 25 to be concerned with more than themselves. A real concern with "the other" is, in my experience, quite rare in any age group. In *The Wretched of the Earth*, Fanon insists that a nation emerging from colonialism must first of all develop its own identity and culture – that nationalism needs to come before the pursuit of "international" culture. I feel quite sure that something analogous to this is true in the case of the development of individual human beings. The self which is strong can reach out to "the other," but the self which is in the process of development may need to look after its own house first. We will explore these issues further in the concluding chapter.

Previous chapters in this book have all had a central core or subject. It is worth pointing out that postcolonial criticism and multiculturalism, like postmodernism, do *not* really have a centre, in an important sense: all three are about throwing off a central authority, and finding local solutions to problems. Although different postcolonial societies may have some features in common, the essential qualities of (for example) Maori and Haida culture may be utterly different. In those cases, to look for solutions to literary or pedagogical problems *on a general plane* may only lead to frustration. But one moral imperative pushing us in the direction of recognizing diversity is well put by Edward Said near the end of *Culture and Imperialism*:

We are mixed in with one another in ways that most national systems of education have not dreamed of. To match knowledge in the arts and sciences with these integrative realities is, I believe, the intellectual and cultural challenge of moment.[9]

This challenge cannot be properly met, in my opinion, simply by expanding the canon and adding more to the current curriculum, although that may be our best first step. We need to accept the responsibility of identifying what will be eliminated to make room for the new material. No one that I know of has a promising solution to this problem, but that is not a reason for abandoning hope that one may yet be found.

Notes:

1. Frantz Fanon, *The Wretched of the Earth* (New York: Grove Press, 1966) 203.

2. Fanon, 80.

3. Fanon, 79.

4. Fanon, 252.

5. Fanon, 161, 163.

6. Edward Said, *Culture and Imperialism* (New York: Knopf, 1993) 222. Said quotes from Angus Calder, *Revolutionary Empire* (London: Cape, 1981) 36.

7. Charles Taylor, "The Politics of Recognition," in Amy Gutman, ed., *Multiculturalism* (Princeton University Press, 1994) 25-73.

8. Taylor, 73.

9. Said, 311.

Suggestions for Further Reading

Frantz Fanon, *The Wretched of the Earth,* trans. Constance Farrington (New York: Grove Press, 1966), first published in French as *Les damnés de la terre* (Paris: Maspero, 1961). This is a passionate appeal for understanding, and a very powerful presentation of the plight of colonized peoples. It has a preface by Jean-Paul Sartre.

Edward Said, *Orientalism* (London: Routledge and Kegan Paul, 1978).

—— *Culture and Imperialism* (New York: Knopf, 1993). This is a rich and complex work, with chapters on European authors (Conrad, Camus, Austen) as well as a discussion of postcolonial nations. Said's main point is that European imperialism worked not just through economic and political means, but also through cultural forms, such as literature. As a result European literature is deeply marked by the colonial project.

Bill Ashcroft, Gareth Griffiths, and Helen Tiffin, *The Empire Writes Back: Theory and Practice in Post-Colonial Literatures* (London and New York: Routledge, 1989). This book contains clear discussions of many of the main issues in postcolonial criticism.

Charles Taylor, "The Politics of Recognition," in Amy Gutman, ed., *Multiculturalism* (Princeton University Press, 1994), 25-73. This is a clear and forceful essay by a philosopher, with a number of references to the politics of the independence movement in Quebec.

CONCLUSION:
Resituating Authority

*I knew too well from experience that it was
impossible to find in the external world that which
was actually located within myself.*

Marcel Proust, Le temps retrouvé

THE CENTRAL THEME OF THIS BOOK has been pluralism in
criticism and the existence of different and incommensurable critical
paradigms. Marxists and feminists (to take two examples) live in different
worlds, and when they read the same book, they see different objects.
This is a problem that is related to the search for authority that all of us
undertake in the course of our lives – and which takes particular forms
for those of us involved in the study of great authors. Who speaks with
authority? Where does authority lie? How do we come to possess
authority?

Paradigm Relativism and the Rise of Modernism

A defining feature of high modernism in literature, as it emerged in the
years following the First World War, was an acute awareness of differing
and conflicting cultural paradigms. Matthew Arnold was able to refer confidently to "the best that has been thought and said," but the modernists
knew that the assurance behind this phrase felt hollow in a world where
culture was not one harmonious whole, but was fragmented along national
lines. "The best" recognized on German or Russian soil was quite different
from "the best" cherished by the English or the French.

For many people concerned with literature this fragmentation did
not pose a problem. It is a relatively rare reader who wants to venture
outside the boundaries of her language, and it can be revealing to ask
why anyone would want to. Curiosity, intellectual ambition, and the
awareness of gaps in one's own culture are all possible reasons for look-

ing further afield. Another reason is the search for authority – and the desire to embark on this search can originate in the feeling that you do not have enough authority "at home," in your own literary heritage and context.

T.S. Eliot, the poet who gave quintessential expression to high modernism in *The Waste Land*, is case in point. Born and raised in St. Louis, Missouri, Eliot clearly did not find the authority he needed or wanted in the American Midwest, or even at Harvard. But because he was an American he was able to approach the culture of Europe as an outsider, with no established commitment to one national paradigm. As a result, he had a kind of access to English, French, Italian, and German literature that was not available to most Englishmen. He acquired an unequalled authority as a spokesman for European modernism partly because he went beyond the national boundaries that effectively contained most Europeans. But it is also clear from his poetry that his ultimate authority was achieved at the price of passing through painful stages of homelessness, rootlessness, and depression, in which he searched in vain, within himself and in the world, for the sources of value, meaning, and authority.

The Parallel with Literary Studies

There are many reasons for the rise of literary theory since the 1960s. One, identified by Roland Barthes, is "the death of the author." He said in his inaugural lecture as professor of literary semiology at the *Collège de France* that "literature [has been] desacralized," that we have a new freedom in dealing with it, because the distinction and the authority of the "great author" have been demystified. Literary theory has spread its wings partly to take charge of, and make use of, this freedom.[1] Since the 1960s there has also been more awareness among critics about the many different kinds of literary criticism. It has become clear that there are significant dangers inherent in being parochial, in remaining within the parish of one kind of criticism. In spite of this, many critics, even today, work happily and productively in biographical criticism for their entire careers. It seems likely that those students and critics who want to look at the whole world of criticism are, as was T.S. Eliot, dissatisfied with the kind of authority that was available (or that they could achieve) within their initial horizon.

There is a problem here of steering between two extremes. The person who is happy with the authority available at home may well stay at home, and lead a contented life, but possibly a narrow life, in which learning more about the rest of the world may play little part. And there is a chance that such a person will miss what he really needs – whether this be a friend, companion, teacher, information, or experience. The explorer, on the other hand, may, like Eliot in the middle of his life, find that she knows a great deal, but does not feel at home anywhere. Of course there is not a right answer to this question, or a single middle course – there is a huge range of possibilities which may suit individual temperaments. Not everyone has the same need for authority, or for a home.

A fundamental assumption of this book, and of reader-response criticism in general, is that in the long run it is desirable that learners become masters – that, as in psychoanalysis and tennis, the job of the teacher is to make himself or herself unnecessary. That is, the authority which is lodged in the teacher comes to reside also in the student, as the student progresses. So the search for authority in the external world is transformed into the discovery of authority in oneself. It is time for a theory of this process.

A Theory of the Search for Authority

The first three of Vico's four stages can help us in drawing a map for the search for authority. We can imagine a time before authority seems necessary, when our spontaneous feelings by themselves carry us forward in the direction we want. This is reminiscent of the Garden of Eden, of falling in love, and of the new-born infant happily nestled in his or her mother's arms. There is a fusion with the outside world that makes authority unnecessary. Wordsworth describes this fusion well:

> Blest the infant Babe,
> (For with my best conjecture I would trace
> Our Being's earthly progress,) blest the Babe,
> Nursed in his Mother's arms, who sinks to sleep
> Rocked on his Mother's breast; who with his soul
> Drinks in the feelings of his Mother's eye!
> For him, in one dear Presence, there exists
> A virtue which irradiates and exalts
> Objects through widest intercourse of sense.
> No outcast he, bewildered and depressed:

Along his infant veins are interfused
The gravitation and the filial bond
Of nature that connect him with the world.[2]

Marcel Proust describes a similar scene, and although it does not involve an infant, it too is a scene of feeding. As a mature man, Proust drinks a spoonful of tea with crumbs of cake mixed in it; the taste is so particular and unusual that it re-immerses him in a moment of childhood, when his aunt used to give him just that particular mixture. The result is something like a mystic experience:

> At the very moment at which the mouthful of tea mixed with crumbs touched my palate, I shuddered, struck by the amazing feelings I had within me. A delicious pleasure had invaded me, and because of its isolation I had no idea what had caused it. Suddenly it made the vicissitudes of life insignificant, its disasters harmless, its briefness an illusion, in the same way that love affects us, by filling me with a precious essence: or rather this essence wasn't in me, it was me. I no longer felt mediocre, contingent, or mortal.[3]

Such presentations of infancy, of mysticism, of the bliss of love or merging with another, are powerful and attractive, and can be motivating at a deep and perhaps unconscious level. Freud says that the child's earliest relation to his or her mother sets the pattern for all future joys, and Proust's experience of *la mémoire involontaire* when drinking the spoonful of tea was crucial to the writing of his novel. But these experiences do not seem to help in working out our conscious relation with people and things in the external world, and one reason for this is that there is no provision for authority.

I want to present a very brief and schematic account of how authority can enter into this scene, so that we can talk about a similar process which can occur in our experience of literature. At some point the infant begins to realize that she is separate from her mother, and that survival depends on maintaining the relation with her. Parents have overwhelming authority – they move like giants through an apparently magical and dangerous world, driving cars, earning money, presiding over PTA meetings, and engaging in conflict. The child needs the support of this authority, and to have this support, she usually has to comply with the rules or guidelines laid down by the parents. At a much later stage, the child tries to acquire the skills that the parents possess, and, with those skills, some of the parents' authority.

We need now to look at an analogous process in the experience of literature, so we can understand how literary theory can play a role in what happens. Two different areas are involved: the first concerns the reader's connection with authors who are important to him, and the second concerns relations with teachers and professors.

I have already alluded to the entrancement certain readers might have with Boris Pasternak as the author of *Dr Zhivago*. This could be a passionate identification in which (as in the relation between infant and mother), the reader is unable to draw a clear line between herself and the author. This could lead to a desire simply to be *near* Pasternak, literally or metaphorically – you might gain some authority by meeting some of Pasternak's relatives in Oxford, or by learning about his life. This seems to be like establishing a metonymic relation with him – touching some things which have touched Pasternak. Or you might try to actually be like him – cultivate a similarly wide range of interests, or try to write nature poetry. In this process, you might feel you came to understand better the reality of what Pasternak did, and find it less mysterious and less exalted.

Several of these themes find expression at the end of Proust's *A la recherche du temps perdu*, which is moving because the author's search for lost time, and the authority of the past, concludes with his realization that the source of power lies within himself. Proust weaves several themes together:

i) The authority of great art lies in its ability to pierce through social conventions to reach a hidden reality beneath;

ii) the work of art is not so much a *creation* as a translation of the artist's inner life into an external physical medium;

iii) we all possess this inner life, and the artist is unusual in the kind of attention he pays to it; and

iv) the distinction between the writer and the reader is not of great significance, because

...in reality, each reader, when he reads, is the reader of himself. The work of literature produced by the writer is only a kind of optical instrument which he offers to the reader in order to allow him to discern that within himself which, without this work of art, he might never have seen.[4]

The grandeur of veritable art...is to recapture, to lay hold of, to make one with ourselves that reality far removed from the one we live in, from which we separate ourselves more and more as the knowledge which we substitute for it acquires a greater solidity and impermeability, a reality we run the risk of never knowing before we die but which is our real, our true life at last revealed and illuminated, the only life which is really lived and which in one sense lives at every moment in all men as well as in the artist.[5]

The whole movement of Proust's novel is toward defining the true value of art; in the process the role of the artist becomes demystified, because what he or she does is potentially accessible to us all. Significantly, Proust reaches this conclusion just as he himself is about to become a mature artist; it allows him to begin writing his great novel, whose very theme is how he came to reach this conclusion.

A similar pattern may be seen in a student's relations with his teachers and professors. At first what the professor does may seem magical (students often say they are surprised by a professor's ability to interpret symbols, for instance). Academic success may depend on acquiring some skills like these, so the student may come to resemble the professor in some ways. This is one area in which literary theory is especially useful. You can acquire these skills much more quickly if you can work out what critical paradigm the professor is using. Literary theory raises this issue right away, and, in doing so, it tends to demystify the process of working with literature.

Many people object to the idea of teaching literary theory to undergraduates because it demystifies authority too soon. Their argument is based on the idea that for healthy growth, a student is better off to accept the mysterious authority of both authors and professors – that she is liable to learn much more that way. Literary theory and demystification ought to come later, according to this view.

This may be true in the cases of particular students. I am certainly not saying that you can never demystify authority too early. But generally speaking, I think the early twenties are a good time to transfer some of the authority from writers and professors to the students themselves. In any case the psyche has its own safeguards; the student who does not want authority demystified will probably put up effective defences.

The Resituating of Authority

Ideally authority migrates from the outside to the inside, as the individual begins to live as an adult among other adults. The speed of this process is variable, and different speeds will feel comfortable for different people. Carl Jung describes how it happened to him very abruptly:

> I was taking the long road to school from Klein-Huningen, where we lived, to Basel, when suddenly for a single moment I had the overwhelming impression of having just emerged from a dense cloud. I knew all at once: now I am *myself*! It was as if a wall of mist were at my back, and behind that wall there was not yet an "I." But at this moment *I came upon myself*. Previously I had existed, too, but everything had merely happened to me. Now I happened to myself. Now I knew: I am myself now, now I exist. Previously I had been willed to do this and that; now *I* willed. This experience seemed to me tremendously important and new: there was "authority" in me.[6]

If this kind of experience happened too early and too completely, it might close an individual off from new experiences and prevent her from learning many things. On the other hand, if this process did not occur, an individual might learn a great deal, but have difficulty in putting what is known to effective use, because the center, or the self, might not be strong enough take action in the world.

This process of internalizing authority often depends on uncontrollable factors – in particular the amount of attention a person gets. A child whose parents listen with love can acquire a strong sense of self early on in life, and later assume authority with ease. A child whose parents cannot or will not listen may find it very difficult to be comfortable while exercising authority. A similar dynamic can be seen in adult life. Knowing that people are listening to you and caring about what you say makes authority seem easy to handle. And of course there are limited supplies of attention in the world. As the British psychiatrist David Smail says, "It helps to be loved, but not many people are."[7] In his view deprivation is the norm rather than the exception.

So the search for authority may be one that some people prefer not to embark on, for understandable reasons. For those who do, a further qualification is in order. The authority that may be acquired is likely to be very different from that which we all observed in some of our most effective teachers, and felt in our most beloved authors. In them it may have looked virtually effortless and absolute. But it rarely feels like that from the inside, because doubts and uncertainties remain for almost everyone; and any reasonable person exercising authority in the real world must be aware of how circumscribed his or her real power is, and how much it is shared with others. The authority that is projected on another seems much more dazzling and complete than the authority which we assume ourselves. That is why we rarely feel we have caught up with our parents or our teachers.

The value of literary theory is that it helps us in our quest for maturity and in our attempts to move beyond the locale where we grew up. It helps us to enter into dialogue with others, and to recognize when dialogue is impossible. It helps us to see that authority is a social construction, that we all play a part in establishing it, and that it is potentially accessible to us all. But literary theory is not meant to be a substitute for reading and loving individual authors; it should enrich, not weaken, our relations with them.

It is not possible to return to the Garden of Eden or the lost paradise, even if we yearn for them at times. But for students of literature a return to a fundamental source of meaning is possible in the act of reading. *If* we had to choose between this nourishment and working with literary theory, then I hope it is clear which I feel is more important. This book, and the real enterprise of literary theory, are based on the assumption that we don't have to choose one over the other.

Notes

1.   Roland Barthes, "Inaugural Lecture," *A Barthes Reader*, ed. Susan Sontag (New York: Hill and Wang, 1982) 475.

2.   William Wordsworth, *The Prelude* (1850) 2.232-44, ed. Ernest de Selincourt, 2nd edition revised by Helen Darbishire (Oxford University Press, 1959) 57.

3. Marcel Proust, *A la recherche du temps perdu* (Paris: Gallimard, 1987) I.44; my translation.

4. Proust, III.895; my translation..

5. Proust, III.897; my translation.

6. Gerhardt Wehr, *Jung: A Biography*, trans. David M. Weeks (Boston and Halifax: Shambhala, 1987) 10.

7. David Smail, *Illusion and Reality* (London: Dent, 1984) 11

Suggestions for Further Reading on Freud and Jung

A good novel which gives a fictional example of Freudian psychoanalysis is *The White Hotel* by D.M. Thomas (New York: Viking, 1981). Freud's *New Introductory Lectures on Psychoanalysis* (Harmondsworth: Penguin, 1973) is easy to read, as is Janet Malcolm's *Psychoanalysis: The Impossible Profession* (New York: Vintage, 1982). Irvin Yalom's *Love's Executioner* (New York: Basic Books, 1989) gives fascinating accounts of ten cases in psychotherapy.

A novel about a Jungian analysis is Robertson Davies's *The Manticore* (Harmondsworth: Penguin, [1972] 1976). Jung's autobiography, *Memories, Dreams, Reflections* presents many of his ideas. Anthony Storr's *Jung* (London: Fontana, 1973) is short and direct. Carol Pearson's *The Hero Within: Six Archetypes We Live By* (San Francisco: Harper Row, 1986) uses Jung's ideas to clarify stages of psychological development. John Sanford's *The Invisible Partners* (New York: Paulist Press, 1980) is a good explanation of the contra-sexual archetypes in men and women – the anima and the animus. Anthony Storr's *The Dynamics of Creation* (Harmondsworth: Penguin, 1976) discusses Freudian and Jungian attitudes toward creation in the arts.

EPILOGUE:

Postmodernism, the Eclipse of Grand Narratives, and the Weakening of Shared Public Meaning

The Short Twentieth Century ended in problems, for which nobody had, or even claimed to have, solutions. As the citizens of the fin-de-siècle tapped their way through the global fog that surrounded them, into the third millennium, all they knew for certain was that an era of history had ended. They knew very little else.

—*Eric Hobsbawm*

WHAT IS THE SPIRIT OF OUR TIMES, in the last decade of the twentieth century? How does our culture differ from that of the 1960s, or the roaring 20s, or the aestheticism of the 1890s? What inheritance will we pass on to the twenty-first century? Questions like these have often intrigued writers and thinkers, in spite of their inherent complexity, and the difficulty of making statements which are fair and representative of something as huge and complex as "our culture." But the attempt to define the present is worthwhile: it is an important part of the quest to find out who we are and what we may become.

If we pay attention to the current debates about contemporary culture, the term most often used to identify avant-garde literature is "postmodern." Whether we like it or not, we live in what is often identified as the postmodern period; and it is fitting to conclude a book about literary theory with a chapter on postmodernism, because theory has played a central role in both the creation of postmodernism and in the defining of our times. Not that our present culture is exclusively postmodern; it is made up of many different strands of thought, some of which can be traced to identifiable historical periods. Our democratic institutions find their beginnings in the Greece of twenty-five hundred years ago; our valuing of romantic love comes from the Middle Ages; the prestige of science has its origins in the Enlightenment; and our fascination with the workings of the unconscious mind became widespread in the early years of this century. All four of these traditions (as well as many others) are vitally alive today, and enrich our culture immeasurably. But postmodernism adds something identifiably new to this mixture.

It is worth pointing out that many people object to the words "modernism" and "postmodernism" because they are inherently inappropriate: the word "modern" comes from a Latin word *modo*, which means "just now." The use of the world "modern" in literary and intellectual history contradicts this meaning. The "modern" period in British and American literature is generally taken to cover the fifteen years running from the end of the First World War to some point early in the 1930s, and its defining authors are Eliot, Joyce, Woolf, Lawrence, and Faulkner. In intellectual history, "the modern period" refers to the much longer era beginning with the Enlightenment and continuing today. What these two movements have in common is that each searches for a foundation, a deeper ground, for the surface manifestations of life. This foundation may be universal reason, or some form of myth, or a story about human progress. What is striking about postmodernism is that it rejects this search for deep structures; it does not seek unity or a shared ground for human culture. Instead it celebrates the diversity, contradiction, and variety which are so clearly present on the surface of our collective life.

What does postmodernism feel like?

I would like to evoke the feeling of postmodernism in three different ways, first by describing a setting, secondly with a fable, and finally with an image. To begin with, imagine you are in the city centre of a large metropolis. Various ethnic communities border on an area dominated by towering downtown skyscrapers. You are aware of being surrounded by several different cultures. People who are obviously wealthy and sophisticated encounter others who are extremely poor. The core feeling you may have as an outsider is one of uncertainty, of floating between different customs and different languages. There is no sign that one of them takes precedence over the others; there is no dominant authority or set of rules. It is hard to know what you might encounter next, or what kind of transaction might be expected of you. It is difficult to know how to distinguish between politeness, indifference, and hostility in the people around you. You may be uncertain about the sex of some of the people who surround you, and about how much power they wield. You may not be able to tell if people are being honest or playing a role which has no sincerity at all.

How would you feel in this setting? Many people would react to it with anxiety, and their first impulse might be to get back to some community which is more safe and predictable, where they know what to expect. And many people feel similarly disoriented and dismayed by postmodern works of literature: they contain such a mixture of styles, genres, and languages that they can seem bewildering. Almost no one wants to live in a world which feels chaotic.

But a very different reaction to the postmodern setting is also imaginable: if you felt secure, you might also feel enormously exhilarated by the variety and the energy in this urban streetscape. New, strange images, sounds, and smells would surround you. You would not feel fenced in by others' expectations; you would feel free; you would (with some knowledge of your environment) be able to choose your way of living to a degree that was unthinkable fifty years ago anywhere in North America. And you could switch back and forth between radically incompatible lifestyles. You could be speaking English one moment, and Cantonese the next. The city could become a friendly labyrinth, offering endless possibilities and strange new combinations of experiences. That might feel like a radical new liberation. The maze of differences might also help you feel protected from the dominating authority of the state. That too would feel liberating, especially for someone who had lived under a totalitarian regime.

A second approach to postmodernism can be found in the following fable from John Fowles's novel *The Magus*.[1] It conveys the confusion and bewilderment which a person can experience when the authority he has trusted collapses, and he is left to make crucial choices between incompatible assumptions about life:

❧ THE PRINCE AND THE MAGICIAN

Once upon a time there was a young prince who believed in all things but three. He did not believe in princesses, he did not believe in islands, he did not believe in God. His father, the king, told him that such things did not exist. As there were no princesses or islands in his father's domaines, and no sign of God, the young prince believed his father. But then, one day, the prince ran away from his palace. He came to the next land. There, to his astonishment, from every coast he saw islands, and on these islands strange and troubling creatures whom he dared not name. As he was searching for a boat, a man in full evening dress approached him along the shore.

"Are those real islands?" asked the prince.

"Of course they are real islands," said the man in evening dress.

"And those strange and troubling creatures?"

"They are all genuine and authentic princesses."

"Then God must also exist!" cried the prince.

"I am God," replied the man in full evening dress, with a bow.

The young prince returned home as quickly as he could.

"So you are back," said his father, the king.

"I have seen islands, I have seen princesses, I have seen God," said the prince reproachfully.

The king was unmoved.

"Neither real islands, nor real princesses, nor a real God, exist."

"I saw them!"

"Tell me how God was dressed."

"God was in full evening dress."

"Were the sleeves of his coat rolled back?"

The prince remembered that they had been.

"That is the uniform of the magician. You have been deceived."

At this, the prince returned to the next land, and went to the same shore, where once again he came upon the man in full evening dress.

"My father, the king, has told me who you are," said the young prince indignantly. "You deceived me last time, but not again. Now I know that those are not real islands and real princesses, because you are a magician."

The man on the shore smiled.

"It is you who are deceived, my boy. In your father's kingdom there are many islands and many princesses. But you are under your father's spell, so you cannot see them."

The prince returned pensively home. When he saw his father, he looked him in the eyes.

"Father, is it true that you are not a real king, but only a magician?"

The king smiled, and rolled back his sleeves.

"Yes, my son, I am only a magician."

"Then the man on the shore was God."

"The man on the shore was another magician."

"I must know the real truth, the truth beyond magic."

"There is no truth beyond magic," said the king.

The prince was full of sadness.

He said, "I will kill myself."

The king by magic caused death to appear. Death stood in the door and beckoned the prince. The prince shuddered. He remembered the beautiful but unreal islands and the unreal but beautiful princesses.

"Very well," he said. "I can bear it."

"You see, my son," said the king, "you too now begin to be a magician."

The postmodern quality of this fable lies in the uncertainty which the prince experiences, and in the shifting frames for interpreting his experience. This quality is increased by the fable's setting within the novel. The protagonist discovers it in an underground bunker on a Greek island. It has been left behind by the troupe of actors who have been used to educate, and at times dupe, him. He is deeply in love (and also furiously angry) with one of the actresses from this troupe. But the fable has no identifiable author, and Nicholas cannot know if it is only an accident that he has discovered it. It is a text without a discernible intention.

A third image to evoke the feeling of postmodernism is to imagine a multicultural bazaar somewhere in the Middle East, a space where merchants and hucksters set up their stalls to do business with a diverse population. There is little shared culture, and few agreed-upon assumptions, beyond the bare minimum needed for security and order. Anything you buy could be unauthentic, a forgery, or a treasure; and the prices could be hugely inflated. The merchants come and go. No one finds a home there; everyone retires to their own community when the day is over.

One feature shared by these three evocations of postmodernity (the city centre, the fable, and the bazaar) is that there is no dominating culture providing a frame for interpretation. They are sites of contradiction and potential conflict, but this makes room for differences to flourish.

A Contrast to Postmodernism: The Unity of a Shared Culture

Life feels very different when you are at home in your own culture: you know what to expect, the rules are clear, and you can trust most of your neighbours. Postmodernists sometimes refer to this kind of experience as one in which there is a shared *grand narrative*. This narrative is a story which evokes a particular culture, tells about the past, and predicts how the future will unfold. Usually it is a story of hope, about how Israel will reach the promised land, or how Christians can build the just city — that is, a loving, fair community.

The two most powerful grand narratives in the Western world today are those which tell the stories of the rise and spread of democracy, and the development of reason and science. Both these stories became very important during the Enlightenment, and they seemed to be confirmed (in politics) by the American and French Revolutions, and (in science and technology) by the success of the Industrial Revolution. They may seem to be further justified in our own times by the disintegration of the Communist bloc in 1991 and by the impressive achievements of science and technology in our culture.

It is worth pausing for a moment to reflect on the matrix in which the Enlightenment began, because it resembles the postmodern condition in some striking ways. Why did mathematics and the scientific method gain enormous prestige in the 18th century? It was precisely because they promised to establish knowledge and culture on a universal common ground, accessible to everyone: clear and dispassionate reason, and the verifiable evidence of the senses. Instead of a myriad of local traditions, customs, and privileges in politics, a single common standard would apply. Instead of the hatred and conflict spawned by religious sects, with their private, mystical revelations and their diverse historical roots, the harmony of a universal rational outlook would be assured. In the light of reason, the narrow, crooked byways of the past would be swept away, and a new era of human happiness would dawn. Wordsworth expressed the passionate excitement felt by many at this time:

> Bliss was it in that dawn to be alive,
> But to be young was very heaven.

The European Enlightenment engendered very powerful hopes for the future of human society.

A grand narrative may exert its force in a general way as an ideology. But it can also be presented in a single book. A striking contemporary example is the highly successful adventure novel by James Redfield published in 1992, *The Celestine Prophecy*, which is focused on a fictional ancient manuscript discovered in Peru.[2] This text contains nine "insights" about human experience, which, the book suggests, are of universal validity, and will occur to every person in the same sequential order. The insights explain things such as the importance of mystical peace, the process of individual character formation, and the achievement of new modes of intense human interaction. This is a grand narrative about the development of human consciousness, apparently universal in its applicability, and infinite in the possibilities it suggests.

Any grand narrative, whether it is that of *The Celestine Prophecy* or the story of human progress implied by the Enlightenment project, suggests a single frame of reference. In contrast, postmodernism rejects the possibility of there being only one frame of reference, and dismisses the idea that anyone can achieve authority by finding an objective, God-like viewpoint, the "view from nowhere," which would guarantee that facts are correct and interpretations valid. According to postmodernism, there is no absolute frame of reference; there are only communities, each operating with its own paradigm. Each has its own "standards of truth," but those standards are only valid within the community.

But postmodernism seems equally hostile to the unity of a shared *local* culture. It emphasizes instead the clashes between interpretations which arise because a single event or text can be interpreted in conflicting ways by seeing it against the background of differing frames of reference. This is, I think, an important aspect of most reflective people's experience of contemporary life. Consider, for instance, the radically different interpretations given to the acquittal of O.J. Simpson in the most publicized trial of the 1990s in North America. Often the unity of a shared culture seems a thing of the past.

Postmodernism and the Weakening of Shared Public Meaning

For the purpose of convenience, we might summarize the ways in which postmodernism differs from modernism as follows:

1. Postmodernism rejects the large scale and lives in particular localities, which often seem like labyrinths in their complexity.

2. It has an innate hostility to grand narratives and the idea of human progress which they imply.

3. It values the surface of things, and doesn't want to search for deep structures.

4. It mixes different styles and genres (combining, for example, realism and fantasy); it rejects the rules governing individual genres.

5. It revels in irony, pastiche, and parody, and the uncertainty and undecidability which these foster.

6. It tends to disconnect signs from the underlying reality they refer to; words tend to float free, detached from what they mean.

7. It seems to accept the overload of information provided by the new electronic technology. In postmodern culture, often many things are happening at once, and somehow the recipient takes in what is necessary.

The conflict between modernism and postmodernism can be described by using Vico's four stages (described in Chapter 9). It is the struggle, or at least the disagreement, between a stage 3 person (who feels she has penetrated beneath the surface of modern life and discovered its inherent properties) and a stage 4 person, who has been much influenced by deconstruction, and "who greets the absurd or meaningless confusion of contemporary existence with a certain numbed or flippant indifference, favouring self-consciously 'depthless' works of literature."[3]

This conflict is well illustrated by a recent Gilbert Adair novel entitled *The Death of the Author*.[4] Its protagonist is a depthless but intriguing character. As a young Frenchman living in Paris during the Second World War, Léopold Sfax writes anti-Semitic articles for a Nazi newspaper under a pseudonym. He does this partly because he feels the Germans will win the war and dominate France for the foreseeable future, but also because he cannot bear to stifle his genius as an author: he wants to write and be recognized as a writer. When the Germans lose the war, he emigrates to the United States, and begins a career as a lecturer in comparative literature, hoping to leave his past, with its burden of guilt, behind him for ever.

He acquires a wide reputation, however, by becoming the chief spokesman for an extreme form of deconstruction, and popularizing its theory that no text can have a determinate meaning:

> The more closely a text is studied the more insidiously it is drained of
> sense or legibility, just as the more fixedly a word is stared at on the page
> the more it too is drained of legibility or sense, striking the increasingly
> bewildered eye as a mere weird disconnected sequence of squiggles.
> Words are far older and fickler and more experienced than the writers
> who suffer under the delusion that they are "using" them. Words *have
> been around*. No one owns them, no one can prescribe how they ought
> to be read, and most certainly not the author.
>
> I proposed that, in every text, there would fatally arrive what I called
> an *aporia*, a terminal impasse, a blank brick wall of impenetrability, an
> ultimatum of indetermination, when its self-contradictory meanings
> could no longer be permitted to coexist in harmony and its fundamental
> "undecidability" would undermine for ever the reader's most
> fundamental presuppositions.

This deconstructionist view is congenial to Sfax, because he can use it to
deny that his pro-Nazi articles have a definite meaning. His theory represents a complete disjunction between literature and life; and death, he
suggests, is only the "displaced name for a linguistic predicament."

But there is a danger: as he rises to academic stardom, it becomes
likely that someone will write his biography, and reveal his ties to the
Nazis — a possibility he cannot bear to contemplate. One of his graduate students, a beautiful young woman, embarks on this project, gets a
major publisher to give her a substantial advance, and plans to go to Paris
to do her primary research on Sfax's early life. The book ends with three
brutal deaths — a colleague of Sfax and the beautiful graduate student
are both murdered, and Sfax apparently commits suicide.

Despite its bloody conclusion, this is a funny and clever book, especially for readers who can see how Sfax's story is modelled on that of the
late Paul de Man, a professor at Yale who also collaborated with the
Nazis and later became an eminent spokesman for deconstruction. It
presents a wryly exaggerated version of poststructuralism, and creates a
protagonist who is amoral, brilliant, sophisticated, and believably self-
contradictory. (One of his most characteristic statements is that "English
has always been for me a language to lie in.") After his death, Sfax speaks
to us from beyond the grave:

Have I any posthumous last words? Not really. As I have discovered to my disappointment, death *is* merely the displaced name for a linguistic predicament, and I rather feel like asking for my money back — as perhaps you do too, Reader, on closing this mendacious and mischievous and meaningless book.

But is this book meaningless? Does it have a sharable public meaning, in spite of the labyrinth of uncertainty created by its protagonist, both through his theory and through the narrative of his life? My answer will surprise no one who has read the rest of *In Search of Authority*: it depends largely on the reader, and the community in which he or she is reading. The book could be seen as an amusing pastiche, a witty afternoon's read for a sophisticated audience. Or, on the other hand, it could be viewed as an eminently moral tale: Sfax has the opportunity, in occupied France, to lead an engaged, authentic life. Instead he betrays his country and his culture repeatedly, and after the war goes into hiding to protect himself. But retribution comes in the end, caused partly by his insatiable need to assert his own superiority to those around him — in a word, his need for fame.

The postmodern quality of this story can be found in the contradictions in Sfax himself: he wants the adulation of his followers (and he receives it), but he despises them; he is a teacher, but he has no sense of community, either with his colleagues or his students; and he promotes the idea that texts are meaningless, while being terrified that the real meaning of texts he has written will come to light. Each of these contradictions rests on confusion about how communities keep their coherence, a subject which postmodernists and deconstructionists, like many stage 4 people, have trouble appreciating.[5]

It may be clear to many of you that this book is motivated by a stage 3 urge toward making sense of life and the world in general, and from this point of view it is possible to see a lot of value in postmodernism without giving up on the stage 3 liking for coherence, understanding, and meaning. Grand narratives are certainly often oppressive, and leave out important details or counter-narratives which don't fit easily into the main story. An enthusiastic history of the rise of the United States to world dominance might easily neglect the fate of the native peoples who were, and still are, badly treated by the invaders from the imperialistic European civilization. The postmodernist urge to include awkward details and counter-traditions is a healthy one, as long as it doesn't completely undermine people's sense of their own identity.

As I come to terms with the conflict between modernism and postmodernism, my basic allegiances are with the modernist side, and so, like an aspiring stage 3 person, I do not want to allow in a degree of postmodernism which will dissolve my community, my language, or my sense of self. Like the prince in Fowles's fable, I think we need to live with an awareness that the standards of our culture are constructed. If we want to avoid the unexamined life (as Socrates proposes we should), we need to acknowledge our role in being members of a community which supports those standards. Inside these communities, a shared public meaning for a work of literature *is* possible, and working it out can be fascinating. Discussion in a literature class can be precisely this process, working on a small but very meaningful scale.

But outside these communities there is no ground on which to construct a shared public meaning; and that is where the real postmodernists live their lives. I don't know how they do it. I imagine them humming the song from the Monty Python film *The Meaning of Life* which outlines the enormous dimensions of our galaxy, and then continues:

> The universe itself goes on expanding and expanding,
>> In all of the directions it can whiz,
> As fast as it can go: the speed of light you know —
>> Ten million miles a minute, and that's the fastest speed there is;
> So remember when you're feeling very small and insecure,
>> How amazingly unlikely was your birth,
> And pray that there's intelligent life somewhere up there in space,
>> Because there's bugger all down here upon the earth.

Notes:

1. John Fowles, *The Magus*, revised edition (New York: Dell, [1965] 1968) 560-2.

2. James Redfield, *The Celestine Prophecy* (New York: Warner, 1992).

3. Chris Baldick, *The Concise Oxford Dictionary of Literary Terms* (Oxford University Press, 1990) 175.

4. Gilbert Adair, *The Death of the Author* (London: Heinemann, 1992). The subsequent quotations are taken from pages 26, 27-8, 29, 45, and 135.

5. Eric Hobsbawm says in *The Age of Extremes: The Short Twentieth Century, 1914-1991* (London: Michael Joseph, 1994):

> What postmodernism produced was ... a (largely generational) gap between those who were repelled by what they saw as the nihilist frivolity of the new mode, and those who thought that taking the arts 'seriously' was just one more relic of the obsolete past. (516)

Suggestions for Further Reading

Andrew Bennett and Nicholas Royle, "The Postmodern," in An Introduction to Literature, Criticism, and Theory: Key Critical Concepts (New York: Prentice Hall, 1995) 178-186. This is an interesting and up-to-date book, with short chapters on twenty-four ideas, such as "Me," "God," "The Performative," and "Pleasure."

Terry Eagleton, "Capitalism, Modernism, and Postmodernism," in *Against the Grain: Selected Essays, 1975-1985* (London: Verso, 1986).

Ihab Hassan, *The Postmodern Turn: Essays in Postmodern Theory and Culture* (Columbus: Ohio State University Press, 1987).

Linda Hutcheon, *A Poetics of Postmodernism: History, Theory, Fiction* (London and New York: Routledge, 1988).

——, *The Politics of Postmodernism* (London and New York: Routledge, 1989).

David Lodge, "Modernism, Antimodernism, Postmodernism," in *Working with Structuralism* (London: Routledge and Kegan Paul, 1981).

INDEX

A

A la recherche du temps perdu 72, 104, 227
A Passage to India 55, 214, 217
Achebe, Chinua 214
actant 154, 159-161
Adair, Gilbert 238
aesthetic movement 37
aestheticism 201, 203
allegory 104-105
Ambassadors, The 157
analepsis 156-157, 161
Animal Farm 104
Anna Karenina 39, 59, 135, 193, 203
Apprenticeship of Duddy Kravitz, The 104
Arnold, Matthew 80, 223
Arrow of God 214, 217
Ashcroft, Bill 221
Atwood, Margaret 193
Auden, W.H. 107
Austen, Jane 193
author-centered criticism 35, 191-192

B

Bakhtin, Mikhail 54-55, 122
Balzac, Honoré de 108, 158, 162, 169, 201
Barthes, Roland 18-19, 21, 72, 111, 117, 147-149, 151, 153, 157, 161-162, 175-176, 204, 224
Bayley, John 16-17, 18
Benjamin, Walter 205
Bennett, Andrew 242
Bible 201
binary distinctions 116
Blake, William 27, 41-42, 204
Bleich, David 180-183, 186
Brecht, Bertolt 41, 150
Burke, Kenneth 53, 56
Byron, George Gordon, Lord 27, 41

C

Camus, Albert 132

canon-formation 41-44
catalytic material 157-159, 161
Cixous, Hélène 194-196
Coleridge, Samuel Taylor 21, 27-28, 30-32, 34, 41, 44, 95, 134, 154, 158
Comedy of Errors, The 133
Conrad, Joseph 141, 155, 193, 207
Copernicus 67
Crowley, Helen 127
Culler, Jonathan 127
Culture and Imperialism 219, 221

D

Dances with Wolves 214
Davies, Robertson 96, 112-113, 116, 125
Death of the Author, The 238
de Man, Paul 239
deconstruction 12, 74, 111-112, 114-115, 136, 151
demystification 150, 203
demythologization 150
Derrida, Jacques 21, 116-117, 125, 127
diachronic relationships 88, 91
dialogism 54, 56
dialogue 47-53, 70-71, 230
discourse 195
Diviners, The 147, 161
Dollimore, Jonathan 172
Donne, John 38
Dr Faustus 105
Dr Zhivago 144, 202, 227
Dürer, Albrecht 50

E

Eagleton, Terry 15, 82, 84, 202, 242
Eliot, T.S. 107, 138, 224-225
Ellis, John M. 18, 171
Empson, William 49
Enlightenment 232

2950168